First Instruments

First Instruments

Teaching Music Through Harmony Signing

NICHOLAS BANNAN

OXFORD
UNIVERSITY PRESS

OXFORD

UNIVERSITY PRESS

Oxford University Press is a department of the University of Oxford. It furthers
the University's objective of excellence in research, scholarship, and education
by publishing worldwide. Oxford is a registered trade mark of Oxford University
Press in the UK and certain other countries.

Published in the United States of America by Oxford University Press
198 Madison Avenue, New York, NY 10016, United States of America.

CIP data is on file at the Library of Congress
ISBN 978-0-19-093205-3 (pbk.)
ISBN 978-0-19-093204-6 (hbk.)

1 3 5 7 9 8 6 4 2

Paperback printed by Marquis, Canada
Hardback printed by Bridgeport National Bindery, Inc., United States of America

Contents

IV: BUILDING CREATIVELY ON HARMONY SIGNING

Illustrations

Figures

Images

Acknowledgements

This book emerged from a lifetime of interest in the relationship between singing and composing that first arose in my earliest childhood experiences. Throughout my teaching and performing career, it has seemed to me self-evident that the physical voice and the capacity for self-expression that is captured in the metaphorical 'voice' of the composer or improvisor are both intimately connected and an aspect of the personality of every human being. The intention to unpack this existing personal perspective, and to protect the approach to teaching that it represents from the sceptical or negative position of colleagues who do not share it, prompted me to investigate the phenomenon in systematic research at the University of Reading in the mid-1990s. This led me into contact with figures in several disciplines who collectively represented to me the fledgling field of Evolutionary Musicology, to which my own work in vocal education has made a contribution. I have benefitted in this journey from the advice and encouragement of Anthony Kemp, Gordon Cox, Steven Mithen, Iain Morley, Ian Cross, Robin Dunbar, Ellen Dissanayake, Bjorn Merker, Jonathan Dunsby, Colwyn Trevarthen, Sheila Woodward, Frank Heuser, Patricia Shehan Campbell, Alan Harvey, Benjamin Smith, Sven Ouzman, Jim Chisholm, Steven Jan, Beatriz Ilari, Tran Quan Hai, Pedro Espi-Sanchis, Dave Dargie, Lori Custodero, Steve Laitz, and Lily Chen-Hafteck.

As a composer and educator, I have at one stage or another received support and encouragement from Malcolm Singer, Graham Elliott, Rolf Gehlhaar, Alexandra Dalton, Josephine McNally, Nigel Osborne, Roger Smalley, Chris Tonkin, James Ledger, Gerard McBurney, Trevor Wishart, Peter Webster, Eirimas Velička, Cecilia Sun, Sarah Collins, Suzanne Wijsman, and Graeme Gilling, and former students Andrew Melvin, Perry Joyce, Eva-Marie Perissinotto, Ilario Colli, Adam Pinto, Joshua Bamford, and John Hails. Administrative and support staff whose contributions have been immense include music librarians Linda Papa and Jenny Wildy; audio and video technicians Mike McMillan, Brian Hayter, Brian Pimley, and Jesse Stack; and music administrators Liz Smith, Daniela Hotolean, Sarah Brittenden, Pip White, and Danielle Loiseau.

Norman Hirschy at Oxford University Press has supervised the shaping of this book from the manuscript stage through to publication and Lauralee Yeary has ably and generously managed every step of the production process. The type-setting team led by Prabhu Chinnasamy ably dealt with the combination of text, music notation, charts, diagrams and images on which the communication of Harmony Signing depends. I am grateful to David Penco and Nik Babic for the cover and in-text images, and to Jesse Stack for his work on the video examples for the companion website.

One person whose contribution to the production of this book is owed more than I can ever repay is my wife, Valerie. She has contributed to every stage of the development of *Harmony Signing* and the sequence of creative projects that have tested and refined its concerns with children of all ages and abilities. In the complex process of producing the musical examples, formatting and proofreading the text, and preparing the book for final submission, she has devoted more hours to this project than I had any right to expect. Her own experience as a singer and music teacher has inspired much of what we have, together, assembled between these covers.

About the Companion Website

www.oup.com/us/firstinstruments

Oxford has created a website to accompany *First Instruments*. Material that cannot be made available in a book, namely videos and audio files of *Harmony Signing* and related performance and pedagogical content, is provided here. The reader is encouraged to consult this resource in conjunction with the musical examples and strategies described in the book.

Introduction

Picture a school in the midwestern United States. Students who are about twelve years old arrive at a music lesson. They immediately begin contributing to a hummed chord, sustaining its texture, and tuning in to one another's contribution. When everyone is present and facing the teacher, she moves her left arm from in front of her body to a vertical position with the fingers pointing upwards. The chord the students are singing with an open 'AH' sound changes in response. Led by a series of related gestures, the class performs a variety of harmonic progressions, carefully discriminating between major and minor and moving between root position triads and their first and second inversions. As the teacher introduces a new set of gestures with her right hand, part of the class responds by adding a melody that complements the chord progression performed by their classmates. On a sign of invitation from the teacher, a boy takes over the leadership of the activity, improvising with hand gestures the combination of melody and three-part accompaniment to which everyone responds fluently and with enthusiasm. After a minute or so, the boy passes on this leadership role to another student, initiating a sequence of different improvisations led by each member of the class. The musical material presents varying styles and turns of phrase that exemplify the element of personal creativity this approach affords. When the teacher intervenes to suggest moving on to a new activity that involves getting out books and laptops, it is the first time for some twenty minutes that anyone has spoken a word.

In Brazil, similar musical procedures engage a mixed-age brass ensemble in warm-up exercises prior to rehearsing a bossa nova arrangement. The group's director combines leading the music-making with presenting a supportive and encouraging response to the challenges individuals negotiate, throwing an approving smile towards one player and patiently waiting for another to successfully adjust his tuning. Again, this is achieved without a word being spoken.

In Singapore, a teacher is working with sixteen-year-olds on writing down a chord progression she performs on the piano. Her students have long experience of aural development through Harmony Signing and are able to access the library of relationships they hold in their aural imagination. The students confidently note down what she plays.

In England, a class of students is divided into groups, each of which is responsible for devising a chorus as part of a musical they are writing collectively. They know that presenting their work through Harmony Signing will permit their contribution to be learned really quickly by the rest of the class and that this permits the trying-out of the material prior to the laborious process of notating it, which will be the next stage before collaborating with their teacher to orchestrate the show.

All over the world, with groups of students from seven years old through to members of an adult community choir, and whatever their mother tongue or the nature of the musical style in which they perform, participants are able to enrich and accelerate their musical learning through the collective leadership that Harmony Signing provides.

This book introduces an approach to music teaching developed by the author over the last twenty years or so that is intended to accelerate and deepen students' acquisition of fluent musicality. It draws on research in neurology, anatomy, and child development to present collective musical activities sequenced as a complement to existing and familiar musical pedagogy (Bannan 2019). *Harmony Signing* focuses on the use of manual gestures to represent and communicate musical ideas. In particular, it seeks to develop students' confident understanding of pitch relationships through improvisation and composition. As the approach has developed, it has proved adaptable to a variety of aspects of musical learning: the development of aural skills such as discrimination, memory, and the discernment of function; the means to test music-theory concepts through practical creative application; and a method of establishing acute listening habits that promote tuning and blend for members of performing ensembles.

The book is laid out in a series of four related parts, each of which contributes to illustrating the potential of *Harmony Signing* as experience builds from primary school to the end of secondary school and the transition to tertiary education. Each section exemplifies and makes explicit its concerns through practical pedagogical strategies that can be incorporated into student practice and reflection. Illustrations throughout the book inform understanding of the concepts addressed and contribute to developing the framework of pedagogy through which *Harmony Signing* can be effectively introduced.

Harmony Signing grew out of practice that placed children's musical creativity at the core of musical learning. The intention was to parallel the ways in which mother-tongue education involves children writing stories and poems, and improvising drama; while in the visual arts, they draw, paint, sculpt, and construct. Strangely, music teaching has often been presented as a purely re-creative activity rather than one in which students are motivated by the opportunity to express their own personal worlds through the art form.

In presenting a complement or alternative to traditional music teaching, this book acknowledges and builds on the work of pioneers in creative and community music education. Exponents of emotive and communicative music-making from the early twentieth century include Zoltan Kodály, Carl Orff, Percy Grainger, and Émile Jaques-Dalcroze. Other influences to whom this book is indebted are composer-educators such as Peter Maxwell Davies, R. Murray Schafer, Nigel Osborne, David Bedford, Alan Ridout, Cornelius Cardew, Wilfrid Mellers, Olli Kortekangas, and Malcolm Singer and current teachers and researchers who have advocated an approach to music education founded on composition and improvisation, such as John Paynter, John Blacking, Pamela Burnard, John Kratus, Peter Webster, Maud Hickey, Panagiotis Kanellopoulos, Jody Kerchner, Patricia Shehan Campbell, and Jolyon Laycock.

Harmony Signing emerged in parallel with investigations into the origins and purpose of human musicality. The journey towards what is presented in this book commenced with an attempt to document the relationship between children's composing and the acquisition of confidence to sing. In seeking support for a method with which to understand this in the psychology literature, as well as related fields such as linguistics and anatomy, I found myself drawn to consider wider questions:

- What is the significance of music to child development and the fulfilment of individual potential?
- How is this transmitted from one generation to another?
- What is the relationship between group music-making and its effect on the individual?
- What are the neural relationships between music and speech?
- What is the role of multimodal learning in the development of musicality, and why do we appear to close off some aspects of musical response (dance, gesture) in the way we organise music teaching?

These questions led to collaborations with scientists across a range of disciplines whose work influenced a series of publications on the evolutionary origins of the human capacity for music and the implications of this agenda for music education (Bannan 1997, 2000, 2003, 2008, 2012b, 2014, 2016, 2019; Bannan & Montgomery-Smith 2008; Bannan & Woodward 2009;). These initiatives were a response to the growing literature that has explored the evolutionary role of music (Hodges 1989; Wallin 1991; Wallin, Merker, & Brown 2000; Benzon 2001; Mithen 2005; Levitin 2006; Malloch & Trevarthen 2009; Ball 2010; Changizi 2013; Morley 2013; Grauer 2011; Jordania 2011; Krause 2012; Tomlinson 2015; Harvey 2017). Throughout the period during which I contributed to the field, its influence shaped the pedagogical experiments it stimulated.

It seemed to me that, as a consequence of exploring this evolutionary perspective, the normal assumptions of school and community music-making represented an incomplete picture if the capacity of individual students for original utterance were not addressed. Music would seem to be older than language. Its instinctive and emotional properties, discernible in the response of the youngest children—and indeed in the womb—suggest a condition closer to animal communication than to language. Do we harness these features fully in the way we teach? If we accord to music the role of an evolutionary bridge between the way animals communicate and the eventual cultural achievement of language, then Ian Cross's (1999) question 'Is music the most important thing we ever did?' takes on a startling resonance: without music, we would not be here. It has been vital to the survival of our species. And yet it is at the same time a medium of children's play and their discovery of the world. How do we reconcile these complex attributes to set out and practice a coherent approach to teaching that prepares students for a lifetime of participation? And, might music-making of this kind contribute to well-being and to physical and psychological health?

Musicality has conferred some extraordinary capacities that we should not take for granted. We are the only species that coordinates rhythmic movement in fully synchronised dance and vocalisation (Merker 2000; Changizi 2013); an ability that we transfer to external tools such as musical instruments (Espi-Sanchis & Bannan 2012). We assign significance to precisely tuned pitch so we can, with continued practice, match and meaningfully complement the pitch of others. We are not the only melodists. Several species of bird and cetacean, for example, share similar abilities, and some even teach and learn from each other. But only humans can achieve this simultaneously in the parameters of both rhythm and pitch. A variety of species displays cooperative behaviours that depend on close synchrony: birds flock and fly in formation; bees swarm; fish shoal. But the distinctive behaviour of human beings is to sing in unison, and in many cultures this is done together by both males and females as well as intergenerationally, with children who sing along at the pitch of their mothers.

We are amazed by the capacity of some bird species to mimic other species and even sound sources such as machines and human music (Taylor 2008; Powys, Taylor, & Probets 2013). But in our wonder at what animals achieve, we overlook our ability to match and even surpass what they are doing in our own capacity for vocal mimicry. Indeed, imitation is at the heart of all vocal learning, whether musical or linguistic.

The attributes of human music-making are, then, both specialised and purposeful. They have clearly played a significant part in the generation of universal social behaviours that have been constructive of human culture for millennia.

But musicality is not only about cooperation and communication. As important, and essential to the development of the capacity for the forms of communication we have considered, is *representation*: how the individual responds to what the senses perceive so as to accord it meaning, file it in memory, and retrieve it as a rehearsed response. This is where infant play forms the basis for the hours of practice that confer mastery on more experienced musicians. Much of this is done alone, and it is with the music itself that the individual develops a dialogue. Musical material can acquire the properties of a 'significant other', a surrogate carer or transitional object (Winnicott 1971; see also Falk 2004) that accompanies the individual through times of loneliness or stress. In addition, the personal sorting of musical ideas in the mind generates new ideas, presenting an internal soundtrack that parallels the emotions and mental state. It evokes memories that sustain our biography in remembered sound.

What *Harmony Signing* has sought to achieve is a synthesis based on recognising the deep capacity for affective engagement through music in a manner that harnesses the instinctive, embodied, and personal nature of these evolved behaviours. The underpinning philosophy that defines the practice assumes the following:

- The voice is our first instrument. It co-evolved with the human auditory system and remains the portal to inner hearing and musical thinking.
- Social vocalisation presents the means whereby participants can both contribute to the phenomenon of absolute unison and, through harmonic and heterophonic means, to a choral texture in which their individual roles are unique.
- Music-making evolved as a multimodal behaviour (Mithen 2005). In several languages, the word for music embraces dance, instrumental playing, and singing as inseparable features. Christopher Small (1999) coined the term 'musicking' to capture this phenomenon in English.
- Gesture is a medium for the exchange and shaping of musical ideas. Participants learn more effectively how such interaction gives rise to musical consequences when they take on a leadership role.
- Gesture can be so much more than the time-keeping of the conventional conductor. It permits musical thinking in real time that can form the basis of collective creativity: composing through *cheironomy*.

- The scaffolding of responses to pitch and harmony arising from a sequenced, practical response to gesture can permit the achievement of complex music-theoretical understanding—polyphony and advanced harmony—without the need for notation.
- The harnessing of gesture to musical response can permit musical exchange independent of language: music teaching and learning without words.

The origins of *Harmony Signing* as a systematic pedagogical tool were largely accidental. I was working in the mid-1990s with members of the Reading University Children's Choir, a choral laboratory of volunteer children aged seven to eleven. The choir was nonauditioned: any children who arrived unable to match pitch learned to do so through a variety of games and activities. The practices of the choir were based on multimodal experience, largely influenced by Dalcroze and Kodály techniques including solfa, and also strategies for mime and improvisation taken from drama education.[1] Notation played a part in what we studied and in how we learned some songs, but the children also acquired repertoire through bringing songs they taught each other,[2] through learning by rote from me or from one of my postgraduate assistants, or through developing improvised arrangements of existing material. An ongoing practice in the choir was for students to create their own songs. Teaching these original compositions to the choir developed our repertoire and accelerated confidence in a way that results noticeably from hearing other people sing music you have created (Davies 1992). We also worked with digital electronics, especially echo/delay systems through which students were able to play with textures and to experience the sense of empowerment with which they responded to the sounds of their amplified voices returning in captured loops (Bannan 1998).

On one occasion, a group of about seven children worked under the direction of a ten-year-old girl to develop a cappella arrangement of the song *Shenandoah*. They had made good progress, but the leader sought me out: 'We know which notes to sing to make chords, but people keep forgetting which chord to go to when we need to change.' I suggested that they devise some clear signs to represent each chord and ensure that the members of her group could follow them. So, we came up with a hand across the chest for the tonic; a movement upwards for the chord of the subdominant (to which, following the melody of this song, one feels a sense of rising); and an opposite movement, pointing downwards, for the dominant—all connected by effective voice-leading. Within five minutes, the group had mastered this system as a means of coordinating the performance they intended. An even more satisfying outcome was that their leader was able instantly to teach the system to members of other groups (who had been working on different songs of their own), permitting a massed performance of *Shenandoah* under her direction by some thirty children. Thus was the seed of Harmony Signing revealed.

These three chord positions became the basis for an elaborate framework of signs and their interpretation that are set out in this book. These simple beginnings that primary

---

[1] We will encounter these throughout this book as the material that both represents a way to prepare initiates for the experience of Harmony Signing and acts as useful warm-ups for ensembles with intermediate and advanced skills.

[2] Since the choir served an international university community, there were always children whose mother tongue was not English who were able to teach songs from their native cultures.

children could handle provided the foundations on which it proved possible to build more elaborate procedures. *Harmony Signing* can now represent aurally and in collective response the complex pitch relationships of nineteenth- and twentieth-century music, supporting the creative, theory, and aural work of upper secondary and tertiary students.

From these first principles, I took every opportunity to develop and test the capacities of the system as it expanded, working with a variety of student groups of different ages and abilities, including transferring the practice from being principally vocal to working with instruments. I shared the system with teachers and with members of community choirs, including patients with Alzheimer's disease (Bannan and Montgomery Smith 2008). Many of the new additions to *Harmony Signing* were inspired by observing the sign language of the deaf, which, like speech and song, conveys a range of emotions and intentions alongside factual information (Sacks 1990). Other ideas were influenced by a variety of vocal practices from other cultures that similarly encourage collective creative responses (Dargie 1988, 1996; Fanshawe 1993).

Perhaps surprisingly, *Harmony Signing* also owes a considerable debt to recent advances in technology. Many of the ideas regarding the transformation and organisation of sound, especially that of which the voice is capable and the relationship between composition and game-playing, were stimulated by the work of Trevor Wishart (1977, 1996) and Rolf Gehlhaar (1991), composers working at the cutting edge of music technology who were keen to share their ideas with educators and music therapists. More generally, in devising a nested hierarchy of signs that convey complex information in real time, the development of *Harmony Signing* has benefitted from observing the effortless familiarity today's children acquire with the architecture and function of computers, mobile phones, and remote control devices. In particular, the way that buttons and keys change function according to context, permitting shortcuts and enhancements that make use of the same basic interface at higher levels, has inspired a great deal of what the method permits, much of which has been spurred by students' advice and suggestions. While *Harmony Signing* may well complement work achieved on keyboards and computers, it is itself an 'unplugged technology'.

A key outcome of developing Harmony Signing has been to recognise its capacity to employ music and gesture as channels of communication that permit one to dispense with language. My realisation of this was confirmed by a negative experience early on. I was leading a session for teachers and adult musicians at which one participant kept interrupting to demand that I explain everything we were doing verbally. I tried to illustrate that she would understand better if she allowed herself to participate through listening to what was happening around her, since other participants were making progress in this way. I said that explanations would come later. But this did not satisfy her. In fact, it led to a Catch-22: We became so distracted from actually proceeding with the musical activities that the rest of the group lost confidence in what they were doing.

Reflecting on this incident, and on the theoretical question of whether verbalisation may actually interfere with or distract from musical processing and alertness, I resolved that the practice of Harmony Signing would involve from the outset inviting participants to enter with me into a world in which we would not employ language. I suggest that the use of language may actually hinder progress, and that allowing the medium of music itself to form the basis of learning leads to richer and more musically instinctive achievements. I have never again had a problem with a participant requiring explanation as we go along, and I would advise teachers to consider establishing these conditions as a foundational advantage of the approach. Indeed, a benefit of adopting this stance has allowed me successfully to lead extensive sessions for groups of Portuguese and Mandarin speakers with whom I do not share a common language. As a consequence, *Harmony Signing* has taken on the description of 'music teaching without words' (Bannan 2005).

A word of explanation is sometimes made necessary where the words 'singing' and 'signing' get confused, especially in print. The pronunciation of these two expressions is distinct enough for this not to be problem; but their spelling can be! As we will see in Parts I and II, *Harmony Signing* proceeds from foundations in sung responses which establish collective participation that directly influences inner musical hearing and thinking. 'Signing' is then the means by which participants can represent their contribution to themselves, exchange information about this with others, and lead activities. All effective music teaching needs to involve singing as the portal to a secure and transferable response to pitch. The innovation in this pedagogy is the 'signing': the employment of gestures to feel, shape, sort, and connect acoustic information so it can be assembled into improvisation and composition or used as an embodied means of analysing music.

In the text that follows, each aspect of *Harmony Signing* and its precursor activities is set out in a sequence that proceeds from the rudimentary to the advanced within each chapter. Different students with different existing experience will be able to participate in activities not according to age, but based on what they are musically ready to learn. Teachers need to select the material that they feel best meets the needs of their classes and ensembles and that complements the activities they normally pursue. *Harmony Signing* has not been designed as a self-sufficient programme, nor as an end in itself. It should be employed as a catalyst to enhance and support strategies for music teaching with which it can interweave.

The ordering of parts and sections does not represent a syllabus or curriculum that should be followed in sequence. Teachers should draw on the games, tasks, and activities in a manner that covers the range of musical learning that they identify as advancing the progress of their students in relation to their own curriculum planning.

In summary, the activities set out in this book aim to develop an additional mode of music-making that complements conventional practice in the classroom and rehearsal studio. The activities endow student participants with enhanced opportunities to learn style and theory through taking on leadership roles that are often restricted to teachers and directors; involve experience of music-making that can be its own reward through sounding effective and raising motivation to succeed; and connect trial-and-error experience to expressive solutions that emerge within the medium itself: *music teaching without words*. Through harnessing the subjectivity, emotional responses, preferences, and musical choices of leaders and participants, they establish a sense of ownership. This complements the left-hemisphere processing of musical elements and sequences, with right-hemisphere brain processes that deepen experiences and encode them more securely in musical memory. In developing the means for creative musical engagement to have a place in the acquisition of performance skills, *Harmony Signing* offers an effective enrichment of the musical experience of students and their teachers.

PART I
WHY SINGING?

1
Musical Foundations

Meaningful human vocalisation commences at birth: the infant's instinctive cry soon becomes shaped by experience as a varied spectrum of vocal responses that represent and convey emotion (Trevarthen 1979; Trehub 2001; Fernald 1992; Falk 2004). Eventually, these become harnessed in play and dialogue (Trevarthen 1994; Dissanayake 2000; Bannan & Woodward 2009) as infants engage with their carers and the acoustic environment in which they find themselves. Babies respond to vocal sounds before birth (Woodward 1993; Lecanuet 1996) and music remains a significant stimulus and palliative, especially in carer-infant interactions (Nelson 1997; Street, Young, Tafuri, & Ilari 2003) that include vocalisation for its own sake in the absence of company. Initially, there is no difference between babbling that suggests speech and that which resembles song (Locke 1996). At some point in the second year (Halliday 1979), these behaviours begin to diverge. Play, trial-and-error, and enjoyment of the sheer fun of vocal production assume a significant part throughout the process of language acquisition (Cook 2000).

A different transition occurs when young children become interested in peer exchange with others of their age, developing play routines distinct from the vocalisations they have shared with carers (Romet 1992). This leads to games and rituals that depend on vocalisation and movement as significant organising principles (Opie & Opie 1985; Chagall 2014).

Children's early participation in informal rehearsal of play routines can endow the foundations of sophisticated skills. Many children arrive at their first formal educational experience already able to sing in tune, clap in time, and move unselfconsciously to music. But some do not, and the initial routines introduced here are intended both to extend the experience of those with existing skills and provide remedial stimuli for those who, for whatever reason, have been less exposed to the opportunity to participate musically.

Circle Games

Harmony Signing can only proceed where musical responses are rapid and confident: the eventual aim is for children to achieve unrehearsed unison even in complex structures that arise from newly devised material. So initial experience needs to be rhythmic, involving the voice, clapping, other body percussion sounds, and combinations of these.

Game A—Passing the Clap Around (1)

The teacher clicks a pulse, and each participant claps once in turn around a circle. When this is working well, a signal can be introduced for reversing the direction, clockwise or anticlockwise.[1] This activity is very simple, but the participants will become better at it as personal and team skills develop. They may become rhythmically more precise, and their clapping more controlled and even. Variants of this activity can include setting different tempi, including the fastest possible[2], and replacing the clap with a vocalised 'pah' sound.

Game B—Passing the Clap Around (2)

This game involves a completely different kind of temporal organisation designed to encourage personal choice and a sense of performance. Where Game A establishes a principle of almost mechanical interaction, Game B is the opposite. Students take turns in sequence, but how and when they perform their single clap is entirely up to them. Even the youngest soon realise that it can be amusing to play with the extremes: as quick as possible after their predecessor or drawing out the suspense. This game involves personal choices that define the overall effect to which others respond, which plays an important part in establishing the condition for an individual role within collective creativity.

Game C—Clapping and 'Unclapping'

While we are focusing on clapping routines, it can be valuable to model successful hand-clapping as a musically expressive activity. Students can sometimes view it as rather uncool, and this militates against rhythmic accuracy as well as any real quality of sound.

A YouTube clip of Steve Reich's *Clapping Music*,[3] or of Flamencan *palmas*[4] that influenced Reich's composition, can illustrate the true potential of purposeful clapping.[5] Observe how the performers in these clips carry out the act of clapping: They take care to present their hands as if they are musical instruments. This is the opposite of the floppy and uncontrolled 'penguin clapping' one sometimes observes, which lacks this sense of commitment. A solution is to teach 'unclapping': a means of acquiring sensitivity and control that can help students to achieve more musically rewarding results. 'Unclapping' was inspired by Japanese women who punctuate their praying with handclaps that bring their hands together, leading immediately to rubbing the hands against one another like a form of vibrato that 'resonates' the sound of the clap. It is worth trying this, because it makes the initial physical point well. Next, the idea of a 'clasp/unclasp' element is introduced to the clapping cycle. This makes students aware of when their hands are in contact and when they are not. The cycle is then divided into

---

[1] Such as a double- click, or the verbal command 'change'.

[2] This can be timed so that one can demonstrate over successive sessions whether the group can improve on their record.

[3] https://www.youtube.com/watch?v=xhhvgdQs_h4 with Reich himself performing; https://www.youtube.com/watch?v=lzkOFJMI5i8 with an animated score to follow; and a third clip featuring a university ensemble: https://www.youtube.com/watch?v=FcFyl8amoEE

[4] https://www.youtube.com/watch?v=laSqUtxV6Kk

[5] An impressive variant of Reich's piece can be viewed that is performed with colour-coded tennis balls: https://www.youtube.com/watch?v=dXhBti625_s

two rhythmically equal parts: the sound-making clap and the silent unclap. Students will notice that this brings about both audible and visual coordination that tightens up the presentation of rhythm.

The next stage is to capture a sound within the 'unclap' phase of the cycle. This can be modelled by reminding participants of the children's game in which two players bring their fingertips together and one tries to slap the back of the hand of the other before it can be withdrawn. Can one play this game on one's own? The element of surprise is, of course, missing, but the idea that a sound can be made immediately from this central, touching position proves useful. If the 'unclap' can be replaced by a clap in this central position just as the hands part, it provides a different sound and a sense of the larger cycle being preserved. Stylistically, this opens up several possibilities, as shown in Figure 1.1.

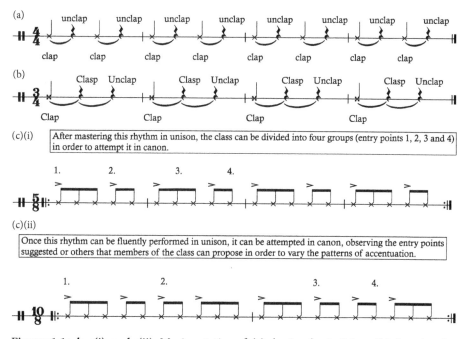

Figures 1.1a, b, c(i), and c(ii) Music notation of: (a) clap/unclap in 2 time; (b) clap, clasp/unclap in 3 time; (c) Greek rhythms (i) and (ii) based on 5- and 10-beat cycles, and the capacity to perform these in canon.

The examples in Figure 1.1 proceed from the simple to the complex, and the canonic potential (as in the Reich piece) of combining these rhythms polyphonically will best be attempted when students have mastered the routines we turn to next.

Game D—Dialogue Clapping (in pairs)

Just as Reich's *Clapping Music* can be performed either by two soloists or by a larger ensemble, we can develop rhythmic skills by working in pairs and then transferring what has been achieved to whole-class performance in a variety of ways. The skills modelled here are those of independence: the foundations of polyphony in which different streams of music are combined.

Students should be paired off and should first practise clapping alternately in a tight and sustainable manner. This can also be replicated in two groups across a whole class. But achieving it in solo pairs develops the interdependence on which coordinated music-making relies. All students should then learn the two-measure rhythm shown in Figure 1.2.

Figure 1.2 Musical example of rhythm with alternating straight and syncopated measures.

From this initial illustration of rhythmic alternation in pair-work, a number of variants could be introduced that present new challenges (Figure 1.3).

Figures 1.3a, b, and c Further musical examples of rhythms that develop pair interaction and class polyphonic performance: (a) a syncopated motto from Tchaikovsky's Sixth Symphony; (b) a round based on duple division in 4/4; (c) a round exploring the properties of 12/8 time.

du - gu   du - gu   du - gu   du - gu   du - gu   du - gu   du - gu   du - gu

du - gu - du du - gu - du du - gu - du du - gu - du   du - gu - du du - gu - du du - gu - du du - gu - du

Du - gu - du du - gu   Du - gu du - gu - du   Du - gu - du du - gu   Du - gu du - gu - du   Du - gu - du du - gu

Du - gu - du du - gu   Du - gu du - gu - du   Du - gu du - gu - du   Du - gu - du du - gu   Du - gu du - gu - du Du!

Du - gu - du du - gu du - gu   Du - gu du - gu - du du - gu   Du - gu du - gu du - gu - du   Du - gu - du du - gu du - gu

Du - gu du - gu du - gu - du   Du - gu du - gu - du du - gu   Du - gu - du du - gu du - gu   Du!

Figures 1.4(a), (b), and (c) Music notation of brain-gym 'tonguing' routines.

This section is titled 'Why Singing?' and yet we appear to have delayed working with the voice itself, but this need not be so. In all of the exercises presented so far, vocalised syllables such as 'pah' can replace clapping. The alternation represented by 'clap/unclap' can be replaced with 'doo-bee'. The vital importance of working first with rhythmic organisation will prove effective in developing confidence and fluency that will benefit the unison and polyphonic singing activities to come.

For more advanced musicians, rhythmic vocalisation can be taken a great deal further. Influenced by the vocal means by which percussion rhythm (*taal*) is taught in North Indian music,[6] and also by the tonguing patterns by which wind and brass players achieve articulation in fast passages, the sequence of vocalised rhythms in Figure 1.4 is presented as a brain gym for developing the kinds of skill introduced with clapping.

---

[6] https://www.youtube.com/watch?v=TXS6UByE_y8

2

The Anatomy of Human Music-Making

The principal anatomical influences on human capacity for music are the consequences of upright posture (Changizi 2013). Our bipedal gait confers an alternating rhythm that defines our sense of how time passes from the moment we stand and learn to walk as children. Later, we vary this through running, marching, hopping, skipping, and galloping, as well as acquiring mastery of the steps of various dances and their relationship to the music associated with them, such as a minuet, rumba, waltz, polka, twist, tango, or cha-cha. Irish dancing focuses almost exclusively on the rhythms of the feet and their audible consequences. But our upright posture leaves our hands free to do other things, including

- hunting, gathering, carrying food or infants as 'work';
- clapping, clicking, patting the thighs or buttocks as 'play';
- playing on a variety of found objects or crafted instruments (Espi-Sanchis & Bannan 2012); or
- in the expressive arm and hand movements of dance.

The pipe organist and kit drummer use all four limbs to produce independent streams of sound that interact to maximise the control of complex textures.

Upright posture has also conferred a specialised arrangement of the respiratory tract and aural system (Morley 2013; Bannan 2003). Among the attributes on which music-making depends are: voluntary breathing; binaural hearing that permits us to mix the sounds we make with those of other participants; a capacity to vary the dynamics and timbre of sustained pitches that leads to almost infinite acoustic productivity; sensitivity to the vocal sounds of others and the capacity for vocal learning through imitation and simultaneous engagement; and emotional response to facial expression and the characteristic sounds associated with it, which maps onto an innate understanding of the features of consonance and dissonance that relate to the phenomenon of the harmonic series. All of these properties of our human anatomy can be linked to the ways in which we make music, and how it affects us.

We can explore the effects of these evolved capacities on phonation in a variety of ways.

Breathing and Vocalisation

Game 1—Maintaining the Group Sound

Every participant sings for as long as possible on a single breath, and then takes a breath as quickly and unnoticeably as possible to sustain their contribution to the overall sound. This can be done in unison but it does not have to be. Students can select their own pitches. Over time, and according to age and experience, this exercise can be employed to improve posture and breathing, aiming to make the latter as effective as possible. Good posture and diaphragmatic breathing should be modelled from time to time in order to illustrate how they permit optimum and relaxed control of the voice.[1] One possibility, if carefully handled, is to encourage participants to time the duration of the longest note participants can sing and keep a record of it. Performance should improve as participants develop the muscles involved. This exercise also teaches participants to connect listening to themselves (in order to sustain the pitch they are singing) to feeling the sensation of resonance and its relationship to breath management.

Game 2—Sustaining While Varying Loudness

This activity builds on Game 1. Starting with notes of manageable length, the pitch is sustained commencing as quietly as possible, loudening to a central point in the overall duration, and returning in a gradual manner to quiet. As students master this, the duration can be increased. A judgement may be made about whether it would be safe to increase the volume of the central target moment. Teachers will need to consider whether all participants are ready for this. It is vital that the relationship between maintaining the exact same pitch and doing so while getting louder or softer is not decoupled.

Game 3—Working on Effective Breathing Over Measured Phases

This activity systematically develops the connection between action and perception involved in Games 1 and 2. The teacher (or, eventually, a student leader) proposes the lengths of time that participants will spend on the in-breath and out-breath (singing), respectively. The idea is to promote relaxed phonation initially by providing plenty of time to breathe and gradually cutting down on this while at the same time increasing the length of the sung note.[2] Each stage can be repeated to make transitions gradual and to build confidence and efficiency. The following chart captures this arrangement:

In-breath	Sung notes
4 beats	4 beats
4 beats	6 beats
4 beats	8 beats
3 beats	8 beats
2 beats	8 beats
2 beats	10 beats
1 beat	10 beats
1 beat	12 beats
Instant breath	12 beats

[1] When appropriate, similar exercises can be developed for players of woodwind and brass instruments.
[2] This can be a unison, a chord, or a cluster, depending on how this activity meshes with other aspects of learning.

Further Rhythmic Coordination Activities

Before focusing on other aspects of vocal development, it pays to have available some further games and warm-ups that develop collective coordination arising from individual creativity. As before, these involve hands, feet, and other body percussion, and accustom participants to close, multimodal interaction that will benefit the transfer of these values and skills to vocalised activities in which instant responses will be vital.

Game 4—Egyptian Clapping

Participants stand in a circle, moving closely together so that they can raise their hands and place them palm-to-palm with each of their immediate neighbours, as in the Ancient Egyptian wall paintings that give this activity its name. The leader sets a manageable tempo with a finger-click. As in Game 1, a clap is passed in strict time, once per beat, around the circle—either clockwise or anticlockwise. But this time, the clap is shared between each successive pair of participants, the right hand of one clapping on the left of the next if proceeding anticlockwise, and the opposite for clockwise. Once everyone is comfortable with this, the 'message' to be passed around can be varied:

(a) According to the overall size of the group, several messages can be sent around 3 to 4 beats apart. Participants need to use both their eyes and their ears to ensure that they are always ready to transmit the next message.

(b) Once this has been achieved, slightly different messages can be sent that require more careful fitting in. It is best to practise these one at a time. Two common variants would be (i) a double-clap that comprises 2 precise half beats; (ii) a single clap on the half beat between the clicks.

(c) When all of these variants can be transmitted successfully, the leader can mix up the messages, so that a more complex overall result is heard that participants can maintain as it winds its way around the circle.

Game 5—Egyptian Stamping

This activity proceeds similarly to Egyptian Clapping, except that the paired response to the beat is carried out through stamping the feet in precise unison. This leaves the hands ready for other things.

If proceeding anticlockwise, Participant 1 raises their right foot as a signal to the person on their right to do the same with their left foot. They stamp at the same time, according to a pulse provided by the leader. Participant 2 (right foot) then stamps in unison with Participant 3 (left foot), and so on. This will probably need to be done at a slower tempo than Game 4 because bigger muscle groups are in action and coordination depends on visual cueing rather than touch. But once it is going well, an increase in tempo should be possible. As with Game 4, several simultaneously stamped 'messages' can travel around the circle separated by 3 to 4 beats.

The next stage is to place a different stream of sound in the free hands; one that that falls between the regular pulses of the shared stamping. The simplest additional element is a half-beat clap that splits the pulse precisely, so that each participant enacts <stamp-clap-stamp> in a chain reaction. When and if the students are ready, they can place two claps between the beats in a triplet pattern, so that the contribution of each is <stamp-clap-clap-stamp>. More advanced students may be able to cope with alternating duplets and triplets against the pulse, or even add further rhythmic variants that the whole group is capable of performing.

Game 6—Body-Percussion Fugues and Concerti

The intention now is to develop a routine out of elements of participants' own invention. This also initiates the establishment of a pattern for relating individual effort over a series of steps to whole-class response (1- 2- 4 - 8 - tutti) that will figure regularly as a strategy for developing the skills of *Harmony Signing*:

(a)   Each student devises a 4-beat pattern that can make use of any safe body- percussion techniques, which may include rests, dotted rhythms, duplets, and triplets. Anything is permitted as long as it can be replicated and fits precisely into 4 beats. They rehearse their 'solo' until it is ready.

(b)   They work next in pairs, teaching their solos to each other so that they can perform both of their inventions in perfect rhythmic unison.

(c)   They aggregate their two synchronised solos into a single 8-beat pattern that they practise performing in its entirety.

(d)   They then form groups of four (formed of two existing pairs). The pairs stand face-to-face to make up a square and combine their 8-beat patterns into a polyphonic texture.

(e)   They then form groups of eight, again rehearsing the resulting more complex texture.

(f)   The work achieved so far is then assembled into an organised whole (a *collage*). This can be planned through the use of a diagram written on a board to which students can contribute. The two most common principles for doing this are:

  (i)   Fugue: material is laid out in overlapping sequences of greater or lesser density, starting with one pair and adding or subtracting the entry of other staggered contributions.

  (ii)   Concerto: a terraced outline of different material is devised around the sequence of 8-bar routines, mixing up solo, duet, group, and tutti elements.

There are several other warm-up strategies that make use of initial Steps (a), (b), or (c), diverging into alternative treatments. For instance, a separate tutti can be devised and learned that has characteristics of its own that are different to what students have devised. This presents greater contrasts with solo and duet material. A signal can be used to control loud and quiet presentations of material to add a different means of contrast.

Another possibility is to alternate tuttis with solo improvisations. Once this has been achieved a call-and-response effect is introduced in which solo improvisations are immediately copied by the whole class. All of these practices contribute to building experience of organising the seed musical material into coherent continuous structures in a manner that reflects a variety of genres of both composed and improvised musics from different world cultures.

3

The Instinctive and the Learned

The parallel research projects that link the development of *Harmony Signing* to investigations into human musicality from the perspective of evolutionary psychology have prompted a quest for pedagogical practices that elicit instinctive responses. This is where the preceding rhythmic warm-ups are essential: They require instant responses if rhythmic continuity is to be maintained. Students who acquire a sense of trust of their nonverbal thinking, and a capacity to process within the medium of music rather than translating experiences into words, will avoid the hesitations and uncertainties that interfere with musical engagement. Building this way of thinking and behaving continues as we make the transition into vocal-gestural associations that will lead us into *Harmony Signing*. Activities involve individuals undergoing experiences for themselves, including expressing themselves to partners and leading groups. Students also become accustomed to making choices and discriminating according to acquired preferences that are consistent with personal creativity. In this respect, learning to feel and to value emotional responses to material is of equal importance to understanding theoretical concepts enshrined in tradition; or, rather, it represents an alternative pathway, shaped by the trial-and-error of individual experience, towards engagement with the existing framework of musical theory and the repertoire it explains.

The following activities include games that can be played by primary children and returned to by older and more musically sophisticated students.

Game 7—Up and Down in Unison

This can first be modelled with a whole group to establish the connection between sound and gesture that it involves. The teacher (or a student leader) stands with both arms horizontally stretched out from the shoulder. This position represents a comfortable note in their mid-range. The group copies both the gesture and the pitch it represents.[1] From this point, the leader signals changes in pitch through upward or downward movement of the arms. It is vital to (a) begin with small, manageable steps that fall within the range of other participants; and (b) achieve this with the smoothest possible *legato*. This promotes a secure sense of tuning together that develops a feeling for intervals and, innately, tonality. The latter will be revealed as we build on this first step.

Once this principle of connecting the visible and felt gesture to the sound has been established, the next step is to split into pairs so that students can focus on developing their skills through a trustful exploratory understanding with a partner. It is vital to

---

[1] Where some students may not yet have mastered matching pitch with others, this activity can contribute to them learning to do so. Further advice on this is provided in Chapter 7, 'Lifelong Participation and Transmission'.

put across the collaborative intention of this task: competition, such as catching one's partner out, is counterproductive. Equally, it is important to request that no-one talk until the activity is completed. What one is setting out to elicit is an exclusive focus on quality of sound and acute listening. Talking is disruptive because it causes a cessation of this focus, which can be inhibiting to others.

The interesting thing that emerges as pairs pursue this activity successfully is that the group as a whole will begin to achieve a semblance of tonality. While standing face to face in order to concentrate on their partners, students will inevitably overhear the performance of other pairs. Unconsciously, they will tend to come into tonal alignment: a further example of instinct at work. Once this begins to happen, it can be instructive to permit a proportion of the class, by turn, to stop and listen to the others. If they also notice this innate tonal organisation, it will play a part in the way they engage with *Harmony Signing* when it is employed intentionally to investigate tonality.

Game 8—Playing With Dynamics and Durations

This activity relates sound to gesture in a different way. It is useful in that it allows every individual to experience leading the group, in order to provide an opportunity to develop their confidence in this role. Working at first with the whole group, a leader initiates a vocal sound. This can be either staccato, signed with a short downward stroke of the hand like the pecking of a bird (to which participants respond together with a very short, pitched vowel sound); or legato, signed with an open hand, palm upwards, with a gesture moving slowly in space to convey continuity (the response to this will be a sustained vowel). Using both hands, these two gestures represent qualities of dynamic volume. With the hands close together, the resultant sound is soft (*piano*). As the hands move apart, the volume rises to *forte*. Performers can choose the pitch at which to sing their staccato and legato contributions and once this decision is made they should stick with the same pitch whatever the leader requires of them.

Once the leader feels sufficiently confident with what has been achieved so far, the option can be taken of dividing the class into two equal groups, left and right. Gestures are now addressed through orientation to one group or the other, allied to using the two hands separately. Volume can now be signed through movement towards or away from the central line of the body. The consequence is that different elements can be combined, offering the first opportunity for leaders to operate in terms of what one will later think of as orchestration. Indeed, this activity can reappear at more advanced levels as an excellent warm-up activity for instrumental ensembles, or as a means of providing initial experience to those directing them for the first time.

Game 9—The Animal Imitation Game

This activity is designed to build musical memory through releasing vocal creativity. A little initial discussion will benefit what occurs next. Participants should understand that the purpose is to imitate the actual sound that animals make (including imaginary and fabulous ones), rather than falling back on linguistic expressions such as 'woof', 'neigh', or 'cockadoodle-doo'. Trying out a few suggestions will confirm this.

The game works on call-and-response lines, but with the additional structural element that all material remains in play. So, whoever volunteers to go first (*1*) makes an animal sound of their choice that is immediately copied as accurately as possible by the whole class (*1: 1¹*). Volunteer (*2*) contributes a different sound, which is then also copied accurately by everyone (*2: 2¹*). Next, the whole sequence available so far is recapped: (*1: 1¹: 2: 2¹*). A third volunteer offers a sound (*3: 3¹*), leading to the aggregate (*1: 1¹: 2: 2¹: 3: 3¹*). This has the benefit of keeping the whole class alert and acquiring experience of one possible way of constructing a composition. As the piece grows, volunteers have to rack their brains to find new animals and the class has to remember an ever-growing sequence. This is where a leader can help, guiding the group in recalling the order of individual solos (through pointing to their originators) and the *tutti* (a two-handed downbeat that confirms that everyone copies the previous sound). I have achieved continuous improvised performances on these lines with classes of well over twenty students who rarely have struggled with this activity. Students rapidly learn how to take on the leadership role.

In terms of outcome, the true value of this game is the variety of range, loudness, timbre, and duration that volunteers offer to represent the animal of their choice. Because they are imitating each other, rather than an adult or the sound of an instrument, they tend to identify with the activity and to unconsciously overcome limitations of range that traditional singing may not address. Similarly, this game can contribute to the release of inhibition and the motivation to respond, which can help to unlock the habitual vocal profile of those who find it difficult to match pitch.

Game 10—The Factory Game

This game has many of the properties of Game 9. It calls on the imagination of participants, elicits vocalisation that can unlock limitations, and links sound to gesture. In addition, this is a movement game with a narrative outcome of sorts.

Volunteer 1 enters a clear space removed from where the class is standing or sitting. He or she adopts a central position and a posture of their choice, making a regular sound that they repeat in association with a physical movement that depicts their role in a machine around which other participants will build. Volunteer 2 next enters the space and places themselves in a form of relationship to what volunteer 1 is doing physically, and commences a different sound and gesture that represents what their complementary part of the machine does. The machine goes on building, physically and acoustically, in this way as each new participant joins in. On a signal, when everyone has made their contribution and the machine is in full operation, participants disengage from their position and movement, while carefully continuing to coordinate their vocal contributions. They slowly move into a choir formation. A leader can then direct how the machine performs: signing crescendos and diminuendos; slowing down and speeding up; cutting off to silence and starting again; and so on. When this has been completed, everyone can rest, at which point the question can be posed: 'What does this machine produce, and what did your part do?'

Game 11—The Unison-Finding Game

This game also links inner hearing to acute listening, controlled performance, and aural analysis. First, every singer imagines a pitch of their choice—high, medium, or low—in which they hear their own voice in their aural memory. On a signal from a leader, they commence singing this pitch, matching what they imagined.[2] This texture is sustained for several seconds so participants can transfer their listening to the blend between their own note and the notes of everyone else. If they need to breathe, they do so as unnoticeably as possible, returning to the same pitch (see Game 1). On a second signal, they commence the process of responding to what they hear so they converge on a group unison by the smallest move(s) possible. This may involve sustaining the pitch they started on if this represents to them a core of the overall sound. Or they may move a step up or down in search of agreeing with others in the room, continuing this until everyone is performing a unison or octave unison. This is sustained for a few seconds to confirm its achievement. After a brief pause, the process can begin again.

This game deals with pitch discrimination at the basic level of 'same/different'. As such, it embraces controlled trial and error as the means of developing the ability to sort dissonance from consonance. The more fine-grained discrimination of precise intervals and functions can be built upon this initial experience. Where students possess the level of aural analysis required, this game can also be played instrumentally.

Game 12—Up and Down in Free Combination

This game builds on the routine involved in Game 7 but liberates the paired singers from having to perform in unison. It helps to develop the skill of 'holding a part'. Participants sing notes of different pitch with confidence and begin to acquire experience of voice-leading and the consequent intervals that make up music in two parts. It can be modelled with the whole class using the procedure of Game 7, but with two leaders, each signing an independent part to half the class. The two leaders execute interacting patterns that develop polyphonic strategies such as:

- 'You move while I sustain'.
- 'Your turn to sustain while I move'.
- 'Let's move in parallel for a while'.
- 'Let's move in contrary motion'.

Needless to say, these instructions can sufficiently be achieved through the gestures themselves. Students should not use language.

Once students are familiar with these strategies, a more effective level of creative exploration can develop from their working in pairs, shaping agreed consequences that can be rehearsed as short compositions.[3] The full consequences of this will

---

[2] We will in due course investigate and elaborate on this phenomenon of matching notes inwardly heard.
[3] As in Game 7, the tendency will be for the activities of the class as a whole to converge on a clear tonal centre. It may prove instructive to illustrate this.

be encountered when we deal with the introduction of species counterpoint in Chapter 14, 'Working in Pairs'. The tendency to sing in tune with one another is an outcome one might trace to an innate response to the properties of the harmonic series (see Chapter 6, 'The Four Elements of Vocal Learning'). This instinctive achievement of blend and tuning will often result when students' experience of singing in two parts emerges from listening to one another, rather than basing their performance on responding to an external sound-source such as the piano or attempting to reconstruct existing music in two parts from notation.

4

Music as 'The Missing Link'

A Distinct Form of Thinking and Feeling

What kind of thinking does music require? Gardner (1983) advocated its distinctness as a form of intelligence in comparison with language, spatial reasoning, and mathematics, though it clearly shares properties and the potential for combination with each of these. Similarly, it relates to social intelligence—the way we infer the state of mind of others—and to bodily intelligence—our capacity for embodied memory that governs the memorisation of movement, whether the choreography of the dancer or the fingerings involved in playing the piano or most other instruments. The interdependence of aspects of music-making with so many other forms of physical and psychological process (both cognitive and emotional) is consistent with the proposal that music-making is far older than language and contributed to the development of the faculties of sound analysis and production on which language depends. This is certainly a view taken by researchers and commentators as varied as Rameau, Rousseau, von Humboldt, Darwin, Helmholtz, Nietszche, Sachs, and Jesperson (see Bannan 1997, 2012a, 2019), leading to the debate of the last forty years or so that has brought attempts at the resolution of this issue to the forefront of speculation about the roles of genetics and culture in human evolution. It presents a solution to what communication theory represents as an equivalent to the 'missing link' in palaeontology as in Bickerton's (1991) definition of the *continuity paradox*, whereby a species that has achieved language is, as a consequence, unable to speculate on the condition of not possessing language. But if a form of musical behavior—what Mithen (2005) refers to as *hmmmm* (a system that is 'holistic, manipulative, multi-modal, musical and mimetic'[1]) represented the state of human representation and communication prior to the subsequent development of grammar, syntax and vocabulary, then we need to recognise that its equivalent still exists as a complementary system today. All humans have both music and language (Harvey 2017).

Can musical engagement in our own time provide evidence that music may have played this evolutionary role? We cannot carry out scientific thought in the medium of song, let alone the drum circle or string quartet. Music as a communicative system serves a different purpose to speech. But we can observe some interesting phenomena that contribute to our case. Children in the womb and immediately after birth respond to both language and music as if they were both music; to continuities and their interruption, to prosody of contour, to overall range (especially the difference between male and female sources), and to dynamics (both specific volume levels and changes between them; Bannan & Woodward 2009). Language is subsequently acquired on these

---

[1] Note the way these descriptors map onto the intelligences of Gardner's 1983 model.

musical foundations. Sensitivity to music retains an emotional and discriminatory dependence on assigning meaning to these elements, both in perception—the effects that listening to music has on all of us—and in production—the extent to which how we perform conveys intentions. These factors can be practised and developed, but their basis is in the instinctive properties of how we analyse and respond to sound. Many of these instincts are shared with a variety of other species that both respond to sound signals and that communicate in a manner that exploits this in others (Scherer 1992; Taylor 2008). Within the human life cycle, the resilience of the neural network for music is remarkable, surviving a variety of conditions that attack other aspects of the brain. The capacity of patients with Alzheimer's disease to continue to sing even when they have lost the capacity for speech, and also to regain elements of language through the medium of song, suggests that the substrates of the brain responsible for music are robust and ancient (Bannan & Montgomery-Smith 2008).

In this chapter, we take an aspect of human vocal ability that one could propose transcends Bickerton's continuity paradox and employ it in practice as the basis for developing specifically musical skills that also illustrate the formation of the prerequisites for language.

Facial Expression and Timbre

Charles Darwin (1872) wrote perceptively about the relationship between facial expression and aural communication. The following exercises explore this relationship as a basis for representing and communicating emotion.

Participants are requested to make a facial expression intended to convey a specific emotion that can be visually discerned by others. They might like to think about this and practise a few distinct responses in front of a mirror at home (or take a selfie for easy reference). In class, they exchange these expressions with partners who then respond with how they 'read' them (a group leader could keep a list for later discussion). Usually, *fear* and *anger* are clear, with *joy/happiness*, possibly *sympathy* ('soothingness'), and maybe *disgust*. *Sadness* and *trust* ('approval') may also be evident, though they may appear as intermediary steps between a neutral expression and *fear* or *joy* respectively (Plutchik 1980). What about *anticipation* or *surprise*? It pays to discuss how these expressions are generated with different facial muscles—around the jaw and lips, certainly, but also the eyes, eyebrows, and forehead. Do the participants feel anything elsewhere—in the throat or tongue, or on the skin of their arms or back? Indeed, an initial discussion of these factors can be significant in understanding where activities such as this can have long-term effects on how students can draw on emotions when conceiving or rehearsing music. How did they elicit the emotional states when practising them? If they used memory or experience in this, did they re-live ('actually feel') the emotion when doing so?[2] And did this occur again when they shared them in class? How about the rest of the body? What posture, stance, hand gestures, or orientation also convey our

---

[2] This can remain a theme in thinking about the effects of music, especially when developing compositional skills. Do we need to feel sad to write or perform a sad song? Why do we enjoy (elicit eventual happiness) performing sad music?

emotional state? How much do we agree on our perception of the expressions of others, and might these reflect cultural conventions or are they universals that represent a deep connection with our evolutionary origins (Ekman 1973)?

The next stage is to make a vocal sound intended to complement each expression. When the face is set to convey *anger*, how does that make us sound? What about the other emotions: joy, trust, fear, sympathy, surprise, anticipation?

A vocabulary of sounds is agreed upon to represent each emotional state. This can be rehearsed as a preparation for employment in performance. Just as in previous games we have practised matching pitch, duration, and volume as aspects of contrast achievable with our voices, we can now add *timbre*. Can we make each of these sounds so similar that the aggregate prevents us from discriminating the contribution of any individual voice?

A variety of options is now open to us to explore technically, creatively, or both:

- Working in pairs, devise 'bridges' that, over some ten seconds, represent a means of turning one sound into another (e.g., *fear* to *joy* or *disgust* to *soothing*.
- Working in pairs, consider ways of presenting two emotions simultaneously. With which emotions/sounds is it possible to achieve this? What does the listener notice? What new feelings about the production of one's voice might this give rise to?
- Working in groups of four, devise a vocal composition on the lines of Game 8, adding this new element of selection and variation of timbre to the procedures available (in addition to duration, volume, range, and changes between them).

The singing teacher Lucie Manén (1974) based her technique for shaping the resonance and healthy production of her students' voices on just such processes:

> Singing is the artistic expression of human emotion in sound. The expression of emotion is a reaction to internal and external stimuli in which the whole system participates: facial expression, gesture and attitude and vocal exclamations, together with heartbeat and breathing, reflecting the internal state of the individual. These reactions occur as reflexes. From the sensory organs—eyes and ears—impulses are carried via the nerves to the muscles which produce attitudes and gestures, to the muscles controlling facial expression, to the muscles of the larynx governing exclamations, to the centre of breathing and to the centres controlling the heartbeat. Chemical substances are poured into the bloodstream to supply the system with all those resources on which the human being unconsciously calls in any given state of emotion, be it hatred, love, joy or pain, fear or aggression. (p. 11)

In terms of the voice development of nonspecialist singers and children, these emotional motivations and their combinations can, under controlled conditions, elicit a range of resonances that, when harnessed to good posture and breathing technique, will help develop vocal range and projection. Some of these can be transferred to instruments in a variety of ways to enhance articulation and modify tone-colour. Once the phenomenon of *timbre* has begun to be systematically explored and discriminated, it becomes a valuable tool for selecting instrumentation and expressive articulation that can be shaped in the musical imagination.

The mechanism by which this can be explained is of great significance to the development of sensitivity to consonance and dissonance that *Harmony Signing* adopts and extends. This is the harmonic series, the set of whole-number ratios that govern the transmission of vibration and, therefore, how sounds are carried to our ears. The harmonic series shaped mammalian hearing millions of years ago and remains the basis of the way we discriminate between sounds according to their character—harsh or charming, soothing or surprising. Changizi (2013) associates this with the survival value of analytical hearing which alerts us to fight or flight responses that could save our lives, or discriminates unthreatening stimuli that permit us to save energy and relax.

Manén (1974) connects these features of the discrimination of timbre to the productive properties of facial and emotional expression:

> In any . . . state of emotion the exclamation of the human voice follows laws common to human beings of all races. For describing events with little emotional content and in a neutral mood, the human voice uses exclamations in its lower range. As soon as the individual changes the emphasis of what he speaks or sings, the pitch of the voice changes. It rises with increasing emotional content. For the expression of pleasure the natural exclamation is 'ah'. The exclamation 'ee' denotes disgust and hatred, while 'oo' denotes fear and horror. (p. 11)

As preparation for the vocal needs of *Harmony Signing*, as well as the acuteness of listening on which the confidence of participants will depend, and the unselfconsciousness of those providing gestural leadership, activities based on the properties of Manén's analysis will extend many of the skills introduced in Games 1 through 12. Further improvisational and compositional strategies could explore the difference between the alarming and the soothing and how these can be expressed in musical structure. They might give rise to two distinct kinds of music. But what if, as in the exercise described in this chapter, a bridge that transformed one into the other were to be devised? Or a piece that combined them at the same time?

A fascination for the qualities of sound and gesture that permit these features to be conveyed with conviction in performance is central to what is learned here. Through learning to express emotion as drama students and dancers do, with all the risks this can entail of 'dropping one's guard' and requiring oneself to transcend everyday behaviour, a further step is taken towards becoming a more creative and confident musician.

5

The Aural Feedback Loop and Inner Hearing

The activities and explanations encountered in the previous section illustrate the evolved relationship between perception and production on which a communication system depends—whether language, music, or gesture. Visual and sensorimotor perception records and analyses movement. For most people and in most cases, music is transmitted to the aural system. Through listening while we perform, we monitor our own acoustic production, mixing and blending what we achieve with the performance of others in duet, group performance, or larger ensembles.

Memory permits us to reconstruct sounds and their significance in the absence of their being presented 'live'. This has clearly played a part in music-making since it first entered the repertoire of human behaviour. It is a skill whose development we can take for granted. But, as with improving our language skills through learning new words and polishing our grammar, it benefits from systematic attention, not least because the phenomenon is central to the aural aspect of music education, which many students find daunting.

In further exploring the development of our voices, we can employ them as templates through which to consciously track the encoding and retrieval of musical memories in a manner that will benefit both vocal performance itself and the acuity of our aural discrimination. We can enhance our understanding of this process through considering initially how we match vocal response to a presented musical stimulus. Some students and adults find it difficult to do this accurately when copying a piano pitch but are more secure responding to other voices. When working with young children, one encounters those who find it difficult to respond to a voice that is in a different octave to their own (e.g., mimicking the performance of an adult male), while for others this seems natural. Some adolescent boys can be confused when responding to the voices of adult female teachers with voices an octave higher than their own. All of these cases can be remedied by being sensitive to the fact that a link needs to be established between what participants hear in others and in their own performance that has yet to be fully explored and consolidated.

As an example, I teach the technique *Whistle/sing* in which participants whistle a distinct pitch and then sing a note at the same pitch in a register comfortable to them. The actual result of doing this may well be two pitches an octave or even two octaves apart. I first devised this as a kind of brain-gym exercise to develop listening habits and fast technical responses. I was surprised to discover that some experienced musicians with secure reading skills could find this very difficult to do. One student would sing a note a fifth below his whistled pitch. This was a fascinating problem to overcome, stressing as it did that we listen for congruence (a perfect fifth is the closest interval to the octave in terms of consonance and quality) and, as in some kind of aural illusion, we can be confused by these properties. A combination of techniques—listening to fifths and octaves on the piano, singing them melodically, and discerning them in the harmonic series of the singer's own voice (see Chapter 6, fig. 6.5)—reorientated the relationship between perception and production and resolved the issue.

Similarly, when employing my adult baritone to teach young children, I have found some who associate mimicking me with the attempt to sing lower than they need to. They are responding to the timbre rather than the pitch contour of what I present. The solution here is simple. I employ one of their peers who has established a secure connection to act as the model instead of me. Once participants become used to singing well in unison with each other, a permanent solution emerges. The opposite problem has existed in several cases I have dealt with of male university students who have had musical *puberphonia*. While their adult speaking voice may have been located (though in limited cases this has required some remedial help as well), they always sang in falsetto. In all cases, this was traceable to their having been taught aural and theory by female secondary school teachers. Again, it takes just a few minutes to help male students to locate their adult singing voices.[1] Techniques include (1) asking them to speak slowly to find and match the pitch they are phonating (counting backwards from 10 is a handy task for this; see Williams 2013) and (2) using a combination of piano illustration to reference their range and my own voice as a model to get them to sustain this focal pitch. As soon as they are confident doing so, one can glide upwards and downwards through semitone and whole-tone steps and commence the exploration of pitch around this focal point. Next, one extends the focal points themselves, performing three- or four-note scales, to provide a musical means of employing this newly discovered instrument. I have found that voices 'liberated' in this way can acquire a two-octave range in a matter of weeks.[2] This is by no means limited to the state of the adolescent male voice. I have frequently encountered girls whose vocal confidence benefited from the application of similar methods in overcoming factors that limited range and self-expression.

These instances of the need to coach students in how to use their voices illustrate the extent to which vocalisation provides evidence of what is in a student's head. Recognition of this plays an important role in the strategies to develop inner hearing that we deal with next.

When dealing with musical information to which we can affix labels such as 'plagal cadence', 'perfect fourth', or 'dominant minor ninth', how do we know that students can hear these phenomena in their heads? Even if they can reproduce them on a keyboard, this does not necessarily provide evidence of the kind of inner hearing we need them to develop. They may have learned how to locate the notes or provide the fingerings that achieve the effect. When we previously considered the evolutionary links and interdependent adaptations which relate (aural) perception to (vocal) production, we recognized that they shaped what we are capable of as a species and therefore permitted the emergence of music, language, and other communicative skills. We need to find

---

[1] This is by no means to suggest intolerance of the counter-tenor range and its means of voice production as a viable performing option. But students need to have an open choice as to how to sing effectively in relation to opportunities available and the usefulness of the activity to other aspects of musical learning.
[2] Interestingly, this rapid development can occur precisely because the student has not already got used to the sound in music of their modal voice and has fewer prejudices regarding what it should be capable of. It is not the ideal position for young men—far better that they undergo voice maturation from being confident trebles towards their adult potential over the ages of 10 to 15 under informed adult guidance.

ways of consolidating this instinctive relationship, exploiting it to ensure that musicality is encoded in students' responses as accurately, securely, confidently, and quickly as possible. Unfortunately, it seems that a combination of waning confidence in their abilities and interrupted habits of concentration can undermine the aural performance of some students as they progress over time. Most music teachers have supported individuals who play with technical precision and expressivity but fail or fear aural and theory assessments. In this context, prevention is undoubtedly better than cure: one has to start young. So, some of the remedies for older students facing difficulties will involve returning to simple game-playing that lays down procedures on which they can rebuild their approach.

The first step in reconstructing and extending students' confidence so they can effectively engage with practices intended to improve their aural capacities is to work on their sense of what this entails as a life decision. This has nothing to do with taking tests and winning marks, and everything to do with approaching musical experience with curiosity and openness to self-motivated learning by reflection, including a constructive approach to trial and error. Aural practice needs to be welcomed into the instrumental practice schedule, both as an element that requires time to be devoted to it and as a means of interfacing with technical and repertoire practice to benefit instrumental skills. Several of the strategies proposed in this chapter need to be engaged regularly and for short but focused periods of time: a minute here, a few seconds there. This will promote progress through experiencing music as a mother tongue, rather than aural skills being treated as something separate from practice and set aside for dealing with only when assessment looms. Practice habits, in addition to singing for its own sake, will exploit interaction with performance on students' personal instrument, singing instrumental passages and employing the instrument to act as a template or as a checking procedure for the practise of vocal material.

A Sequence of Musical Tasks

The teacher can introduce a sequence of tasks that can be modified and developed over time. Once students begin to discern the benefits of these tasks, they can take responsibility for varying and extending them to meet their identified needs.

Task 1

Imagine a note, focusing on a constructed memory based on hearing it in the mind's ear performed as successfully as possible. Sing the note, aiming to match the pitch previously imagined. Reflect on the success of doing so. Did the pitch appear to match?[3] Did the process lead to a satisfactory vocal performance?

---

[3] No-one else will ever know!

Task 2

Repeat Task 1. Then find on your instrument the pitch at which you believe you sang. Check this by alternating playing and singing.

Task 3

Imagine a note a semitone higher than the pitch in Task 2 and imagine yourself performing it as well as possible. Sing it. Then check this by playing the new note (a semitone higher than Task 2) on your instrument.

Task 4

Imagine alternating the two notes that were employed in Tasks 2 and 3 a semitone apart. Sing a copy of this exercise. Then play the same sequence. Reflect on how accurately you are doing this.

Task 5

This commences building, step by step, towards performing the complete chromatic array that is captured in the following notated exercise (fig. 5.1). Transpose it if necessary, writing it out in notation so it suits your personal instrument.[4]

Figure 5.1 Music notation of ascending chromatic scale with accompaniment.

Take each pair of pitches in turn, going back to revise your ability to perform and discriminate between each of the expanding intervals encountered:

Minor second
Major second
Minor third
Major third

---

[4] Younger students can experiment just with the diatonic major in the most appropriate keys.

Perfect fourth
Augmented fourth/Diminished fifth (tritone)
Minor sixth
Major sixth
Minor seventh
Octave

This exercise is, at this point, about performing the material and building an aural template of each interval through both vocal and instrumental performance. We will later introduce strategies for more deeply experiencing and sorting the difference between intervals, placing them in context, and developing a subjective sense of their impact and potential through creative ploys (see Chapter 13, 'Working on Your Own').

An alternative way of consolidating this experience in the whole-class context is to work in two parts following a leader (teacher or student) who is employing both hands to convey intervals through Kodály hand signs. This exercise covers the entire 12-tone chromatic array. Both parts experience horizontal movement between the two notes that make up each interval and the vertical result, from both 'upper' and 'lower' aural perspectives. Each interval can be repeated several times in a continuous improvised sequence in which attention should be paid to tuning and the blend between the two streams of sound. Alternation of 'who moves first' helps keep participants focused.

RH: Doh – Di – Doh - - - - - - -	Doh - - - - - - - - Ray – Doh
LH: Doh - - - - - - - - - Di – Doh	Do – Ray – Doh - - - - - - -
Doh – Ma – Doh - - - - - - - - -	Doh - - - - - - - - Me – Doh
Doh - - - - - - - - - - - Ma – Doh	Doh – Me – Doh - - - - - - -
Doh – Fa – Doh - - - - - - - - -	Doh - - - - - - - - Fi – Doh
Doh - - - - - - - - - - - Fa – Doh	Doh – Fi – Doh - - - - - - -
Doh – Ma – Soh - - - - - - - - -	Doh - - - - - - - - Si – Doh
Doh - - - - - - - - - - - Soh – Doh	Doh – Si – Doh - - - - - - -
Doh – La – Doh - - - - - - - - -	Doh - - - - - - - - Ta – Doh
Doh - - - - - - - - - - - La – Doh	Doh – Ta – Doh - - - - - - -
Doh – Ti – Doh - - - - - - - - -	Doh - - - - - - - - Doh⁺ – Doh⁺
Doh - - - - - - - - - - - Ti – Doh	Doh – Doh⁺ – Doh⁺ - - - - - - -

Chart 5.1

Task 6

Working with intervals in this systematic way is one thing. Acquiring confidence in their aural discrimination is another. An effective addition to the practice routine to build towards this essential skill and achieve greater vocal flexibility is as follows: Randomly select an interval, play it on your instrument, repeat it vocally, and then check its performance on your instrument. This pattern <play—sing—play again> can be employed in a variety of circumstances, including scales, the first octave span of major and minor arpeggios, and short passages from the repertoire you are learning.

Task 7

As the saying goes, what goes up must come down. Fifty percent of music involves descending intervals, though many practice routines seem to ignore this with the result that students' handling of the tuning and discrimination of descending intervals is often much less confident and accurate than their ascending work (see fig. 5.2).

Figure 5.2 Music notation of descending chromatic scale with accompaniment.

Continue to apply all of the variants of Tasks 5 and 6, eventually randomising ascending and descending features so that each can be instrumentally performed and sung with fluency and immediacy.

Task 8

We now return to a different pathway out of Task 1, this time without employing an instrument (unless a keyboard is available and proves useful for checking). The purpose of these variants is to encourage imaginative inner hearing.

Imagine any pitch you like, as long as it can be heard in your inner ear, being played on a trumpet.[5] Try to hear it in your head playing a clear note *mf* for about six seconds. Next, imagine, one step at a time, this sequence of variants:

---

[5] It would perhaps be a good idea for trumpet players to select an instrument that they do not play, such as the violin or clarinet.

- The note starts quietly and crescendos to *ff*.
- The note rises a semitone and falls back to the original note.
- The note starts quietly, crescendos to *f*, rises a semitone, and diminuendos to *p*.
- The original note is joined by another note, also on the trumpet, a major third higher (it may help to imagine two players).
- Both notes together proceed through a crescendo from *p* to *ff* and a diminuendo back to *p*.
- Both notes, playing *mf*, rise at the same time a half step, and then fall again.
- The two notes are sounded as before, a major third apart. The two trumpets move in opposite directions, the top falling, the lower rising, crossing in contrary motion through a unison and ending up, having exchanged parts, performing the original major third.

The purpose of these kinds of instruction is to encourage the aural imagination. By definition, a teacher or third party cannot tell whether students succeed at these activities because they are silently enacted in students' heads. But even so, attempts at them will open up a new approach to thinking about aural development, removing it from the abstraction of virtual notes to be added to blank paper, and siting it more definitely in this imaginary version of hearing real notes in performance. Students will trust themselves on whether they carry out these tasks with adequate care and are able to discern consequences in their subsequent aural performance.

Task 9

Where Task 8 largely focused on opening up the inner hearing of pitch movement and intervals, one can also adopt these techniques to sharpen rhythmic processing. The material to be varied in the inner ear is the duration of notes and rests.

One can begin with a simple four-note melody of pitched notes of equal length in 4/4 time. This should play in the head to represent a retrievable memory. Then a variation with rhythmic consequences should be imagined. It could be the doubling of the length of one of the notes, replacing a note with silence, or introducing a dotted rhythm that lengthens one note at the expense of the next. The new version should 'play' for a couple of repetitions prior to a further variation being introduced.

This can carry on for several steps and is likely to end in a melody that is noticeably different to the original one. The steps can be reversed or some other set of variants employed to try and return to the condition of the original melody. The whole game can be attempted on other occasions starting out with different rhythmic conditions (e.g., in 3/4, 6/8, or 3/2 time, and so on).

Task 10

All of these tasks will also contribute to the essential skill of committing musical material to memory. This plays such an important part in communicative performance that it benefits from being exercised multimodally. Performance preparation will tend to encode musical memories in muscular and sense memory, which is vital to fluent technical accomplishment. But the backup of inner hearing and vocalisation can deepen and confirm performative encoding, as we have seen with previous tasks and games.

There are several ways in which this skill can be addressed:

- You practise on your instrument a phrase you are learning, copying it in your voice. By alternating singing and playing and looking away from the music to ensure that the material is committed to memory, this technique is employed to acquire as long and continuous a representation of the notated music as possible. Subsequent to the practice session, the phrase or passage is repeated in the aural imagination, away from the instrument. In the next practice session, prior to playing it on the instrument, the passage is sung from memory.
- Commencing with a simple, short phrase (as in Task 9), you ensure that you can both sing and play it equally well. The phrase should then be extended, note by note, at each stage both playing and singing the new version (the process of introducing material can alternate between singing and playing). The task need not be played to exhaustion. The focus should be the process of tracking development in memory and the activity should cease while it is still successful.

Task 11

An activity related to Task 10 is playing by ear. Where students have mastered the previous tasks, this will prove less hit-and-miss than it might otherwise be. You listen first, repeatedly, to a recording of material that you intend to play, such as a song or passage from an instrumental work. This is first committed to memory in sung form, using scat techniques for articulation and rhythmic clarity. Once the intended amount of material has been learned, it is transferred to instrumental performance. Over time the aim is to make this more effective, so that what one can sing, one can immediately play.

Task 12

An activity that relates to Task 11 is *imitation*, which has the benefit of being carried out with a partner, either a teacher or a peer. One participant plays a passage for the other to imitate immediately. If the imitated version is correct, they can exchange roles, or move on to another example or a different activity. Learning how to help one another by detecting mistakes and modelling their correction makes a valuable contribution to the kind of interactive musical thinking that *Harmony Signing* requires.

Task 13

This represents a different variant that occurs frequently across a variety of genres and styles. A short passage is played and sung. Then, starting a step higher or lower, it is sung in transposition. It is then played at the new pitch. Here, the voice is employed as a template with which to externalise inner hearing of the original example so the technical changes involved in performing in transposition can be accurately applied. As students succeed in this task, the interval of transposition can be widened.

Task 14

This is a companion to Task 13, but it operates in a more continuous fashion consistent with practice in a great deal of Baroque and Classical music. A short passage with a distinct contour is mastered. Then, starting with its precise repetition, it is taken as the first element of a *sequence* that replicates the original passage in a pattern of rising or falling transposed steps (see fig. 5.3).

Figures 5.3a and b Examples of sequences in music notation (a) and (b).

Task 15

Once they have been worked through as distinct procedures, combinations of Tasks 1 through 14 in imagined variations can open up a link to free improvisation. The strategy of alternating singing and playing should continue to be employed as a means of ensuring the multimodal encoding of musical material to develop memory and the fluency of connection between perception, recall, repetition, and instrumental technique.

Summing Up

Tasks 1 through 15 support many of the activities that will be introduced to permit the effective representation and exchange of musical material in *Harmony Signing*. These routines build on the games in previous chapters and are intended to promote speed and accuracy of response, as well as clarity of recall and the retention of concentration. Where these continue to be practised regularly alongside *Harmony Signing*, as warm-ups and a means of extending the specific skill that each task addresses, they will help overcome the tendency to hesitation and slow response that undermines collective musical engagement. While it is essential that activities are carried out at realistic tempi to develop confidence, it is even more important to model the way that musical thinking needs to deliver immediate reaction. Thinking in sound needs also to represent thinking in time, and a late response is (in terms of aural recall, for instance) a wrong note. Students often develop ways of reading music and recalling information that are halting and provisional (as if enacting the implied question 'is this right?'). It is far better that they make loud and confident mistakes from which they can learn!

None of the games and tasks introduced so far have necessitated the use of notation. This has been deliberate. The activities have required sensitive, often complex musical thinking and feeling. But the intention to illustrate that these values can be developed independent of notation is consistent with the idea that music is what we carry in our heads. Its temporary transfer to the medium of writing on paper is a means of recalling what is (or has been) already there, in someone's head (whether Bach, Beethoven or the Beatles), rather than a musical event itself.

However, as students engage with the preceding games and tasks, they will increasingly encounter musical responses reflective of explicit knowledge of intervals; rhythms; and patterns of growth, repetition, and variation. All of these can, of course, be captured in notation and there is no conflict here between different ways of teaching these phenomena. I chose to deal with the inner hearing of these tasks because the most direct way to make responses instinctive is through sound itself, rather than as a recollection of notation. Students who master these tasks will reach a stage at which teachers can introduce a complementary method to deepen musical understanding.

All fifteen tasks could also be carried out on paper, which might well represent an additional strategy for linking this form of aural training to composition practice. The step this represents is also desirable: We want students to be able to hear notation in their heads too. These strategies will have prepared the way.

6

The Four Elements of Vocal Learning

It is a happy coincidence that the means by which digital technology represents and controls the elements of sound maps onto the way our ears and voices have mutually evolved. Sound thus breaks down into the four components of pitch, duration, volume, and timbre (fig. 6.1). One could pose these as questions:

Which?
How long?
How loud?
What?

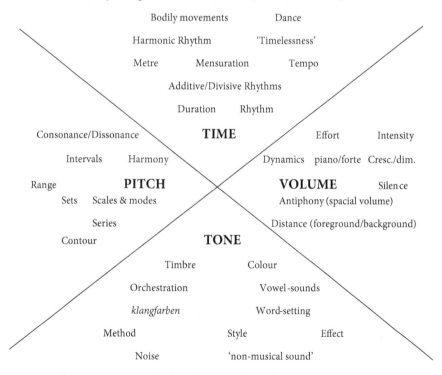

Materials for composition

('Play or sing a note': 'when?'; 'which?'; 'how?'; 'how loud?')

Bodily movements   Dance

Harmonic Rhythm   'Timelessness'

Metre   Mensuration   Tempo

Additive/Divisive Rhythms

Duration   Rhythm

TIME

Consonance/Dissonance   Effort   Intensity

Intervals   Harmony   Dynamics   piano/forte   Cresc./dim.

Range   **PITCH**   **VOLUME**   Silence

Sets   Scales & modes   Antiphony (spacial volume)

Series   Distance (foreground/background)

Contour   **TONE**

Timbre   Colour

Orchestration   Vowel-sounds

klangfarben   Word-setting

Method   Style   Effect

Noise   'non-musical sound'

Figure 6.1 Chart representing the four elements of vocal learning.

As we have seen, changes to each of these elements can convey meaning. These changes are the ingredients from which all music is made.

Each element can be modelled vocally. We have already begun to do this. Game 7, for instance, together with subsequent variants, involved controlling and sharing pitched vocalisation, whereas Game 3 addressed differences in duration and Game 2 worked with the important human ability to vary loudness without affecting the maintenance of the same pitch. We have also explored the relationship between emotion, facial expression, and timbre. In this chapter, we further explore the way these elements of musical continuity and significance may be experienced.

The Sense of Pitch

We will deal first with pitch. When we practised Game 7, and especially its variant in Game 12, we did not specify which pitches were involved. Rather, we moved from experiencing change through up and down glissandi and employed this as a basis for improvised polyphony. But students will be well aware that music universally adopts fixed pitch relationships; that is, scales and modes that provide the scaffolding onto which melodies are mapped (Podlipniak 2016).

Kodály note names can be employed as the means of exploring pitch.[1] Numbers can also prove useful:

Degree of scale:	1	2	3	4	5
Kodály note name:	Doh	Ray	Me	Fa	Soh

Letter names can also be used, as long as they are associated with the precise notes they represent:

C	D	E	F	G

However, all of these draw on mental connections dependent on words or verbal-graphic symbolism (numbers, too, are words: 'one, two, three . . .'). This can both embrace sounds that are disruptive of musical vocalisation (e.g., 'three'; <F>) and load the brain with an additional pattern of representation that is open to mistakes and, therefore, to cautious or hesitant singing. Similarly, the array of different vowel sounds that one may want to combine into chords inhibits good tuning. So it can be musically effective to repeat any musical location tasks that involve the use of letters, names, or numbers with versions that employ an uninterrupted vocal sound such as <aaahh>. This teaches participants how to listen to such combinations and perform them with respect for blend and tuning. Eventually, the use of Kodály gestures can be liberated from the need to pronounce the note names. In turn, this permits Kodály signs to be employed to lead instrumental music.

---

[1] *Harmony Signing* makes extensive use of Kodály gestures, so these will need to be introduced at some stage.

A significant first step towards the methods of *Harmony Signing* is assembling these representations of pitch into chords. The class or group is divided into three equal parts:

Group (a) sings   1 - 2 - 3 - 4 - 5

Group (b) sings   1 - 2 - 3 - - - - -   [or 1 - (1) - (1) - 2 - 3]

Group (c) sings   1 - - - - - - - - - -

The combination of these forms the eventual triad. Membership of the groups should be revolved so that everyone gains experience of all three roles.

Other explorations of pitch and its properties can make use of Kodály hand signs to convey melodies of participants' own invention. Everyone should be given the chance to lead this in order to develop and consolidate knowledge and application of the signs.

Both *Harmony Signing* and Kodály gestures work to embody the sense of pitch *location* that is central to the development of inner hearing and the technical, analytical, and creative skills that its further consolidation relies upon. This theme will be referred to at several stages, as new perspectives on the achievement of *location* emerge from the sequence of activities to come.

Initially, as a basis for the fuller sense of tonality that will be addressed through conveying patterns of related chords, we need to establish a secure sense of the role of each note of the major scale. All participants need to learn the full array of diatonic Kodály signs:

Doh – Ray – Me – Fa – Soh – La – Ti – Doh$^+$

The relationship by interval and range of each can then be performed and consigned to memory:

Do – Ray – Doh – Me – Doh – Fa – Doh – Soh – Doh – La – Doh – Ti – Doh – Doh$^+$ – Doh

This should then be repeated to <Aaahh> so that the purely musical, connected experience is established, as well as the association between sign (which everyone mirrors) and sound.

A subsequent stage will be to practise all the *downward* intervals, commencing on the upper tonic:

Doh$^+$ – Ti – Doh$^+$ – La – Doh$^+$ – Soh – Doh$^+$ – Fa – Doh$^+$ – Me – Doh$^+$ – Ray – Doh$^+$ – Doh

Again, this should be signed by everyone and also practised to <Aaahh>. Attention should be paid especially to the tuning of the two semitone steps Me - Fa (both up and down) and Ti - Doh'.

A really effective way of then extending participants' handling of *location* is to introduce 'replacement'. This provides an insight into the nature of *modulation* that will feature strongly at more advanced stages. At this point, it ought to represent an assimilable means of consolidating the ability of participants to assign significance to the tonic—to hear the relative functions of the degrees of the scale in the inner ear—which they will be able both to respond to and lead. 'Replacement' involves signing with one hand a set of pitches related to a given tonic, and then with the other hand concealing the latest sign so that it can be replaced by something else:

Doh - Ray - Me (conceal Me) = Doh . . . - Ray - Me

Students will get used to adjusting the placement of tones and semitones that permits this to be achieved. It is, again, important that each one of them, over time, has an opportunity to lead. Leading the activity involves hearing what one intends and confirming that the group has achieved it, which are vital experiences within the pedagogy of *Harmony Signing*.

Here is a more complex and extended routine involving 'replacement' (see fig. 6.2):

Doh – Ray – Me=Doh – Ray – Me – Fah=Soh – Fah – Me – Ray=Ti – Doh – Ti – La – Soh=Doh

Figure 6.2 The 'replacement' routine in music notation.

These explorations of pitch will serve to illustrate the overwhelming significance of confidently and creatively handling this property of music.

Exploring Duration

The clapping and body percussion games introduced previously can still act as warm-ups for rhythmic development. We can build on this by focusing on the implication of duration for vocal exploration, both in terms of rhythmic values and articulation. It is important for students to understand duration both as a measure of audible sound, and as a means of meaningfully controlling periods of silence.

One means of doing this is beat-boxing, which can develop rhythmic experience both solo and in groups. In solo performance, the aim is to represent as completely as possible all the strands of a drum-kit pattern through layering different vocalisations that approximate the timbre and relative range of the principal instruments (bass drum, snare, hi-hat) and additional features such as bongos, cowbell, or claves. Students can plan the sounds they intend to incorporate and then assemble them into a signature rhythm.

A way of developing this in groups is to employ it as a mean of analysing and reproducing the preset rhythms available on keyboards, sequencing programs and drum machines. While they listen to the selected model, each member of a group of five is assigned an instrument to 'track' through imitating its sound, and the group collectively maps their vocal performance onto the sample. When the model is switched off, the vocal version continues.

In developing the ability to perform confidently while processing creative responses, it is important to work on sustained vocalisation to which ideas of duration can be applied. So that this does not (literally!) appear monotonous, it can be combined with a limited selection of pitches. This helps to differentiate streams of sound and provides the challenge of performing in a controlled manner. The idea is then to work vocally with a variety of rhythmic patterns that provide experience of the most common time signatures and possibilities available within them.

Each subphrase (separated by the double bar lines in fig. 6.3) can be performed vocally so as to work with the specific durations of which it is comprised, employing scat presentation such as <pah> or <doo-bee>. Solfège rhythm names (ta, ti-ti, etc.) can also play a part in developing performance of the material. Then the whole of each melody can be performed straight through to a sustained <Aaahh>. Each of the examples work either as a round, with each subgroup making staggered entries as indicated, or as a texture made up of ostinati derived from each phrase. When students are ready to work with instruments, these exercises can also be employed to develop blend, articulation, phrasing, and tuning in ensembles.

Figures 6.3a and b Music notation of a variety of rhythmic patterns that can be performed as rounds.

Investigating Volume

Students will have had initial experience of the potential of volume through engagement with Game 2. The value at this point can be to combine the parameter of volume with the other elements (pitch and duration) that have been explored in this chapter. In terms of developing vocal skills, we can consider: (a) contrasts in volume, such as echo effects, and (b) gradual changes in volume—crescendos and diminuendos. The effect and meaning of these can be quite different. The purpose of considering them here is both to build their experience into students' creative imaginations, as elements to be drawn on in composition and improvisation, and to ensure that the performance skills involved can be mastered so that they match expectation.

For instance, we can take the beat-boxing routine described earlier and perform it as if the listener is walking towards the sound source, hearing it build from barely audible to as loud as possible. Or the canonic patterns can be sung to terraced dynamics (e.g., soft, medium, loud), changing from one to another on a given signal. All work achieved in the preceding games and tasks can be revisited to explore the element of controlled dynamics.

Working With the Phenomenon of Timbre

Timbre is arguably the least commonly explored feature of the elements of music, and its role in understanding the basis of *Harmony Signing* will be investigated thoroughly, since in many ways it links together our experience of the other three elements. If we refer to it as 'choice of instrument', this appears so obvious as to be taken for granted. But timbre also embraces

- the difference in sound of the vowels to which we sing and that are essential to discriminating meaning in speech;
- the relative effect on us of the spectrum of sounds that represent different levels of consonance and dissonance;
- the effect on our experience of music of other features of pitch, such as range, use of vibrato, and tone production; and
- the density of combinations of sounds.

When we think about music notation, we tend to focus on the representation of pitch and duration. We often subsequently add markings that determine how a sound is presented (*sfzpp*; *flutter-tongued*). But this does not represent what the listener hears. If you turn the radio on, the first thing that strikes the ear is not the way the music is written down, but the quality of sound, whether it is being played by a military band or on a church organ or harpsichord. Our hearing has evolved to discriminate what is causing sounds, and in the case of acoustic music this remains of interest: Was that an oboe playing that tune? Is this song in Russian? How was that interesting effect achieved? Discrimination of timbre is the fastest response of all the ways our brains process music.

A means of developing sensitivity to timbre that also underpins the development of pitch location and our response to the potential of harmony is to carry out a thorough investigation of how we can listen to the harmonic series in our own vocal production. We can begin with language. How do we learn to speak so as to exchange precise meanings based on perceiving and pronouncing sounds in the same way as one another? If we focus on the vowel sounds on which speech depends, we will recognise how important it is to have a system that discriminates dependably between a range of similar sounds.

In acquiring language, the reliability with which we learn vowels relates to whether we can reproduce them sufficiently distinctly to avoid confusing listeners. The 'raw material' that vowel production embraces can be set out as a sequence of steps, each of which is a variant of its predecessor. Phoneticians and singing teachers refer to this as the 'vowel circle', because the physical adjustments involved can link the final element back to the starting place, like a snake swallowing its tail. Here it is set out in a horizontal sequence:

oo - oa - or - o - ar - a - e - é - i - ee - ü

To perform this and elicit *harmonics* involves progressive shaping of the lips and tongue position, moving from narrow/suppressed via open/enriched to narrow/enriched. The tongue needs to be at the front of the mouth, and all sounds produced in a 'forward' position just above the front teeth, so that a sense of resonance is captured in the hard palate (the roof of the mouth).

We can learn to discern audible harmonics by moving delicately between pairs of vowels that are adjacent in the sequence, for example:

oa . . . or
oh . . . ar.

The important thing is to preserve a controlled stream of air, and to make the tiniest of vertical movements of the lips to turn one sound into the next. Listening acutely to the consequences, one should begin to hear distinct pitches, much higher in range than the pitch of the monotone that is being sustained.

Figure 6.4 conveys why a variety of distinct vowel classes is essential to the unambiguous conveyance of the meaning of otherwise similar words. Thinking of these initially as words, we will employ their pronunciation to develop our understanding of the way that telling the difference between them relies on musical properties.

In this presentation, the words in the left-hand column illustrate how each subsequent vowel maps onto that generated by the next harmonic, beginning with the dull sound of <boot>, in which harmonic activation is suppressed by the narrowing of the lips, and gradually 'opening out' to the harmonic-rich front vowels. The words in the centre column represent those whose vowel colour does not fall within this harmonic series sequence, but which is achieved by alternative means. The right-hand column contains examples of *diphthongs* (pairs of vowels linked in sequence).

This list presents ten words in standard English, plus a couple of proper names and some regional variants: in all, 18 short words which begin with [b] and end in [t] and can only be distinguished from one another as a consequence of the clear production and discrimination of the quality of the central target vowel. The means by which we

The Main Vowels in English		
(Illustrated by words and names beginning with a **B** sound and ending with a **T** sound)		
Boot (English)		
Boat		Boo-wot (British Geordie)
Bought		
Bott		
Bart	Burt	Bite
Bat	Beart	
Bet	But	
Bate		
Bit		
Beet		
Boot		Bute
But (Scottish 'boot')		

Figure 6.4 The main vowels in English.

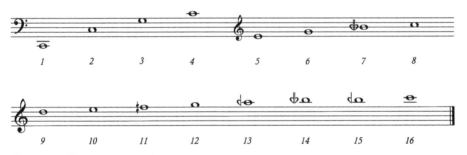

Figure 6.5 The harmonic series.

communicate effectively with those around us depends entirely on our ability to perceive such subtle differences in sound. The perception of language depends on the precise discrimination of these phenomena, but the origin of this ability emerged from our sensitivity to the properties of harmony and their musical potential.

The words in the left-hand column can be read downwards in the manner we practised, making incremental changes of vocal timbre. The words in the centre and right-hand columns are produced in ways which form slight exceptions to this pattern, including diphthongs. If one tries to sing the sequence in the left-hand column, the colour of each vowel stands out as a distinct musical phenomenon. This is all the more clear if one gets rid of the consonants and creates an uninterrupted vocalisation on a sustained pitch. The resulting sequence of vowels elides vocally into a continuous stream. As each new vowel emerges in the order *oo - oa - or - o - ar - a - e - é - i - ee - ü*, a different harmonic will become audible. The pattern of harmonics is shown in Figure 6.5.

Close and acute attention to the way we hear and produce sounds can transform the impression we have of how music works. Rather than requiring access to a keyboard in order to listen to the effects of intervals, we carry our capacity to discriminate between them with us, and this forms the basis of the way we speak. If we can learn to discriminate between a set of intervals as described here, we need only then listen to our own carefully modulated singing to discern the differences between the harmonics as the templates for the natural intervals that we can learn to recognise, for example:

1:2	the octave
2:3	the perfect fifth
3:4	the perfect fourth
4:5	the major third
5:6	the minor third
6:7	a narrower version of the minor third associated with the dominant seventh
7:8	the step to the next octave of (1)
8:9	a large major second
9:10	a smaller major second

Notice that within this the clear reappearance of pitches in the next octave is predictable if one applies the frequency ratios logically:

1:2	2:4	4:8	8:16	are all octaves
2:3	4:6	8:12		are all perfect fifths
3:4	6:8	12:16		are all perfect fourths
4:5	8:10			are both major thirds
5:6	10:12			are both minor thirds

The experience we can gain from listening to our performance of these pitch relationships can then be internally stored. We can encode the memory of the harmonic series in our inner ear and rely on its recall in aural and creative contexts in which it can supply an accurate template for discriminating consonant and dissonant relationships.

In turn, harmonic series properties govern other aspects of our response to timbre. 'Open' and 'closed' sounds achieved through the use of mutes and different bowing and plucking techniques can be associated with different vowel sounds, or the more or less nasal resonance achieved. We can learn to hear in the combination of pitches the presence of unperformed notes that respond to the acoustic properties of adding together different frequencies, or that respond to the resonance of instruments and room acoustics. The greater the sensitivity that these experiences bring to our hearing, the more we will understand the phenomenon of tonality and its application. Students could then investigate the role of the harmonic series in the techniques of sound production and modification of the instruments they play and be asked to demonstrate these to the class.

7

Lifelong Participation and Transmission

The achievement of sophisticated control of the four properties of vocal learning that underpin musical knowledge and creativity—pitch, duration, volume, and timbre—is important not only for the development of skills on which individuals may depend but also for the establishment of musical communities. In Western societies, there would seem to be a far higher incidence of the condition known as 'tone-deafness' than would appear to be present in hunter-gatherer societies in which everyone sings and dances and is treated as entitled to participate in collective behaviour. Why might this be so? From the cases I have dealt with as a teacher, it comes down to the negative experiences, whether of omission or commission, that result in the switching off of the capacity to enjoy music in the early years of life. Teachers who detect signs of inhibited performance can, as with the acquisition and extension of any skill, provide remedial and supportive strategies to ensure that students have the confidence and experience to continue to participate. But many students are left to flounder, or, worse, are treated as unmusical and not worth the effort to help by precisely the people who ought to exhibit the skills and commitment to make a positive difference.

Where the behaviour of an adult or peer can have a negative effect on the preparedness of a child to participate in music-making, the effects can be long term. Researchers such as Susan Knight (2011, 2013), who are committed to the principal that every child is musical and can be taught to sing, reveal the kind of biographical narrative by which subjects in later life recall the exact incidents which led them to consider themselves nonmusicians. Knight's research began with the development of strategies to reverse this imposed lack of perceived musicality, even late in life, in adults who proved able to acquire the ability to sing in tune even after fifty years or more of musical silence. In my own teaching career, none of my students have remained 'tone-deaf'.

Yet the expectation that some children are musical while others are not remains widespread (Ruddock 2008), and the position is not helped by school policies which demand that teachers should be selective, or by curriculum provision that takes no account of the value to later education and socialisation of musical experience in early life for every child. These negative positions fly in the face both of evolutionary models and of the evidence of cultures in which a high value is placed on ensuring that all children are given the opportunity to make music well and are provided with skilled teachers dedicated to this outcome.

Creative and aural development have a central role in vocalisation and, given the number of young students who present themselves in our music classes who do not appear to have sung at home or been encouraged in early education to do so, it pays to have strategies available to aid and accelerate the achievement of singing in tune.

Exercises to Remedy Poorly Developed Pitch-Matching

The following section is designed to provide guidance to teachers who need to help poor-pitch singers to develop their skills so they can participate in and benefit from *Harmony Signing*. Many of these activities will also contribute to the vocal development and capacity for free vocal production of all students. Indeed, I incorporate some of these activities in warm-ups and extension strategies for experienced choral singers. Some can be especially helpful as practice strategies for individuals who need additional support.

The following are the most common factors that student teachers report as suggesting a lack of musical ability that they find challenging to address:

- inability to locate pitch at all, or even to match the contour of a phrase
- a tendency to sing lower than the target material
- a tendency to sing higher than the target material
- a tendency to 'fall off' target pitches, which commence accurately but then glide downwards, often dramatically, to lower pitches

We will deal with these 'symptoms' in sequence, proposing a variety of activities that can contribute to remedying their effects and may with perseverance confer the ability to sing in tune.

The singing voice exploits anatomical features that were shaped by the evolutionary achievement of upright posture and the instinctive responses to which this gave rise. Upright posture has shaped both an aural system and a respiratory tract that are unique to our species and represent the prerequisites to which the neural control of pitch-matching has had to adapt. At the front of the human throat, behind the Adam's apple, is a highly complex neural and muscular junction box. It involves systems for a variety of independent functions: secure breathing, whereby the vocal folds protect the vertical airway from intrusion; the swallowing of food in a manner that does not compromise breathing; instinctive facial expressions, including those motivated by the strong emotional correlates of the 'fight or flight' mechanism; voluntary facial expressions, such as smiling, frowning, and those by which we render ourselves attractive; preparation for defence, at least as a last resort; and phonation, including whistling as well as a variety of registers of vocal-fold activation that permit song and speech.[1] The disgust reflex, for instance, which can save lives by preventing associates from eating noxious substances, is hard to produce artificially. Its work is done instinctively, because hesitation could be fatal. So what happens if singing has led to a sense of self-disgust? How might this affect our ability to make sounds and enjoy doing so (Bannan 2000)?

Boys who sing into adulthood have to acquire mastery of the system twice. First in infancy and again during adolescence. Changes to several of the variables that affect the junction box behind the Adam's apple (muscular, hormonal, psychological, proportional) ensure that the adult voice will emerge with characteristics quite different to those developed from birth to the teenage years, some of which may take time to

---

[1] Vocal tract flexibility also proves essential to the mastery of wind and brass instruments (Scavone, Lefebvre, & da Silva 2008; Wolfe, Garnier, & Smith 2009; Fréour & Scavone 2010).

recognise as 'belonging' to their owner. Girls can experience something broadly similar (Gackle 2000), but in most cases to a much lesser extent. And girls whose voices undergo change during adolescence may need reassurance just as much as boys.

The expressive harnessing of all the properties of this set of overlapping systems is highly vulnerable to the effects of critical timing mechanisms in the brain, including those resulting from nervousness or lack of self-esteem, or associated with emotional states. For instance, stammering (stuttering) has been recognised as a speech impediment for which one typical strategy is to treat the speaking voice as if singing, since many stammerers are excellent singers. The twin benefits of rhythmic performance and smooth, continuous phonation contribute to the achievement of improved capacity for speech.[2]

Most of the students who require our focused help are those who believe that they speak adequately but cannot sing. The teacher needs to diagnose the nature of their individual vocal profile. One can begin by ascertaining whether phonation is occurring effectively by asking the student to attempt a sustained *Ah* sound maintained for as long as possible. This will yield two kinds of information: how stable the capacity is to sustain the same note over time, and how effective the breath management is that makes this possible. In order to follow this with procedures that investigate the relationship between the student's hearing of the pitch they produce and the actual sound, one needs to match the pitch of the student's performance to an appropriate model, such as one's own voice or an instrument. Gender differences between teachers and students can present a challenge, especially where teachers themselves lack vocal confidence or flexibility. Sometimes teaching a student alongside a trusted friend, whose voice and ability offer a useful model, can be the best solution. Developing a trustful interaction between the student's voice and our own is usually the best way forward. Otherwise, we employ whatever techniques we can: using piano or, since the percussive attack of the piano can present a confusing signal to some inexperienced children, the sustaining settings of a keyboard or organ; employing, if male and able, falsetto; or teaching the student how to respond to sounds that are an octave higher or lower than the note they have 'found'.

Initial investigations into this issue prove very helpful. The problem may be traceable to the act of breathing, especially if it is tight and clavicular. The symptoms of this are raised shoulders, a consequent lack of supported airflow, and an inhibited vibratory sensation in the upper chest due to muscle constriction.[3] Our perception of our own singing relies on the 'feel' of the experience as much as on heard sounds,[4] so it pays to deal with the postural and body-use issues that shallow breathing represents. Effective musical breathing can indeed be usefully taught to the whole class, since it will benefit all participants. Upright posture is, after all, the foundational stance that brought about these abilities in the deep evolutionary history of our species.

---

[2] A talented musician I once knew had great difficulties speaking in his mother tongue, English, but in the tonal languages such as Mandarin, which he learned at university, he was entirely free of the problem. The contrast between speech conditions in tonal and nontonal languages provides several clues to the neural control of speech and song (Welch & Murao 1994; Jordania 2011).

[3] Many singers with beautifully in-tune voices may display similar breathing habits that can inhibit future development.

[4] Deaf musicians such as Evelyn Glennie and Liz Varloe employ a variety of means of sensing sound, but the brain area that sorts these and permits musical response is the same as for hearing people.

Proficient breathing contributes, to use Tinbergen's (1951) term for instinctive behaviour, to the <release> of the voice (the clinically informed German singing teacher Hustler preferred the term <unlocking>; see Hustler & Rodd-Marling 1965). Development of posture and breathing in groups in which some members already pitch well can elicit swift progress in pitch-matching for some students. But for others, the causes may be more complex and one will need to be patient and provide a variety of further strategies.

A key inhibition that may also have evolutionary origins is the 'fight or flight' reflex. This imposes, under conditions of emotional stress, a muscular contraction of the jaw and root of the tongue that has the effect of turning the voice into a transposing instrument. The singer seems to hear the target note accurately, but their phonatory production is compromised in a manner that prevents them from producing the same pitch. For inexperienced teachers, this can appear to be an insoluble problem. But dramatic improvement can ensue if the muscular tension causing this distorting effect can be removed. The following strategies can help to achieve this.

The 'transposition' effect often comes with a history. The student may in fact be quite sensitive to sound, often playing other instruments with flair. The inability to match pitch can therefore be all the more painful to their self-esteem. It can emerge that previous attempts to respond to adult or peer stimulus have made things worse by increasing their sense of helplessness. Several steps may be required in order to begin to remedy the phonatory profile they present. One needs to discern which muscles may be responsible for the tension that prevents free association between the target pitch and the student's response. Why does there appear to be a ceiling on the student's attempts to move their voice to the heard target? The first step one needs to take is to further extend the sense of relaxation in muscle structures that may be responsible for tension, working from the top of the head downwards through the attachments to the jaw muscles that wrap around the cheeks and temples, down through the lips and tongue to the attachments that link the lower jaw to the larynx, and onwards to the muscles that spread across the upper chest. At the same time, one needs to observe the postural features whereby the head is suspended as an extension of the spine above the neck. Tension can arise both from the neck being tipped forward; or from it being angled backwards and upwards, especially when doing this is associated with achieving an extension of range.

There is a set of muscles that in our evolutionary history was anchored in our distant ancestors to pronounced ridges on the crest of the skull and to the brow ridges above our eyes. Both of these anchor points are invisible or much diminished in modern humans but they have left traces on our behaviour in the way they can still be activated which can be evident in their involvement in biting and chewing. Muscles involved in aggression and the mastication of food are strongly anchored at the chin and jawbone. These muscles contract in the gritting of teeth as an emotional response to threat, which can be the cause of problems in singing.

Students need to be aware of these muscles and to learn consciously to 'switch them off'. A means of doing this is to imagine the head and torso as a wax dummy which can be shaped with hot hands. The hands are placed together on top of the skull, and then moved down slowly over the temples, cheeks and, finally, the jaw, 'melting' the muscles into relaxation. This will have the additional effect of presenting the instrument to the touch of our hands as one that is long and vertical in its shape, rather than squat and horizontal. The student, having achieved this, needs to see this form of facial posture as the default on which they can rely, and to which they can effortlessly return, as further strategies are attempted. Students can be encouraged to practise in front of a mirror, monitoring whether this strategy is visibly beginning to make any difference, in terms of sensations in these parts of the body and the resulting sound.

Following from achievement of these postural adjustments, one monitors whether there are resultant improvements in breathing and phonation. This is done by employing the same pitch-matching strategies as noted previously. Achievement of the 'targets' may still be incomplete, but if quantifiable progress is evident it can be maintained and built upon.

If there is already discernible progress in the student's singing, this will be a cause for satisfaction. But experience tells that the level of inhibition experienced by some individuals can go very deep. Fortunately, further strategies are available. The next two suggestions relate to tension in the jaw muscles, which can transmit to the larynx and rob the student of the experience of hearing the pitches they anticipate, and tension in the tongue.

As in the result of the 'wax dummy' procedure, the jaw needs to hang loose, and the bite mechanism must be entirely disengaged. The lips should then be rounded to form an <ooo> shape, as if blowing bubbles through a straw into a thick milkshake.[5] This forms the optimum starting position for vowel formation, as we have already seen when introducing vocal harmonics. It promotes freedom from the constrictive muscular effects of the permanent smile (rictus) that some teachers advise in order to make singers look happy—a mistake that is itself responsible for creating nonsingers! It also achieves a larger mouth cavity that will promote resonance and provides room for the tongue to sit inactively on the floor of the mouth. Aiming for this <ooo> shape can therefore help to switch off the muscles that are transferring tension to the vocal folds and turning them into a transposing instrument. A further advantage of this form of facial relaxation is that it opens up the space just in front of and below the earlobes, enabling both more sensitive musical hearing and a clearer capacity to 'mix' the incoming signal of the voices of others with the sensory loop of perceiving one's own voice, which is partly achieved through bone conduction. It renders our ears more alert.

The steps taken so far will have ameliorated inhibited phonation in some students, who may already have shown sufficient improvement to be singing in tune with their peers. There may still be others, though, whose fear of singing is so deep that further strategies are required. It should be borne in mind that the strategies proposed so far can be equally useful in general warm-ups as a means of establishing healthy practice that will protect the voices of all students.

Rigidity of the tongue is a tricky problem because the organ is in normal circumstances virtually invisible. Indeed, concealment of the tongue, and its compression back into the throat, often seems to be associated with the set of symptoms that poor-pitch singers exhibit. Experienced teachers can hear this effect immediately. But the student will be habituated to it: it represents to them *their voice* as they normally

---

[5] A strategy for achieving this has been developed by the voice researcher Ingo Titze and can be accessed on YouTube: https://www.youtube.com/watch?v=asDg7T-WT-0

experience it, including in adequate, sometimes even expressive, speech. They may at first be unaware of any tension until it arises when attempting to sing.

The root of the tongue is attached to the vocal folds, so careful achievement of independent function needs to be exercised. Where the tongue is free to work optimally, it is responsible for the variations of resonance, filtering, and timing that allow us to perceive and produce the distinctions between similar vowels, as well as the voiced/unvoiced consonant pairs <b/p>, <d/t>, and <g/c>. If the tongue is clenched in a position similar to that required for swallowing, it can change the vibratory profile of the vocal folds altogether, and also affects the resonance of sounds as heard by the singer.

In my experience, remediation of the habitual functions of these sensitive muscular and neural connections requires one to access 'the child within' (Bannan 2000). A playful, trusting response is essential to progress, not least because the negative experience that has locked the voice up in this way in the first place almost certainly occurred in early childhood.

The tongue needs to be exercised freely, in a variety of operations. The aim is to create in the nasopharynx conditions that represent to the singer that their voice is an instrument that extends throughout the head and torso. The tendency to tighten and withdraw needs to be overcome. From the top of the skull down to the top ribs where they join the sternum, the capacity to vibrate needs to be activated in order to release resonance. In order to monitor and promote this, one hand can be placed against the sternum, acting as a reminder that it should be normal to feel vibrations there. The other hand can be placed experimentally, and only *very* gently without any pressure, to monitor whether vibrations can be detected in various resonating positions beneath and around the skull: with the finger and thumb on each side of the larynx; with finger and thumb each side of the bridge of the nose; and with flat of the hand against either the crest of the skull or the back of the head just above the neck. A vibrating instrument is a healthy one.

In order to free up the tongue and its functions, the singer should commence with 'tut' sounds at the front of the mouth, like talking to a chipmunk. Phonation should then be attempted on a rolled <r>. Singers who can normally roll an <r>, can sometimes at this point encounter a real breakthrough. Suddenly, because it is impossible to roll an <r> with a tense tongue, one hears one's voice free of the constriction to which it has become habituated. I have found that singers' response to my vocalisation on a rolled <r> can elicit perfectly matched pitch.

However, students with vocal constriction may well be among those who are unable to roll an <r> in speech. An alternative strategy that can yield the same outcome of liberation from tension is to place the tongue outside the mouth altogether, and vocalise while licking upper and lower lips in quick succession employing a circular, sweeping movement. It is very important that this is achieved without any movement of the lower jaw, which should hang loose and still. It is worth checking in a mirror that this is the case. The tongue movement should then be sped up until it is as fast as possible. The addition of a sustained phonation on any convenient pitch will result in something that sounds like 'lebble-ebble-lebble-ebble.' Once this can be produced consistently, through swift and agile movements of the tip of the tongue, it can be employed to discover whether it makes for more accurate pitch-matching. The next step is to try and move the pitch up and down in steady glissandi, widening the range as it proves possible to. Students may find they can only make the required tongue movements slowly at first, but should aim, through practice over time, to increase the speed and freedom with which the 'lebble-ebble' sound can be produced. To test progress, the teacher, using the 'lebble-ebble' noise at the same pitch as the student, can aim to illustrate the quality of unison they can achieve. Once this is in place, it should be possible for both in unison to move up and down a step. The focus on it being a shared experience is important if this technique is to be reinforced psychologically and physically. Greater flexibility in the tongue should thus begin to develop. Alongside the respiratory and postural strategies modelled previously, some progress should now be evident. If so, this can be built upon as confidence grows, since it may take several repetitions of these therapies for progress to be consolidated.

It is important to recognise, while helping students in this way, that the so-called tone-deafness of such individuals represents a highly inaccurate term to employ for their inability to match pitch. Rather, the muscular tension and psychological state which they had been accustomed to in their attempts to sing will have been responsible for the fact that they were unable to locate the same pitch with their voice that they could hear prior to phonation.

A less commonly encountered problem is the student who presents with the condition that they sing higher than the target pitch, as if having inhaled helium. Many of the strategies already introduced can help, including a focus on calming. In preadolescent boys, over-high singing can be a response to the impression that this is the timbre with which their singing voice ought to be produced, in contrast to the low and deep sounds of the adult male. I have had my suspicions, on the occasions when I have encountered this phenomenon, that the student concerned may have been exposed to live singing only where the adult role-models in their experience were drunk or otherwise overexcited, and this impression of uninhibitedness has been carried into their own attempts to perform in the same way. Some of the postural issues that can relate to this and other problems can be dealt with by singing lying on one's back. This relaxed position removes some of the conditions in which the recalled overstimulus affects the phonatory system.

A further strategy for lessening the fixed physical mechanism of inexperienced singers is to model sustained singing through imitating a piece of machinery, such as a hedge trimmer, which is efficient only if its operation is continuous. Trimming an imaginary hedge through singing a continuous buzzing sound such as <zzz> or <djj> while moving one's arms to mimic the operation, one follows contours up, down, and sustained on the same pitch without interrupting the flow of air or resultant sound.

Another characteristic associated with poor-pitch singing is the tendency to 'fall off' target pitches, which commence accurately but then descend, often to much lower pitches. In children, I have found this to be a response to copying the percussive effect of the piano, which has a loud and immediate attack followed by a rapid decay which they respond to by falling away in pitch. I have also encountered this in adult choral singers. Some well-known performers have made their careers out of this technique, notably the great Bob Dylan. But when it becomes habitual and pronounced in a young singer, it can lead to being deemed unfit for involvement in choirs and music learning. 'Holding a part' depends on being able to sustain pitch that is stable. This is a matter of both perceptive listening and 'feel', whereby the sensations of resonance also guide the stream of sound. The activities already covered here and in the initial games and tasks will help with this. A further set has been devised with the intention of promoting the singing voice as a distinct medium with properties different from—and in many ways superior to—the speaking voice. Some of these strategies have been designed to appeal to younger children, but in the spirit of drawing on the response of 'the child within', they also have much to offer older students and adult choral singers.

We can begin through extending our experience of the postural and breathing-related values discussed earlier. Many of these transfer to the playing of instruments, and good practice in both singing and playing is essential to both physical health and convincing performance.

Expressive and healthy singing depends absolutely on a well-managed supply of air. Good practice represents both the act of breathing in and the vital sensations felt and heard in relation to the special form of exhalation that singing represents. Key to the effectiveness of musical exhalation is to optimise *resonance*, the sense and acoustic result associated with getting the most and best sound out of the least breath use (Howard 1995; Titze 1989). The goal is to maintain continuity of phonation over extended periods: breathy or tense singing leads to vocal tiredness and, at worst, dysfunction. The practice of feeling for resonance with the hands played a part in developing this sense when addressing the issue of poor-pitch singing and it can be employed to develop tone and projection in all singers. Most of the body parts responsible are invisible, so we need to find a noninvasive but informative means of accessing them in order to find out what they do, and of experimenting in ways that may improve performance.

Variation and improvement in resonance depends on the posture of the nasopharynx (Kayes 2000), the location in which vibrations are amplified and enriched after air has passed through the vocal folds. The focal area is the soft palate, which we need to learn to lift in order to give more space for sounds to 'echo'—the 'cathedral of the mouth'. But it is hard to explain this, especially to children. Indeed, talking about vocal anatomy can be misleading even to those who understand it factually. A game can provide insight into function and potential more quickly and accurately.

The family of the children's cartoon character Peppa Pig includes Father, Mother, and Baby Brother. Each of them announces themselves with a signature pig snort on the in-breath, making four distinct pitches of snort: one could think of them as Soprano, Alto, Tenor, and Bass. If one snorts like a pig and then immediately sings, one can be aware of the sensation in the roof of the mouth, where the snort was achieved, giving a sense of the resonance where the singing voice is now being directed. This is the soft palate, immediately behind the hard palate that helps project the voice out of the mouth. So, let's see if we can produce the four different snorts of Peppa's family and associate them with four different pitches on which we produce the most comfortable sung *Ah* sound using, immediately, the air we have just 'snorted' in.

This kind of game can be instructive in developing vocal self-knowledge and the capacity to vary habits that may be preventing us from developing the way we sing. Next, we can consider the relationship between sound and sensation involved in singing an *ee* sound on a medium-high note and gently pinching the nose. Can we sustain the pitch? Does the *ee* sound appear audibly different to us when pinching the nose and releasing it again? If we listen to someone else doing this, can we also hear the same difference? What happens if we try the same thing while singing the following sounds?

Oo - Ah - jjj - vvv - mmm

This illustrates (yes, *mmm* is impossible!—sorry) that when singing words it is essential to imbue as much of the language content as possible with the musical values of vowels. We need to pitch the consonants as often and contiguously with surrounding vowels as we can. Using **boldfaced** type for voiced sounds (vowels in upper case and consonants in lower) and *italic* for sounds that contain no pitch, we can analyse the alphabet in terms of the capacity of the letters it represents to generate sounds consistent with musical phonation:

A b *c* **d** **E** *f* **g** *h* **I** *j* **k** **l** **m** **n** **O** *p* **q** *r* *s* *t* **U** **v** **w** *x* **Y** *z* [6]

Students can experiment with the letters of the alphabet and evaluate which can be employed to sing a melody. This is both instructive in its own right and conducive of good vocal practice. In turn, they can be encouraged to aim to sing as smoothly as possible the transitions between vowels and consonants; stressing and resonating on voiced consonants while passing through the obstruction represented by unvoiced consonants as quickly and lightly as possible. This agility of placing unvoiced consonants between vowels depends on the stress-free posture and forward tongue position that we have sought to establish. The exercises in Figures 7.1 and 7.2 can be used to practise rendering consonants musical.

Central to the development of the voice in infants is the quality of *play*, and it is my experience that only through playfulness (Bannan 2000, 1998) can vocal development be reactivated in students in which it has been interrupted. This is why we have identified the sense of wonder that can be associated with attempting to sing harmonics and the inner calm that can ensue. Contrasting with this have been the opportunities shared that embrace the silliness of imitating animals, beat-boxing, and developing vocal sensation through glissando and other techniques that do not normally occur in the standard song repertoire. While the voice can be put to the most serious use—political speeches, prayer, solo or collective singing, vows and promises—the mechanism itself is relatively neutral, even though it is open to swift and highly differentiated motivation through the stimulus of real or mimicked emotional states. Where motivation elicits memories of unpleasant experience, this can manifest in phonation being inhibited or compromised. Actors and singers have to take care in this respect. Humour, relaxedness and open-mindedness all play a vital part in achieving release from these negative associations.

Figure 7.1 Musical example of *Llamas love many zoos*.

<hr />

[6] It is the *sounds* represented by the letters that need to be performed, not their names.

Figure 7.2 Musical example of *Thirty thousand feathers on a thirsty thrush's throat*.

Teachers and ensemble directors have a vital role in achieving these conditions, from which participants benefit enormously. The final suggestions in this section arise from the spirit of play that remains a factor in the entire *Harmony Signing* project.

The Peppa Pig snorting strategy was intended to encourage resonance through raising the soft palate. Another means of achieving this, and of further exercising the tongue and its access to different parts of the oral cavity, is to practise the tongue clicks that are employed as consonants in Southern African languages such as Xhosa. As with rolling the <r> or making the *lebble-ebble* sound, the tongue can only move to the position in which these can be achieved if it is free to do so. Starting with the click that is closest to a European consonant, we can focus on producing the loudest possible 'tut' sound (like a normal <t> but given greater emphasis as in the 'tut' of disapproval), with the tip of the tongue pressed against the front of the palate and released quickly. The most characteristic of the Xhosa clicks can be accessed from here, though it may require practice for those whose tongues have been habitually stiffened. The tongue is drawn back slightly over the palate, though still in a forward position, and 'spread' to produce a vacuum across its entire width. Releasing this produces a loud 'plop' akin to opening a champagne bottle or performance on a wood block (stories exist of this sound being deceitfully used in cricket to fool umpires into believing that a player has hit the ball and should be given out 'caught behind'). A third tongue click is made further back in the mouth, the tongue curled to whip backwards before coming forwards again, producing the sound we use to imitate the clucking of chickens. Both of these, the 'plop' and the 'cluck', activate the resonance of the mouth: one can pitch them so as to perform staccato melodies. A fourth type of tongue click releases suction created by the side of the tongue against the back teeth on one side of the mouth. This is the click employed in giving instructions to horses and camels.

Aside from their potential for flexible tongue development without which these clicks are not possible, they have the side benefit of illustrating the posture of the mouth and tongue that gives rise to optimum resonance—the achievement of the 'cathedral of the mouth'. In order to experience this, students should follow each of the four clicks with an immediately sung *Ah* vowel, as in the consonant-vowel pairs of their mother tongue, but with a musically sustained consequent. Listening carefully to the result illustrates the influence of each tongue click on the quality and resonance of the following vowel. Mastery of the 'plop' tends to lead to the most 'open' and efficient singing. As an addition to the repertoire of vocal beat-boxing (see the section, 'Exploring Duration'), these sounds can help exercise the voice and develop self-knowledge of how we employ its evolved anatomic structures.

A variety of spoken and sing-song strategies can also liberate the voice from fixed habits. *Talking like a Pirate* is a popular meme that has spread in the wake of recent Hollywood movies and has the advantage of exploiting new resonances, as well as the continuity of phonation involved in performing the requisite *Aaaaarrrrrgggghhhh*! Cartoon voices (Mickey Mouse; robots; manga characters; monsters; Transformers, etc.) can also profitably extend the range and register of students' voices. One can take a line of poetry or a song and, employing flash cards or PowerPoint slides or images, lead an ensemble in collective response to capturing the vocal performance of the sample material in the variety of ways displayed. This is a collective activity, with the group aiming to match in unison the vocal characteristics suggested. An individual variant that can help release vocal creativity and flexibility is to have students provide the voices to glove puppets: animals, the handsome prince, wicked witches, and so on.

The Vocal Template

Part I has focused on why singing is central to the vision of music education that *Harmony Signing* embraces. We have considered the factors of child development and play through which the speaking and singing voices are initially acquired in infancy, and how these can be revisited in remediating vocal problems in later life. We have considered especially some means of helping the performance of poor-pitch singers, fired by the belief that no normal human is 'tone-deaf'. We have achieved these developments through humour and playfulness that are in many ways inseparable from the human impulse to create. We have transferred these 'external' developments to the 'inner ear', illustrating the aural benefits of recalling the sound of our own voice in silent singing and in relating our experience of performance to its recall. In this way, we have recognised the essential factor of aural development that feeds on vocal learning.

Harmony Signing exploits and extends all of these experiences. It provides the means to deepen musical understanding that will allow fluent improvisation and the experience of collective composition that can inspire individual achievement. Through the techniques encountered so far, students will have the means to attempt scat 'cover versions' of songs and instrumental works of their choice and to make vocal arrangements of them. Part II deals with how such processes can be accelerated, and their role in learning made more memorable and fluent, through the use of gesture.

PART II
WHY SIGNING?

8

Representation and Communication

The story of how *Harmony Signing* commenced almost by accident was told in the Introduction. The students aged seven to eleven who first stumbled on its potential were ready to do so because they had already experienced leading collective song through the use of Kodály signs and through playing a variety of musical games that linked sound to gesture. Fortune favours the prepared mind. Reflection on why this form of interactive pedagogy developed so quickly as a representation of more extensive musical thinking and on what the explanations may be for this led to the formation of a number of connections among concurrent research in neuroscience, child development, semiotics, and evolutionary psychology.

The two most significant factors at play in *Harmony Signing* are: (1) the multimodal, embodied manner in which gestures encode musical structures as information that develops musical knowledge; and (2) the capacity to convey intentions emerging from such knowledge to others who share understanding of the system in operation and are able to respond both cognitively and expressively in real time.

While notation can and does carry out the first function, it cannot achieve the second. The value of this second attribute of *Harmony Signing* is that it represents both an alternative mode to notation for the communication of musical information and an alternative to speech. All interaction thus takes place within the same integrated musical system, rather than crossing into a separate medium such as language. It continues to feed on and develop the instant, instinctive responses that were required by the games and tasks introduced in Part I, permitting simultaneous participation that amplifies and intensifies the musical intentions of the person leading, feeding back to them the consequences of their actions as the basis for developing fluency and confidence. This feedback loop carries two kinds of information: the cognitive (the musical information determined by selection and shaping of the potential of the system) and the affective (the emotional motivation both bound up in the selection of content and communicated in the manner in which gestures are presented). Figure 8.1 captures these relationships.

Figure 8.1 sets out to convey what is happening in the minds of leaders and participants when *Harmony Signing* is proceeding effectively. The process involved is virtually instant: while one relationship depends on another, the anticipation of outcomes by all participants results in the simultaneous action of everyone involved. Of course, mistakes are made that can interrupt or slow down progress or stop it altogether (inclusion of a sign yet to be learned or ambiguously presented; changes of sign carried out at too fast a tempo; hesitation that results in lack of momentum). Indeed, trial-and-error learning plays a healthy part in the development of the pedagogy, shaping the sense of consequence that the signer feels that can spur greater clarity and the expressiveness that results. The role of the teacher is vital in this. Teachers have the great responsibility of modelling the fluent and effective practice of *Harmony Signing* in the first place, and can often intervene to help overcome problems as they occur. However,

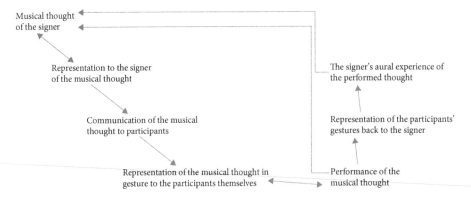

Figure 8.1 The multisensory feedback loop of *Harmony Signing.*

the more students themselves take on the leader role, the more evenly this skill will be distributed throughout the class or ensemble and the greater the incidence of intrinsic motivation shared by both leader and participants.

The factors of intrinsic and extrinsic motivation (Kohn 1999; Hallam 2002) operate differently in *Harmony Signing*, largely as a result of the transfer of leadership to students. As we will see, an aspect of this is the minimising of comment and evaluation in language that the pedagogy admits. When a group performs a musically coherent passage that meets with mutual approval that is detectable in the quality of performance, this is the 'reward in itself' that needs no explanation. A gesture of acknowledgement by the signer—a nod or thumbs-up sign—may have its place, essentially as a means of conveying that a 'turn' is over and that leadership is being transferred to another participant. But the kinds of competitive reflection ('I preferred Jo's to Keith's'; 'You forgot to include a minor chord') that students offer as criticism has no place in *Harmony Signing*.

The teacher's role is, then, classically more that of facilitator and expert participant than either instructor or director. Conceding leadership of an ensemble on a regular basis to potentially every member of a class, choir, or ensemble may represent a step beyond what some teachers will initially find comfortable. One can only hope that in the relationships they set out to build with their students and the manner in which this is achieved in intrinsically musical and mutually respectful ways, teachers recognise the value and motivational potential of this approach.

The teacher remains in control in regard to how much time is given to *Harmony Signing* and how to combine it with other musical practices in the curriculum. *Harmony Signing* is not itself a curriculum, though it has been designed to integrate developmentally with a wide range of aspects of music education. Former students and other practitioners who employ the approach over time tend to incorporate *Harmony Signing* as a warm-up, as supportive of aural and theory development, and as a means of exploring creative options leading to composing and arranging. This leaves a great deal that teachers select from in, especially, the secondary classroom: notation and its teaching; keyboard work; the use of music technology at individual workstations; individual and group instrumental lessons; music history. For *Harmony Signing* to succeed, it needs to be viewed by both teacher and students as contributing to their success. It must never appear to be an end in itself.

Returning for a moment to reflecting on the processes conveyed in Figure 8.1, one might consider how these could be equally present in, say, harmony taught by other means. What similarities might exist if work of this kind were achieved in a keyboard class or a guitar ensemble, for example?[1]

I have led, participated in, and modelled similar parallels with students. There are, and should be, suitable ways of working on these lines with students who play a variety of instruments. But there are differences. To begin with, the performative modelling of material cannot be achieved in the same way. In *Harmony Signing* gross bodily gestures communicate information. In playing guitar or piano, performance is achieved by relatively small movements of the fingers. To model this to a group, one has to rely upon alternatives; for example, a 'call and response' sequence in which participants mimic the teacher *after* the initial presentation, or a form of counting that elicits simultaneity. What about selection of information? In *Harmony Signing*, this is simultaneous by design. It would be difficult for such simultaneous performance to be possible with guitar or piano. One might imagine a camera on the teacher's hands projecting an image of what they are doing onto a big screen. This could permit students to decode what the teacher models in something close to real time. But what would be lost here is contact with the teacher's face, especially their eyes. The quality of expressivity would be difficult to convey, and the empathy between leader and participants lessened. Focus would be divided and, one suspects, language would be relied upon to bridge the gaps.

Such reflections illustrate why we rely on notation. Written musical instructions stand in for the visual modelling of what our hands do, where we have learned what the notation indicates (whether TAB and chord symbols or stave notation). So, what would be lost in this case? Clearly, it is the capacity for spontaneity: for the leader to invent and communicate musical thoughts to which participants can respond in real time.

There is another important difference between our vocal *Harmony Signing* group and a keyboard or guitar ensemble. Human beings can only sing one fundamental pitch at a time. This means that, in contributing to the performance of a signed passage, each individual must select, according to conventions of voice-leading, a single line of music which only makes sense in combination with the performance of others. No individual can perform 'the whole'. So, a foundational strength of *Harmony Signing* is social and musical dependence on others and the sense of trust and collective effort this involves. By comparison, a chord progression on piano or guitar can be presented in its entirety by the teacher and mimicked in its entirety. Instrumental performance in such groups represents a transfer of skill achieved through its accurate copying. There is intrinsic motivation in the amplified performance to which this gives rise, but it is different to the interpersonal cooperation that provides a buzz in *Harmony Signing*.

Before we leave this point, it is important to mention that the voice-leading principles which permit the mutual intelligibility on which successful *Harmony Signing* depends are themselves formative of musical understanding. The sense of *location* built through engagement with these processes is different to the more global selection of complete

---

[1] We will set to one side the replacement of voices in *Harmony Signing* with the use of instruments. This is a desirable outcome that will be advocated in due course. All of my experience, including deliberate experiments with leaving out the vocal education stage, points to the fact that instrumental work is only effective when participants have first learned the required skills through singing.

chords that the fingerings of piano and guitar equivalents determine. In an ideal world, music learners would have all three experiences while benefitting from the different perspectives they afford.

What this comparison between different ways of learning harmonic function has illustrated is the potential interrelationship between *Harmony Signing* and other complementary musical practices. While *Harmony Signing* need not depend on understanding of notation, it can valuably support it. On a great many occasions, students have volunteered the advice that a concept they found difficult to understand has been clarified through the practical experience *Harmony Signing* involves. Instances of this include suspension, modulation, the creation of a variety of ninth chords, and the role of the *tièrce de Picardie*. Where our students are using notation already in their instrumental or vocal lessons and ensemble experience, *Harmony Signing* presents a supportive means of making what is known in notation available to creative and personal experiment that can accelerate and deepen understanding. Within school practice that deals less thoroughly with notation, *Harmony Signing* can provide a means of understanding musical continuity that is not reliant on written symbols.

A further element evident in Figure 8.1 is that signing conveys both cognitive and expressive information, and this is at the heart of the intrinsic motivation and sense of collective achievement we can set out to develop. By cognitive information, I imply factual information—that which is essentially right or wrong; that is, the chord or melodic line presented by the signer, whose capacity for continued action depends on it being performed correctly. The capacity for expression is bound up in the quality of signing—of timing, gestural clarity and elegance—that participants also perceive and respond to in their performance. This dual factor is shared by what all conductors achieve as well as by most communicative systems, certainly in language and in the interpretation of music in all genres. It reflects the bicameral structure of the human brain and the multitasking of which we are consequently capable. Nevertheless, the precise formulation of the gestures of harmony signing also owes a great deal to the observation of deaf sign language. While working at the University of Reading, I became familiar with the research of colleagues who ran a dedicated course in Theatre for the Deaf. It was a revelation to me that the text of, say, a Shakespeare play could be communicated in British Sign Language by actors who could convey the emotion their roles required with a force and clarity equal to their speaking equivalents. In mixed spoken/signed productions, one relied, as a nonreader of Sign, on this factor in order to follow the plot and the interaction between characters. Oliver Sacks (1990) brilliantly accounts for this phenomenon and its implications in a book that I found as influential as his later writings about the neuroscience of music itself (1998, 2007).

This factor of the dual-purpose channel that signing represents in music is also the basis of the advice I offer that *Harmony Signing* should be learned through vocal interaction prior to any eventual transfer of leadership skills to instrumental ensembles. To explore this further, we can consider the developments in psychology and pedagogy of the last generation or so that have questioned the assumption that education should address and assess only logical, mathematical, and linguistic processing. Antonio Damasio's (1994) labelling of this opening-out of how we learn and behave calls upon us to recognise 'Descartes' Error': the assumption that the rational is the principal representation of the self, captured in the statement 'I think, therefore I am'. Damasio argues strongly for the role of emotion both as a parallel system to cognition in terms of thought and recall, and also as a more rapid form of response to experience that acts as a gatekeeper to rationalisation. The brain works best in balance. Neurologically, this opposition is seen as mapped onto the two hemispheres of the brain. The left side, in the majority of us, is responsible for guiding the use of our dominant hand and eye and the right side cross-laterally motivates the left-hand side of the body. Two further models of how we learn and behave outline similar concerns regarding a limited cognitive approach to brain function: Howard Gardner's (1983) theory of *Frames of Mind*, a suite of varying responses to what our senses inform us of; and the division into Visual, Aural, and Kinaesthetic *learning styles* (Dunn & Dunn 1978) that are taken to co-exist in different balance in each human individual.

We can reflect briefly on some aspects of *Harmony Signing* that are consistent with these theoretical frameworks. Foremost is the harnessing of emotional response as a reliable and formative aspect of how we process music. For instance, *Harmony Signing* assumes a qualitative rather than quantitative means of, for example, discriminating between intervals, aiming to teach them as a set of unique experiences with distinct effects on the listener. Contrast this with the means many teachers employ of having students count semitones, or degrees of the scale, as their method of 'measuring' intervals, whether in written dictation tasks or oral performance. The practices we will employ in relation to intervals will strongly advocate the value of acquiring confidence in our emotional responses.

This in turn plays a part in the 'discovery learning' that underpins the place of improvisation in *Harmony Signing*. Again, using the example of intervals: Rather than viewing them as analytical constructs, students employ them to understand their potential in musical utterances of their own creation; they operate preference and choice. This is one of the reasons that singing of the harmonic series has been proposed strongly as a means of learning to train the ear through the properties of the voice. The sense of awe and magic that many students experience in learning to achieve this empowers them in a manner that contrasts sharply with teacher direction regarding what they ought to hear.[2]

Similarly, teachers can be wary of exploring emotional response for two possible reasons. First, they fear its unreliability, relating to factors such as taste and preference, and to outcomes different to the teacher's own experience. Second, they are concerned about the inconsistency that may result from the hormonal mood swings of adolescence. I have on many occasions discussed these features with serving and preservice teachers, and am usually able to allay their concerns. *Harmony Signing*, and creative teaching generally, adopts feeling and its evocation as a purpose of music, the inhibition of which undermines motivation and removes the personal identification on which deep experience depends.

Gardner's 'Frames of Mind' (1983) provide a further illustration of desirable attributes of *Harmony Signing* that accord also with personal learning style. The multimodal thinking bound up in simultaneous vocal performance and its representation in

---

[2] It would be my observation that the many computer apps that claim to aid in the teaching of aural are limited to the assumption that discrimination is based on quantification. While they can reward correct answers, they have little to offer a student who is wrong.

gesture bridges two distinct 'chapels of the mind' (Mithen 1996): the musical (aural) and the kinaesthetic (feelingful), which deepen the encoding in memory of the information involved. But there is a further dimension to this musical engagement. Gardner argued for an independent *social intelligence* that is associated with our understanding of the needs of others, the effect of our behaviour upon them, and our capacity for collective agreement. The intentions behind *Harmony Signing* have been to maximise students' capacity for collaborative engagement and lessen the element of competition in order to exploit the means that collective performance establishes for musical engagement that brings a sense of mutual achievement. Commentators have considered the attainment of this to represent a key turning point in the evolution of human culture (Merker 2000), and to embody a view of music as a medium for the alignment of minds (Livingstone & Thompson 2009; Harvey 2017). It is for this reason above all that *Harmony Signing* proceeds most effectively where students themselves take leadership roles. The group as a whole develops a culture of learning in which every individual benefits.

9

The Two Hemispheres of the Brain

Multimodal Musical Response: Mirror-Neurons at Work

A model of sensory integration that has developed in the last twenty years in neuroscience helps to illustrate what is happening when *Harmony Signing* proceeds successfully, especially at more advanced levels. Italian scientists in the 1990s discovered fascinating neural responses in monkeys which suggested that the mind contains networks that are active both when an action is carried out and when it is merely observed (Iacoboni 2009; Kohler et al. 2002). The networks involved were dubbed *mirror neurons*. More recent research has attributed to mirror neurons the capacity for coordinated action, the acquisition of language, and an explanation for the nature of human music-making (Molnar-Szakacs & Overy 2006).

However, the exploitation by *Harmony Signing* of the two channels of gesture and musical vocalisation places a specific and focused load on the brain, taking in aural, kinaesthetic, and social recognition systems. It is for this reason that I have found it helpful to propose that language is to be avoided while engaging in *Harmony Signing*. Thinking in the additional system of words invades the aural-productive networks that are involved in representation and communicative participation. This can be both distracting and inhibiting.

Musical Thinking and Feeling

We have considered some aspects of the relationship between cognition and emotion in music-making that emerge from the evolved bicameral architecture of the brain. Another outcome of hemispherical balance with consequences for *Harmony Signing* is handedness and the integration of our anatomical potential.

Even in the simplest forms of *Harmony Signing*, leaders deal with using the two hands for different roles. Initially, the left controls the signalling of chord selection (the *what*), while the right indicates starting, stopping, and continuity so as to coordinate the *when* and, to an extent, the *how*. As skills develop, a greater load of information can be conveyed through a variety of shortcuts and substitutions. Once it proves possible to combine melody (RH) with harmony (LH), the body divides these roles in a manner that replicates those of playing the piano accordion.

But a further set of gestural combinations offers a variety of means to control texture within the ensemble and lead different musical outcomes:

- adding a bassline in the RH to a chord progression signed with the LH
- directing a two-part, polyphonic texture through employing Kodály hand signs in both hands

- employing both hands to signal more complex harmonic operations, such as *inversion* and the signing of dissonant chords and their relationships
- employing both hands to signal functions such as modulation

Working in this manner with two hands over time, simultaneously conveying two streams of sound that can be performed by participants, develops musical instincts and an understanding of function and style that can be achieved in no other way.

When working with students and classes, I often find that left-handed participants request permission to reverse the roles of the two hands. Where they are comfortable themselves with this arrangement, it is by far the best way for them to lead, and coparticipants rarely notice that they are doing so in mirror-image. What works much less well in terms of establishing clear practice is for individuals to vary what they do from time to time. Participants rapidly appraise hesitation or lack of conviction in signers, and this is as much about whether the signs provided are clear, unambiguous, and timed to permit effective reading as it is about which hand is used. Just occasionally, the model of clear, well-formed gestures may need to be reestablished. As in any activity, but particularly in one that relies on clarity combined with conviction, sloppy or reluctant gestures lead to poor results.

10
Wordless Musicking

Returning to the theme we have already mentioned of why it is important not to talk during *Harmony Signing* engagement, it is clearly the role of the teacher to model this. Facial expression is vital if one is to guide behaviour without adopting the linguistic instruction on which we rely most of the time. I adopt the formula: 'For the next *x* minutes, I am not going to use language, and I would be grateful if everyone could do the same. Try to clear your mind of words so that we can focus exclusively on thinking in music.'

In addition, one needs, in order to preserve this position, to devise nonmusical signs that indicate readiness and such things as:

- 'would someone like to take over from me at this point?'
- 'thank you, let's have someone else take a turn'
- 'are you happy to go next?'
- 'that didn't quite work, but we will do it again'

I find that turn-taking revolves far more quickly and efficiently when it is done silently and without breaking the atmosphere through relying on language. Students can begin to operate these same conventions. When students lead, I always participate alongside the class or ensemble. The effective *Harmony Signing* class is one in which a visitor might not immediately detect who is doing the teaching.

More on Aural *Location*

Some practical activities that act as a bridge between the games and tasks already experienced and the *Harmony Signing* proper that we will commence in Part III employ the combination of Kodály signs with drones in order to create the simplest and arguably oldest and most universal form of accompaniment. Melody conveyed in the RH using Kodály hand signs is accompanied by a sustained drone on a pitch selected to be signed with the LH. Using this procedure, the relationship between notes of the scale and the drone can be explored in a manner that recalls the Alap of Indian music. The first Alap given in Figure 10.1 is diatonic, and should be mastered by every participant as they perform one of the two roles—melody or drone—into which they have been divided. The roles can then be exchanged. Either way, everyone should develop their representation of the experience by using both hands.

This exercise reveals an important aspect of each note of the scale: whether it is stable (consonances on the third, fifth, and octave) or unstable (dissonances on the second and seventh; and the intervals of the fourth and sixth). The latter divide into those in which the instability is resolved by falling (second, fourth, sixth) and the seventh, which rises to the octave (it is, after all, the *leading note*).

Figure 10.1 Music notation of a diatonic *Alap*.

Figure 10.2 Music notation of a chromatic *Alap*.

When participants are ready, a second Alap can be employed at a later stage that sets out the notes of the chromatic scale over a drone (fig. 10.2).

Again, the qualities of stability and instability can be discerned and the routes towards resolution compared: both the minor and major second fall to the tonic; the minor third rises to the major; the augmented fourth rises to the perfect fifth; both the minor and the major sixths fall to the fifth, and so does the minor seventh, taking two steps to do so.

Listening acutely to these qualities of implied movement or stability while gaining experience of performing these under the leadership of a signer whose gestures one mimics, makes a vital contribution to acquiring a strong sense of the *location* of specific pitches in relation to the drone.

Leadership Skills and Student Independent Learning

This Alap exercise provides the first experience of leading harmonically coherent music employing both hands. Crucial to the value of this step is the freedom to test rhythmic and sequential possibilities through unprepared direction. While the horizon remains limited, this experience represents a valuable basis for the more complex creative choices that will be built upon it.

PART III
PATTERNS OF LEADERSHIP
AND INTERACTION

11
Collective Creativity

This chapter lays out the first formal elements of *Harmony Signing* proper: the ordering of chords based on good voice-leading from which everything grows. The basics steps of *Harmony Signing* reveal and explore the relationships between the three primary triads. This begins with establishing a comfortable and resonant tonic chord. One might employ the strategy provided in Chapter 6 ('The Four Elements of Vocal Learning') to achieve this. But participants need to become accustomed to making chords in which they are divided into three parts that perform notes 1, 3, and 5 respectively: Doh, Me, and Soh. This chord is signed with the left arm placed horizontally across the chest, the flat hand palm downwards. It mirrors the Kodály sign for the note Me. This is deliberate since the major character of the chord is dependent on this pitch. Visually, this presents a very clear image around which every other gesture revolves. Imagine that the three notes of the tonic triad are like three positions. For the moment, we could imagine dividing the horizontal arm into three critical points: the elbow, the wrist, and the fingertips. These do not represent fixed pitches, but rather qualities of potential movement from these points. What happens next results from assigning meaning to the movements that link chords together.

The first progression we will then make will link this tonic chord to the subdominant by the following means:

> The left arm moves from its horizontal position, with palm downwards across the chest, to one in which the fingertips are pointing upwards—a gesture that covers a right angle.
>
> The elbow, representing the *anchor note* of the unchanging tonic (doh/1), remains where it was.
>
> The wrist, representing the semitone rise from Me to Fa (3–4), moves   to a new position by a small step;
>
> The fingertips, representing the whole tone rise from Soh to La (5--6), moves to a new position by a larger step.

One can represent this as follows, captured also in music notation in Figure 11.1:

One can represent this as follows:

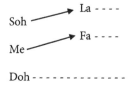

Figure 11.1 Music notation of the initial *Harmony Signing* move from tonic to subdominant.

Different students can then play with this relationship, rising and falling between the two positions, as well as cutting off to silence on either chord so as to repeat chords or re-enter on either. Even with a repertoire of only two chords, a range of possibilities is presented. One can set up rhythmic patterns based on the chords being of differing lengths. For instance, in the theme from *Chariots of Fire*, Vangelis accompanies the melody with a pattern that sounds the tonic for three beats and the subdominant for one.

The mirror of moving to the subdominant is accessing the dominant. This time, the arm descends through a right angle to a position in which the fingertips point vertically downwards, as illustrated in fig. 11.2:

> The elbow, representing the *anchor note* of the unchanging dominant (soh/5), remains where it was;
> The fingertips, representing the whole tone fall from Me to Ray (3–2) move to a new position by a larger step;
> The wrist, representing the semitone fall from Doh to Ti^{+} (1–7) moves to a new position by a small step.

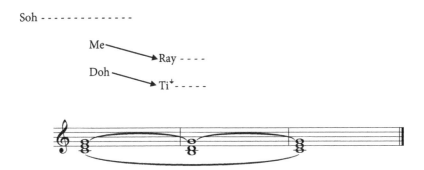

Figure 11.2 Music notation of the *Harmony Signing* move from tonic to dominant.

Recall that the arm movements represent the *property of voice-leading* rather than exchanging specific positions of the wrist, elbow, or fingertips. The interchangeability is captured by the overall direction of movement (tonic to subdominant requires upwards voice-leading; tonic to dominant, downwards), and by the clarity and opposing functions of the two new positions. A misunderstanding that can arise even with teachers and able students is that the two arm movements signal a generalised 'up' and 'down': this results in the response to the move to the subdominant being the provision of Ray (note 2 of the scale) where participants have failed to maintain the anchor note,

Doh. At worst, the outcome is chord ii if this interpretation dominates. Similarly, in the move towards V, participants can follow the herd and move from Soh to Fa, producing a chord vii/diminished triad. Two strategies can clarify the appropriate intentions and ensure that these errors are eliminated: one nonverbal, the other conveyed in language.

The nonverbal technique, one that proves highly effective as a teaching tool at every level of *Harmony Signing*, is to repeat the progression containing the mistake while signalling clearly with the right hand the Kodály sign for the anchor note that binds together the two chords in question. Sometimes this ploy can be reinforced through the leader singing this pitch while signalling the chord change, so as to illustrate that participants performing this role do not move. This is an example of conveying thinking-in-sound that can achieve the desired improvement both as an immediate remedy, and as an example of how students should be listening to the function their voice part represents, which helps to develop location.

For that reason, the nonverbal solution should always be attempted first. Subsequently, the theoretical underpinning can be explained or made clear in music notation. At that stage, the point can also be made that chords ii and vii will be introduced later as additional elements of the harmonic family in which they also have a place. But the vital aim in the initial exploration of the primary triads is that they are established as the bedrock of confident and reliable response on which all later elaborations can build.

The habit of performing the moves that outline the relationship of the primary triads to a sustained 'Aaahh' sound rather than to note names or numbers should be established as soon as possible. This will allow the quality of sound, and of blend and tuning, to become the principal association of performing these chords. On any suitable future occasions, when it may help with location or the introduction of new information, Kodály names or numbers can be reintroduced. But the ideal in *Harmony Signing* is to match pure sound to gesture. This will be especially the case when routines are transferred from voices to instruments, and the habits which will permit this need to be laid down from the beginning.

Two questions tend to be posed when I work with teachers and experienced students who encounter *Harmony Signing* for the first time: (1) Why move to the subdominant first? and (2) Why place the subdominant in the 'superior' position and the dominant in the 'inferior' one?

These questions tend to suggest that training in music history and theory has fixed in people's minds the idea that music moves to the dominant as its likeliest structural destination. Certainly, this is true of the conventional plan of Baroque dance forms and of major-key works conceived in relation to the Classical sonata principle. But a great deal of music from the medieval and Renaissance periods, as well as folk music around the world, favours the subdominant relationship. Equally, people think of the dominant as 'above' the tonic because this is its position in the scale; the subdominant is 'below' because the tonic occupies the fifth position in the subdominant scale. Many of these impressions result from the patterns of scale practice to which young pianists and other instrumentalists are introduced.

But let's listen to the acoustic leanings bound up in the relationships between these chords and captured in Figures 11.1 and 11.2. The answer lies in the acute aural sense we seek to establish. When we set out to produce vocal harmonics, we noticed that a pronounced dominant seventh has a place in the harmonic series.[1] If the harmonic series contains a dissonance of this kind, then it suggests that all music is, in a sense, on an infinite quest towards incomplete resolution: Each dominant seventh on the tonic demands a modulation to its subdominant, only for the process to require repetition as the seventh harmonic over the new tonic becomes audible! Of course, we have learned to tolerate this effect, and composers mitigate it in the ways in which they underline the ends of movements through strongly orchestrated unisons and other ploys. But it is enough, for me, for this to distinguish the sense of movement that places the subdominant in the position demonstrated, and to favour introducing it first, especially when dealing with younger participants. By clear visible and acoustic contrast, the dominant occupies the opposite position and function. When we consider the nature of modulation practices that *Harmony Signing* makes possible, we will encounter further confirmatory reasons for this arrangement in space, sound, and representation.

We have now achieved an initial handling of the primary triads (I, IV, V) and the capacity to move between them. We have modelled I - IV and I - V. The next step is to move between IV and V directly, allowing the common progression I - IV - V - I.

Presenting the move IV - V provides the first real opportunity for the wordless introduction of a new possibility through employing the method itself as the teaching process. Having ensured that the sounds of moving between I and IV and I and V respectively are being achieved cleanly and without hesitation, the leader can move directly from IV to V at a carefully measured pace. For me, this can be the first 'breakthrough moment' in teaching *Harmony Signing*, and successful outcomes are instructive. It is worth characterising this, because responses can be varied. Where students have some existing musical experience and vocal confidence, the move IV - V will be performed successfully, though one will notice smiles—either of satisfaction, in which the potential of what has been achieved is conveyed or of relief. In cases where the move confuses, the discernible response can be that participants recognised the intention but needed reassurance in carrying it out. If this is the case, simply repeating it can work immediately—and one tends then to encounter the same smiles of satisfaction as for those who 'got it' the first time. Where participants require further help, the progression can be remodelled using Kodály signs to convey the voice-leading route of each of the three parts. Achieving the completion of the three-chord progression nonverbally will elicit the emotional responses identified. Stopping to explain it in words renders the experience in facts, in which such a quality of experience is missing.

One further move is, of course, also available: V - IV, the characteristic sequence that defines blues and the rock and popular styles descended from this African American tradition. This should be practised for two reasons: (1) it provides a further and discernibly different experience of the potential of the primary triads that will aid the development of location and fluent participation in general; (2) it acknowledges the foundational contribution of a genre that will appeal to students keen to write or arrange songs within the traditions that have arisen from it. As our understanding of *Harmony Signing* proceeds, we will develop further and more elaborate responses to the potential of the blues progression.

---

[1] It is audible in the pronounced <r> sound following an <a> vowel in some speakers with a midwestern US or Canadian accent.

Some Characteristic Progressions as a Basis for Analysis and Creative Work

We have illustrated the means of signing the progressions I→IV→V→I and I→V→IV→I. But there are many more options in addition to this apparent choice of pathway, for example:

> I→IV→I→V→I
> I→V→I→IV→I

Every participant should be given the chance to model a progression of their choice from these ingredients and lead it with the class. This will consolidate collective knowledge and effectiveness, while also providing participants with an initial opportunity to experience the accelerated understanding obtained from taking the leader role. However, it will also become evident that the creative choices are somewhat limited. A simple additional action can render them very much more varied and applicable to a wide range of stylistic possibilities.

The new 'move' does not involve further harmonic choices, but the rhythmic liberation of current practice from undifferentiated continuity. This permits the establishment of *harmonic rhythm*—the characteristic sense of weight and movement that is associated with a variety of dance and song forms and other existing procedures. It also confers the ability to shape phrases, and thus commence for leaders a sense of responsibility for expression, as well as for the relationship between phrase length and the breathing capacity of participants.

The signalling of rhythm is thus a significant development: both the rate of movement and the replacement of chords with silence. Leaders need to begin to use the right (or nondominant) hand, so that there is a clear distinction between functions: one hand signing choices of chord and the other controlling rhythmic features.

Right hand functions introduce a new skill. This requires practice for the relationship between signer and participants to employ it successfully. The main functions to focus upon at this stage are:

> starting,
> stopping, and
> creating a sense of phrase (continuity).

Starting is achieved in the conventional manner, through providing a preparatory upbeat followed by a downbeat that elicits a response from participants. It is vital that signers learn to provide the anticipatory upbeat that gives participants the opportunity to breathe and prepare. Stopping is also achieved conventionally, as in the conductor's cut-off. This introduces periods of measured silence (rests) that, as we will see in some of the examples provided, can give a new flavour to a progression. During such silences, the left arm signal for the next chord can be changed, so that participants are able to locate their contribution while awaiting the leader's direction to join in again.

The right hand can also be employed to shape phrases expressively, sustaining continuity in order to create a sense of phrase. To achieve this, one needs to avoid using signs that may be confused with other specific functions—and there are a great many new signs to come. The gesture that will work both at this stage, as well as in more complex and elaborate signing, employs the right hand with palm open and fingers spread upwards to express a feeling of connection between chords. This gesture can be helpful for three principal reasons. (1) It prevents singers from 'thinking with the breath,' or stopping and starting habitually between chords. (2) It helps develop a sense of musical direction because if the signer is signalling that participants should *not* breathe, then he or she is responsible for shaping a phrase in which an opportunity to breathe occurs later, prior to the point where the music collapses.[2] (3) It begins to permit stylistic and expressive choices to be made—greater or lesser legato, a sense of rubato within rhythmically consistent progression, and dynamic change.

All participants should be encouraged to develop these true directing skills, since the enhanced sense of expressive communication will prepare the group for meaningful and sensitive engagement with the more elaborate creative possibilities that advanced *Harmony Signing* will introduce. Above all, signer-leaders need to both listen to and observe the response of participants, since not only the musical results but also the capacity for the group to perform at all resides with them. The sense of responsibility this should confer is an important aspect of the social integration and mutual dependence that this approach both relies on and develops. Signers learn that, as they control what is performed, the theoretical underpinning of the musical results is being acquired unconsciously by the whole ensemble, and they share responsibility for this progress.

As leaders have their turn to operate in this way, their learning is best developed by exercising free exploration. This allows choices and decisions to be made in real time that feed and respond to the musical imaginings of the inner ear. But an available alternative is to apply the *Harmony Signing* skill acquired as an analytical tool, permitting participants to generate the accompaniments to some well-known musical examples, as captured in fig. 11.3.[3]

1 *Wimoweh*
2 Bernstein 'One Hand, One Heart', from *West Side Story* (opening chord progression)
3 Schumann, *Frauenliebe und leben* No. 1, 'Seit ich ihn gesehen' (opening chord progression)
4 *Silent Night*
5 Chopin's Etude in E Major, Op. 10, no. 3 'Tristesse' (opening)

Examples of this kind can be experienced in a variety of ways:

- 'Tracked' in response to the music: participants gesture the chords while listening to a recording
- Performed live as an accompaniment to the melody sung (or played instrumentally) by an individual (who could be the teacher) or subgroup

---

[2] This teaches signers to listen, observe, and monitor whether they can perform what they are signing, and by doing so earn the trust of participants.
[3] These are simplified arrangements, adapted for representation and performance through the limited strategies we have so far learned and which represent the spirit of these examples.

This arrangement of the Chopin sets out to capture the effect of the original, of which it is not a precise transcription. Rather, it conveys with the resources so far available an impression of the harmonic progression that underpins Chopin's melody.

Figure 11.3 Examples 1 through 5 in music notation.

- At a later stage, led by a signer who simultaneously handles both the melodic and harmonic streams (see the section, 'Working in Groups').

Building next on the skills and analytical understanding these experiences develop, suitably inquisitive students can be encouraged to bring their own examples of accompaniments to melodies that they would like to try out with the class. Since a great deal of music from a wide range of genres makes no greater harmonic demands than the use of the primary triads, there is an infinite amount of musical material that can be explored in this manner. (Three rounds that exploit the primary triads are available in the Appendix.)

The blues progression is also ripe for exploration (fig. 11.4)[4]:

Roman numeral presentation				Harmonic function			
I	I	I	I	T	T	T	T
IV	IV	I	I	S	S	T	T
V	IV	I	V^7	D	S	T	D^7

Figure 11.4 The blues in music notation.

Further popular styles can also be conjured from these same ingredients—for instance, the world of Mariachi can be represented with the three chords in the order I, IV, V if we assign the syncopated rhythms of the style and add the upper part Doh-La-Ti (fig. 11.5).

Figure 11.5 A mariachi progression in music notation.

[4] Note that in teaching the blues I have favoured completing the twelve-bar sequence with a dominant seventh chord. This indeed occurs in a proportion of authentic blues examples, but my reason for doing this at this stage is that it helps students to track where they have reached and to signal the return to the beginning of the cycle. We will soon learn the additional sign required to add the seventh.

This takes us to Mexico, but also to the fusion of rock and Latin style that characterised the song *La Bamba* made famous by Ritchie Valens.[5]

The *Quixote* Gesture, Liberation of Range, and the Development of 'Location'

The voice-leading routines on which experience of the primary triads have so far depended have been fixed. Students should be given the opportunity to exchange the roles defined by their selection of starting note (Doh, Me, or Soh) and to experience the different pathways through the three possibilities that arise. This provides the necessary performance experience of the whole chordal array on which understanding and capacity of consistent location relies. However, the textures that result may seem limited. One possibility that should be attempted is to set the starting tonic at a variety of ranges to decouple the capacity of the ensemble to perform accurately from any associations with specific keys or vocal registers. Equally valuable is to distribute responsibility for different pitches around the class, so that all participants acquire the ability to hold a part without depending on sharing this with the person next to them. This can relate to working in small groups, even trios, in order to practice this level of independence.

The next routine that contributes to establishing a feel for location, and that liberates from fixed positions and limited range, is named after the character Don Quixote, famous for his assault on windmills he mistook for giants in the novel by Cervantes. The *Quixote* gesture recalls the circular motion of the arms of the windmill and is carried out with the right hand as a means of controlling how the chord conveyed by the left hand is to be sung. When this gesture is made, and the arm is in motion, all participants move at whatever rate they wish up and down the arpeggio of the chord being signed. The following provides examples of this for each chord position:

Tonic:	Doh - Soh$^↓$ - Doh - Me - Soh$^↑$ - Me - Soh - Doh$^↑$
Subdominant:	Doh - La$^↓$ - Doh - Fa - La$^↑$ - Fa - La$^↑$ - Doh$^↑$ - La
Dominant:	Ti$^↓$ - Ray - Soh$^↑$ - Ray - Soh - Ti$^↑$ - Ray$^↑$- Ti - Soh

These are the pitches that could be in play, though rather than singing the note names vocalisation should be to 'Aaahh' in order to promote blend, tuning, a smooth transition from pitch to pitch, and an overall evenness of effect. The result should preserve a clear sense of the chord intended, while being based on each individual tracing their own free pathway through the pitches that make up the triad, selecting durations that can be as varied—fast, slow, long, short—as they wish.

Whenever the leader's right arm comes to a stop, participants respond by sustaining whatever note they have reached. This permits them to listen to and judge the overall effect. An extension of what occurs at these sustained moments is that every participant signs with one hand or other the pitch they are currently singing. This forms the perceptual basis of being able to succeed in the next step we will encounter: inversion.

During their response to the *Quixote* gesture, participants will quit their original note and explore the available pitches within their range that they are able to contribute to the chord. When the chord changes to another of the primary triads as signalled by the leader, every participant has to fit in with the tonal requirement irrespective of where they find themselves. Succeeding in this both depends on and develops acute listening (the *Quixote* gesture can, for this reason, remain available as a means of developing understanding of more complicated chords and sequences to be introduced later). What this experience will have provided is a secure basis for immediately understanding and coping with the principle of chord inversion.

Inversion

Chord inversion permits harmony to be varied without introducing new chords. Indeed, the techniques of *Harmony Signing* provide a means of learning to discriminate between 'chords that are the same but inverted' and 'chords that are based on different degrees of the scale', which I had found in the past that some students could not easily identify or discriminate between.

The right hand gesture that controls inversion is similar to that for encouraging legato performance, but it is used in conjunction with the left hand to convey a specific movement by all voices. The right hand is held palm upwards towards the class, but with the fingers together, and movement up and down draws the voices of participants in parallel into the desired inversion of the chord:

(1)   Soh – Doh⁺– Me⁺– Doh⁺– Soh – Me – Soh

(2)   Me – Soh – Doh – Soh – Me – Doh – Me

(3)   Doh – Me – Soh – Me – Doh – Soh⁺– Doh

Figure 11.6 Inversion of the tonic chord in music notation.

The sign for inversion (as in fig. 11.6) can be related to any chord, as was the case with the *Quixote* gesture. A class that is ready to do so should be able to rehearse the passage in Figure 11.7, beginning slowly one chord at a time, then each phrase separated by the dotted bar lines, and finally the whole passage, increasing speed and continuity.

This passage should be commenced slowly, stopping on the chords marked with pauses, and gradually revealing more of the sequence until the whole can be sung continuously. At this point, the tempo can be increased, and the pauses ignored, so that the whole passage can be performed with confidence in a single breath.

The entire process can be employed again when transferring this level of activity to instrumental ensembles.

Figure 11.7 Music notation of 'Inversion in Action' employing the primary triads.

An indication of the liberation that inversion represents is to employ it to test the location experience of participants. For instance, can everyone assimilate and correctly perform the following (fig. 11.8)?

(1)   Soh – La – Soh – Doh⁺ - - - - - - - - Ti – Doh - - - - La – Soh - -

(2)   Me – Fa – Me – Soh – La – Soh - - - - - - - - - La – Fa – Me - -

(3)   Doh - - - - - - - - Me – Fa – Me – Ray – Me – Fa – Doh - - - - -

Chord: I   IV   I   I⁺   IV   I   V   I   IV   IV⁺   I

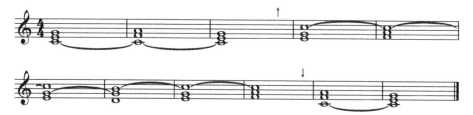

Figure 11.8 Music notation of a passage that explores the primary triads through inversion.

Again, so that all participants can fully experience this procedure, it is important that all have their turn in leading activities in which they feel the effect of inversion through conveying it in passages improvised on these lines.

What this exercise reveals clearly is a link between the 'horizontal' construction of melody from the notes of the triad and the 'vertical' performance of the same pitches as constituents of a chord. One might discuss this with the class: in origins, is harmony 'frozen melody' or is melody harmony that has thawed so that it flows? A tune in which this relationship comes across most clearly is the opening theme of *The Blue Danube Waltz* by Johann Strauss (fig. 11.9):

(1)	Doh - Doh - Me - Soh - Soh	Soh - Soh	Me - Me
(2)		Me - Me	Doh - Doh
(3)		Doh - Doh	Soh⁺ - Soh⁺
	Melody_____		Chords

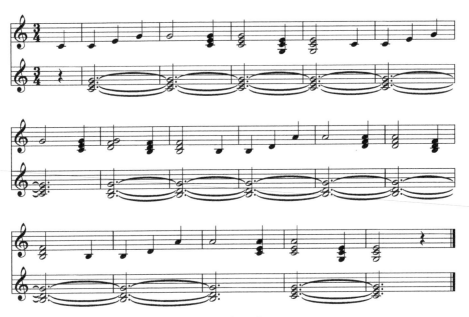

Figure 11.9 Music notation of the *Blue Danube* waltz.

Tonicising, Family Relationships, and Replacement of the Tonic

The new capacity for greater mobility made possible by inverting chords, which has extended harmonic scope and range, leads to another means of widening our musical horizons, this time through commencing journeys away from the tonic. As with many aspects of *Harmony Signing*, this is achieved by borrowing techniques from digital information processing: in this case, cutting and pasting.

The sign ✂ can be made with the fingers of the right hand to represent scissors that can be placed against the wrist of the left hand to indicate that participants should continue to sing the pitches represented while the entire chord is moved to be placed in another position. This is the harmonic equivalent of the concealment of individual Kodály hand signs that we introduced in Chapter 6. This time, instead of replacing one pitch with another, we move chords from their current function to a different one.

For instance, let's imagine moving from I to IV in the usual manner, and then use the scissors sign to 'pull' chord IV into the tonic position. At this point, we now treat it as if it *is* the tonic. This implies that there is a new subdominant awaiting discovery in its appropriate position. We will also become aware that, as a result of our manoeuvre, the old tonic has now entered the dominant position.

It is dealing with the 'new' chord IV and its implications for secure location and performance that represents the new challenge. Here is the process spelled out (fig. 11.10):

[sign ✂ and Drag]

(1)	Soh – La	Me (of new I) – 'new' Fa	
(2)	Me – Fa	Doh (of new I) – (remains on Doh)	
(3)	Doh ___	Soh (of new I) – 'new' La	
Chord	I IV - becomes 'new' -	I IV	

(cut and paste)

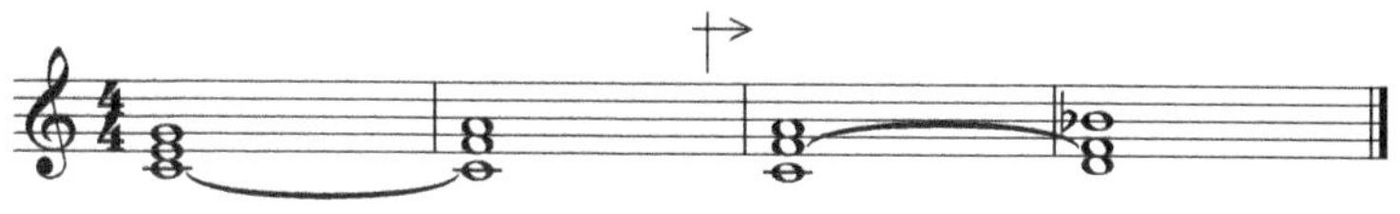

Figure 11.10 Music notation of 'cutting-and-pasting' chords to move their position.

Achieving tonic replacement by cutting and pasting is the first step towards understanding the structural and expressive function of modulation, which we will deal with in detail in due course. What it depends on is a response to the family relationship represented by the primary triads, and its key role in establishing a sense of tonality, together with all that flows from this in terms of creative opportunity and aural discrimination. This family relationship can be seen to arise from our account of harmonic implications emerging from the 'grain' of the harmonic series, and it is worth taking a brief detour to further explore this metaphor and its significance for developing a secure response to tonality, especially in terms that younger participants may understand.

Structure and Family Relations: A Detour Into Analogy

The approach we have taken to the phenomenon of harmony has been to relate its perception and musical employment to the harmonic series. We have sung and explored this in order that its existence and implications are entirely familiar. In developing *Harmony Signing*, we have aimed to lay down strong, habitual responses to the critical difference between the roles of subdominant and dominant as points of departure from the tonic. As a consequence, we set out to establish a sense of tonality in which the primary triads and their relationship are the crucial means by which we locate ourselves in the flow of a piece of music, whether it is one that we are composing or imagining or one that we are listening to or performing.

Why should this be so? From the cut-and-paste task that permits us to replace one tonic with another, we encounter a sense of travelling through musical space, of both range and perceived 'otherness', a process we engage with as performers that relies on both cognitive understanding (singing the correct notes) and emotional response. How might this be explained?

I sought an analogy that even young children would understand—not least because these processes were beginning to be explored in choral composition by seven-year-old children. The link that offered a model I could adapt was provided by music theorists Lerdahl and Jackendoff (1985), who explored the *generative* properties of tonality. We all understand the concept of generations, even the youngest children, whose pets, dolls, and toys represent a kind of 'next generation' for which they are responsible.

So, *Harmony Signing* operates on the basis of audible tonal relationships that have the characteristics of biological generations. This idea works for both girls and boys,[6] and just as well with older students as younger ones.

Let's begin by thinking of oneself as the tonic. It is not just 'home': it is 'me'. I will be the subject of the musical journeys that occur. All of us know that we emerged from a previous generation and that the survival of our family (or species) is dependent on a next generation. Going 'with the grain' of the cycle of fifths, as we have argued is determined by the harmonic series, we can then apply this as a form of 'time's arrow' that provides the sense of direction to our generational analogy. The usual way in which we imagine both sides of the relationship that defines 'me' is to place ourselves *between* generations. We need to see ourselves both as real or virtual 'parents' and as (real) children. From this perspective, 'me' relates both to 'grandparents' and succeeding 'children'. The cycle of fifths mirrors the cycle of life.

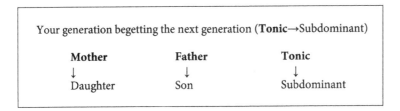

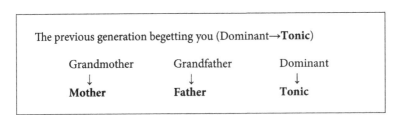

This model of tonal generation provides a sense of potential movement through harmonic function that is analogous to time travel. Moving 'forwards' through subdominants [→→→] is like experiencing the future. Moving 'backwards' through dominant relationships [←←←] is like revisiting the past. The relation 'grandparent-parent-me' represents the process by which every member of the human race has come into being (Dawkins 2004; Rutherford 2016). Why might a story like this help? Because the

---

[6] It is essential to maintain equal opportunity in musical generation. This is important for the role modelling of both girl and boy composers.

evidence coming from music psychology and neuroscience is that music works on our thought and emotions in a manner that plays with our sense of space, scale, and time. If our purpose in teaching music is to support students in experiencing its effects deeply, and responding to them in their own creativity, then exploration of these qualities has its place in music education.

So, to summarise: All tonics are the consequence of dominants and all tonics can produce subdominants. These principles are what we have experienced in mastering moving chords around through cutting and pasting. Their effects will prove essential when we embark on tonal journeys through addressing the more radical processes involved in modulation.

Modes and the Secondary Triads

There is still more that can be explored at this stage within the orbit of the primary triads. Our experience of harmony in general has emerged exclusively from the major properties of the harmonic series. This has led to the exploration of chords I, IV, and V, but there are other chords we can derive. In turn, the alternatives to the diatonic major this introduces prompt the investigation of other scales. Indeed, musical history and experience of styles across the independent cultures of the world illustrates that modes other than the major (Ionian) have often emerged as the preferred means of pitch organisation.

We can begin by considering adaptations of the primary triads, each of which can be presented in partnership with a secondary triad that can be derived from it, and which is minor in mood (fig. 11.11):

(1)   Soh – La -   La - - - - - -   Soh - - - - - -

(2)   Me - - - - -   Fa - - - - - -   Ray – Me - -

(3)   Doh - - - - -   Doh – Ray-   Ti$^+$ - - - - - -

Chord I   vi   IV   ii   V   iii

Figure 11.11 Music notation of the production of secondary triads.

Figure 11.12 and image 11.1 illustrate a progression that consolidates these chord choices and which it is useful for all students to be able to sign.

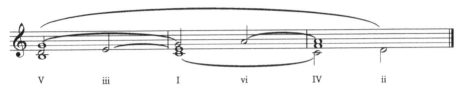

V   iii   I   vi   IV   ii

Figure 11.12 A model progression that employs all primary and secondary triads.

Images 11.1a–f A model progression that employs all primary and secondary triads.

Images 11.1a–f Continued

Images 11.1a–f Continued

Each of these pairs (I/vi; IV/ii; V/iii)[7] involves a single voice raising its pitch by one step. The pairings also map onto those that define the bond <relative major—relative minor>. To make these close associations clear, the sign for turning the major into the minor is created by balling the fist and moving the arm in a direction that captures

[7] Minors are conveyed in lowercase in both numerical notation (iii) and letters (e.g., the chord of d).

the moving part which accounts for the new chord. In the case of I → vi, the flat hand becomes a fist while moving a little to the right. For the move IV → ii, the flat hand is raised a little as the fist is formed. For the move V → iii, the fist is again raised from the low vertical position. These moves seem to capture these qualities of adaptation well. They should be learned in this sequence one at a time and then feely explored. They provide a widened harmonic vocabulary that can be discovered through improvisation and also, as before, as an analytical tool for capturing the progressions of existing music.

Several new progressions now become available, including those that are familiar from Baroque and Renaissance music, others associated with the Great American Songbook, especially the popular music of the 1950s and 1960s.

The progression I - vi - IV - V will be familiar from the simple piano duet sometimes referred to as 'Chopsticks'[8] that generations of young pianists have taught each other—sometimes to the disapproval of their teachers (fig. 11.13).

Sung in response to *Harmony Signing*, this progression is conveyed through effective voice-leading that is characteristic of vocal music from the Renaissance onwards. This

Since this is an aurally transmitted piece, there are doubtless a great many variants. This is, as I recall, the version I encountered as a schoolboy in Canterbury, UK, circa 1963.

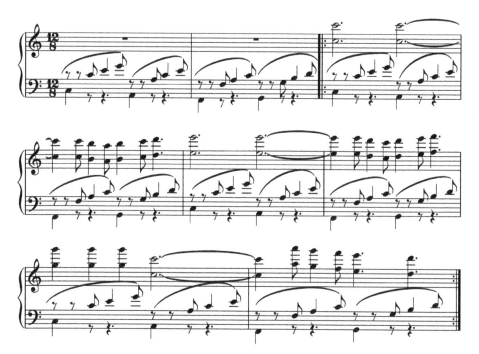

Figure 11.13 The typical piano duet version of *Chopsticks* that students transmit to each other.

[8] Also known as the 'Chopsticks Waltz,' though it is in two time, transmitted from child to child around the world and quite different to the composition written in 1877 by the British composer Euphemia Allen under the pseudonym Arthur de Lulli that commences with the repeated whole tone f/g and is accompanied by alternating dominant and tonic chords, and that is a genuine waltz in 3/4 time.

Figure 11.14 Music notation of this characteristic progression featuring chord ii.

Figure 11.15 Music notation of the *Nutcracker* theme.

'Chopsticks' progression introduces chord vi. Chord ii features characteristically in the related progression I - vi - ii - V (fig. 11.14).

Two well-known songs that employ this progression, and that could be performed through *Harmony Signing* with the melody carried by Kodály signs in the right hand, are Hoagy Carmichael's 'Heart and Soul' and Richard Rodgers's 'Blue Moon'.

Chord iii is often associated with chord vi, as in this progression from Tchaikovsky's *Nutcracker* (fig. 11.15).

More Elaborate Progressions Using These Chords

With six chords to play with, we can call up a wide range of progressions that composers have devised for songs and instrumental works. Students leading these examples will both develop their understanding of the original material and gain confidence to explore their own invention of new progressions. Pachelbel's *Canon in D* can be conveyed as:

I - V - vi - iii - IV - I - IV – V- (I)

The bassline that defines it can also be signed to complement this harmony presented with suitable voice-leading (fig. 11.16):

Doh' - Soh - La - Me - Fa - Doh¹- Fa - Soh - (Doh')

Figure 11.16 Music notation of Pachelbel's *Canon* progression.

The opening of Henry Mancini's 'Moon River' is also now accessible, since it too employs the progression I - vi - IV - I, but we will need to learn the positions for some additional chords, including added sevenths, to progress further into the song. A task that a suitably experienced class could be set would be to bring other examples using chords ii, iii, and iv from the song repertoire that they have sought out, which they can prepare to lead.

Each of chords IV, V, ii, iii, and vi can be the resting place ('final') of a mode. This experience can be captured without needing to move any of them to the central tonic position, which is reserved for the true tonic of the major-minor system that has evolved since the Baroque period out of the old Ionian mode. The modes relate to their initial notes as follows:

ii	Dorian
iii	Phrygian
IV	Lydian
V	Mixolydian
vi	Aeolian

We will not at this point deal with the properties of the Lochrian mode on the seventh degree of the scale, but will explore it within the realm of chromaticism when we consider the diminished triads.

An insight into the character of each mode can emerge from improvisation similar to the Alaps we have proposed for exploring the properties of scales. This involves both hands employing Kodály signs. A leader selects a particular mode and signs its final with the left hand. A group within the class performs this as a drone that is sustained throughout. The rest of the class follows an improvised melody beginning also on the final, which moves in patterns up and down by steps, testing the placement of tones and semitones that provide the unique signature of the mode. All participants mirror the gestures of the leader with both hands to fully experience the different intervallic relationships involved and further develop the sense of location this affords. This can act as a warm-up over several sessions, each student having the opportunity to select a different mode of their choice. It can also be usefully incorporated into any ensemble preparation for performance of a work based on a given mode.

Each mode gives rise to relationships between the triad on its *final* and other chords from which characteristic progressions can be derived that are suitable to its properties. These do not tend to be the direct equivalent of the pattern I - IV - V. For instance, one could experiment with the following patterns as the basis for accompaniments to melodies:

ii - IV - vi
iii - IV - V
IV - vi - I
V - I - ii
vi - IV - iii

Students could select their own 3–4 chord progressions and try them out, comparing the sense of coherence and character to which they give rise. We will later consider how we can add a *tièrce de Picardie* to allow a minor-mode piece to finish on a major cadence. We will also consider some of the properties of modes that can be explored through employing two-handed Kodály signing to achieve species counterpoint.

Working With Major-Minor Substitution

A further variant of the primary triads can be introduced that gives rise to minor chords by the means of substitution. In this case, each of the major chords, I, IV, and V, can be turned into a minor in the same position (they become chords i, iv, and v). The means by which this is done is that the flat hand employed for the major is turned so that the palm faces the participants. It seems a little like a warning sign, and this is not unhelpful. This procedure should first be introduced by turning I into i. It is important that only the third of the chord moves, from Me to Ma, while the outlined perfect fifth is sustained (fig. 11.17).

Next, after moving from I to IV, IV is turned into iv by the same process. It may be noticeable that the progression <I - IV - iv - I> is recognised as occurring in music familiar to the participants.

Finally, the minor version of V can be introduced, using the progression: <I - V - v - V - I>. The way that these minor chords can form the basis of a variety of minor key and modal variants will be dealt with in Chapter 15, 'Next Steps: Chromaticism and Modulation'.

A significant aspect of the way we will deal with the minor distinguishes practice based on the Aeolian mode from that of thinking of the minor as an adaptation of the major; that is, 'Doh minor'. In a great deal of nineteenth-century music, from Schubert via Brahms and Dvorak to Mahler and Strauss, major and minor are interchangeable. This can occur between verses of the same song (e.g., Schubert's *Gute Nacht*, no. 1 of *Winterreise*); or within a phrase (Dvorak's *Slavonic Dance No. 8 in g minor*; Brahms's *Symphony No. 3* opening of the first movement; and the cadences that colour the opening of Richard Strauss's *Also Sprach Zarathustra*).[9] Clearly the same tonic, Doh, operates for both the major and the minor (we do not feel that Doh has been replaced with La). For this reason, we will advocate adopting the same three positions of the arm for the primary triads of both major and minor. In each case, I and i, IV and iv, and V and v occupy the same space, though with the significant difference in hand-shape presentation that we have introduced.

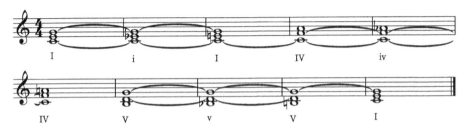

I   i   I   IV   iv

IV   V   v   V   I

Figure 11.17 Music notation of major-minor substitution.

---

[9] The class can contribute to compiling a log of music they encounter in any style that employs major-minor substitution on these lines.

Further Exercises for Combining the Vertical and the Horizontal

We are approaching the completion of our investigation of the primary triads and their nearest variants and relatives, which is the first major stage of the *Harmony Signing* agenda. Before dealing with more complex chords and harmonic relationships, we will look at some ways to further investigate the signs we have learned and preparing the ground for supporting the operations to come. We will also take a further look at the properties of melody construction and counterpoint that will prepare us for the voice-leading assumptions which will permit the combination of melody and harmony. Prior to completing this chapter, we can gain a glimpse of what this all leads to by employing strategies we have already experienced.

We should by now have an entirely fluent sense of the movement between the primary triads. Using the right hand, we can experience some functions of voice-leading within harmonic practice by capturing a given part and temporarily 'liberating' it in order to illustrate the properties of neighbour-note inflection, suspension, and anticipation.

Here are examples of how this works. The 'captured' note is given in bold type (fig. 11.18):

Figure 11.18 Music notation of 'captured' right-hand melody notes.

Subsequent to signing these examples for the class, one can discuss the properties of *suspension* and *anticipation* that they introduce, and then encourage students to prepare some phrases of their own that contain these properties that can be led using these same techniques. This will present a first important step towards students being able to think polyphonically and to lead the results in real time.

12

Signs About Signs

The Notation of *Harmony Signing*

This chapter presents proposals for how the gestures of *Harmony Signing* can be notated in pencil-and-paper fashion, or, as here, using available text symbols and keyboard access to extended shapes and patterns available online through Word symbols and Wingdings.

It was not part of the original development of *Harmony Signing* to include a means of notating it. Indeed, given that much of its purpose and elaboration has been to communicate musical ideas without reliance on verbalisation or staff notation, it may seem perverse to suggest that a further graphic system may have a place at all. But a significant aspect of the action research activities and reflection that have given rise to the approach has involved embracing what students and peers contribute and evaluating how their contributions may prove effective.

It became clear that leaders who had planned solutions to tasks in which they prepared the signing of progressions and musical passages were devising their own notations. These comprised 'workings out' on which they could rely for sorting ideas and 'scores' that they could follow when leading performance. Initially sceptical, I carefully weighed the pros and cons of adopting these processes into my teaching. In my own work, I had always relied either on the link between kinaesthetic and musical memory or the ability to translate directly into *Harmony Signing* from music notation.[1] Eventually, the evidence that notated homework represented a valuable prop to students convinced me of its potential. The clinching feature was realising that once leaders had employed it to support their initial engagement with participants, one could often successfully remove it in subsequent rehearsal. It fulfilled a similar function to stave notation as a means of working out and memorising the sounds desired.

Thus, a system for representing *Harmony Signing* on paper was born. I can now feely admit that, as more complex applications demanded additional signs and combinations that needed to be consistent and unambiguous, the discipline of employing notation in this way made its contribution to the process. However, I cannot stress strongly enough that *Harmony Signing* should never be taught from these graphic symbols. It is not, in fact, a system of music notation at all. True music notation directly conveys the sounds that result from its interpretation and their relationships in time; or simply, what the listener is intended to hear. It provides little information about how this is achieved technically. By contrast, what has been devised for *Harmony Signing* is a *tablature* that represents the movements the signer makes to guide performers, who in turn supply the musical interpretation of what they do as individuals in order to achieve the overall

---

[1] It is largely for this reason that musical examples in staff notation have been provided throughout this book.

result. In some respects, such a tablature resembles that used for instruments such as the lute and guitar, with the critical difference that the latter are intended to be read *in toto* by individual performers. *Harmony Signing* communicates information that has to be divided into different strands to which each performer responds appropriately through a sense of their contribution to the whole.

In some respects, this is also similar to Benesh[2] and Laban[3] notations that have been devised to permit the accurate recording of choreography. There is again a difference. Choreographers employing these notations are mapping the dancers' position and movements directly into the system for recording them, and vice versa. Choreographers leading a group or modelling the performance of soloists may well use their own bodies as templates for transferring this knowledge. In this process there is no equivalent of the intermediate step involved in *Harmony Signing* in which the leader's gestures communicate information that performers interpret. It is important to accept that of the two, the gestural system and its graphic representation, it is the former that is at the core of teaching and learning.

So, teachers are genuinely invited to consider taking no recourse to the notations at all. If they find themselves or their students in need of them, this chapter remains available to provide this support.

The initial graphic signs represent parts of the body in use. O is the shoulder of the signing hand, around which the arm moves up or down. —■ represents the arm (—) and hand (■). Thus o—■ is the tonic major chord (I), whose shape can be moved into the subdominant and dominant positions. Here is the progression I→IV→V→I:

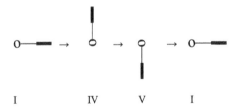

The three secondary triads on ii, iii, and vi all require the fist to be balled in contrast to the flat hand of I, IV, and V. The sign for this is ʘ. We can now practise leading progressions that contain these chords:

(a) (see Fig.11.13: *Chopsticks*)

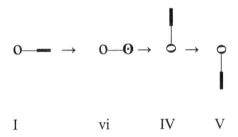

---

[2] https://www.rad.org.uk/study/Benesh
[3] http://user.uni-frankfurt.de/~griesbec/LABANE.HTML

(b) (see Fig.11.14: *Blue Moon*)

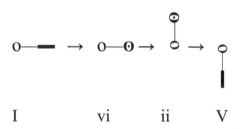

I   vi   ii   V

(c) (see Fig.11.15: Tchaikovsky, *The Nutcracker*)

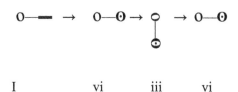

I   vi   iii   vi

Here is the progression for Pachelbel's *Canon*:

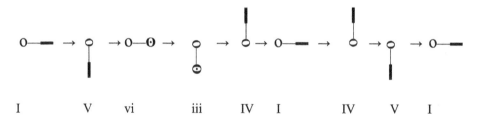

I   V   vi   iii   IV   I   IV   V   I

Up and down arrows (⁺⁺) apply to right hand signing changes of inversion, up or down. The sign ═ o indicates that the right hand is held palm upwards. The following illustrates the inversion of the tonic:

o—▬   ═o.⁺ ↓ ↑ ↑ ↓ ↓ ↓ ↑
                    · · · · · · · ···

Left hand   Right hand

(vocalisation continues through changes of chord inversion up and down)

A right hand symbol (⌣) is the *tonicising sign*, which illustrates that a modulation has taken place and that the **next** chord to be performed should be the new tonic anticipated in the sense of tonal movement undergone (see Chapter15, 'Working in Groups', for modulation to the subdominant and dominant).

The rest of this chapter introduces signs which represent harmonic functions that we have not yet covered. The musical options they convey will form the basis of what follows in this book, and the graphic notations in this section will be referred to and elaborated upon as each topic arises.

Image 12.1 The sign for adding a minor seventh.

Adding sevenths to existing chords is achieved by making the round 'OK' sign with the opposing left hand thumb and forefinger (see Image 12.1). This is represented graphically by adding an open circle (°) to the chord sign. Sevenths can be added to any chords. This sign indicates *minor* sevenths that render major chords as dominant sevenths and thus demand the possibility of modulation dependent on the use of the *tonicising sign* . A seventh added to a minor triad in this way does not change it.

The following examples illustrate the formation of seventh chords in this way:

o——°   Tonic with seventh – I^7

o—♠ °   Tonic minor with (minor) seventh – i^7

o—o°   Submediant with seventh – vi^7

Modulation can be achieved either by adding the 'OK' sign to an existing chord, or by showing the sign for a chord outside the prevailing key and then employing the *tonicising sign* to confirm the modulation implied, and thus prepare for 'arrival' in the new key. The most common modulations are to the subdominant, dominant, and to the relative minor (see Chapter 15, 'Working in Groups'), and we will confirm the signs for these as we proceed.

The sign for introducing the pivot chord though which modulation to the dominant is achieved is highly specific, since this is aurally a radical change to previous practice and it needs to be 'read' unambiguously. It introduces a 'new' chord outside the orbit of what we have thus far encountered. The left hand moves out across the chest to a position in which it extends to the left, with a hand sign that simultaneously represents a 'thumbs up' gesture (see Image 12.2). The new hand sign is associated with this chord—the sharpened form of Chord II of the 'old' key—being outside the prevailing tonality. It also carries the useful association of being the sign for Fi in Kodály signing, the sharpened fourth, which is the third of the chord. The written notation for this new hand sign is:

Note that, for the first time, the sign for a chord is represented by a movement 'outside' the body, with the hand position to the *left* of the elbow.

Image 12.2 The sign for the major version of chord II.

So we can now notate the signs for a modulating progression (fig. 12.1):

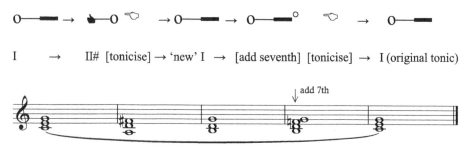

In fact, this progression modulates twice: *away* from the tonic, replacing it with the dominant, and back to the 'old' tonic, by adding a seventh to the new tonic, which makes its function unstable. So we should end up where we started. This little progression is worth mastering with complete confidence, with every participant being able to perform all possible 'routes' through its voice-leading, and everyone having practised directing it using these gestures. Not only does it provide clear experience of the two most common modulations in music: it is, as a tiny 'piece' in its own right,[4] a kind of building block for

---

[4] A microscopic sonata, perhaps.

the larger-scale processes that underlie a great many musical works of all styles. Where the original positions of the primary triads were represented by a triangular presentation that defined the tonic through consciousness of its immediate satellites, modulations of this kind introduce the hierarchical 'nesting'—akin to the Russian doll effect—whereby each journey through tonal space can be tracked through some form of relationship within the cycle of fifths, whether 'close' (as in the above) or more distant. The distant relationships that we will encounter in due course rely on these same extended 'triads of triads' founded on temporary (or 'passing') I - IV - V - I relationships.

The signing of the modulation to the relative minor requires the use of both hands. Where this occurs, it is conveyed graphically though the use of the forward slash (/) to confirm this and to delineate which hand carries which function. The pivot chord that achieves this modulation is the sharp version of chord III—the dominant of the new minor tonic to which we are moving (fig. 12.2)[5]:

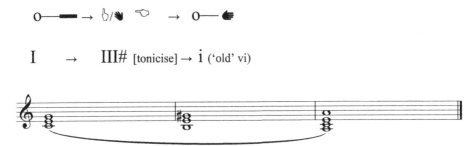

Figure 12.2 Music notation of modulation to the relative minor.

Image 12.3 The combination of Kodály signs required for this modulation.

---

[5] Once this has been confidently learned, the final chord could be replaced by others: within the original key, the pivot can be treated as a chromatic decoration through which we can colourfully proceed to chord vi or chord IV; or the final chord could be major (VI), which represents a shortcut across the cycle of fifths.

In all direction of harmonic progressions that requires the use of both hands to represent Kodály signs in this way, the third part sustains the pitch it is already performing. In this case, it is the note Me (third) of the original tonic, which in fact acts as a pivot connecting all three chords in this particular progression.

In this brief illustration of the potential offered by diagrammatic representation of chord progressions, graphic symbols have been employed that may support learning and practice as further harmonic possibilities are introduced. These notations parallel and complement the musical presentation in performance of each new step, and new notational signs for additional gestures will be introduced as required. For further guidance, the video clips of the *Harmony Signing* website present these steps in sequence.

13
Working on Your Own

In the games, tasks, and initial functions of *Harmony Signing* we have encountered, we have focused on the means by which low-level decision-making, within restricted options, provides the basis for step-by-step development of additional individual and collective skills that enable a wider range of increasingly personal and expressive aesthetic choices. The role of collective engagement and peer-learning has been essential to the formation of this level of achievement. Before introducing the next range of *Harmony Signing* procedures in which leaders work with whole classes or ensembles, we will model some activities for individuals and pairs that will deepen musical understanding and fluency.

Understanding Intervals

Intervals are the building blocks of pitched music, responsible for the shape and tonal unfolding of melody and the colour and functional implications of chords. In teaching and assessing students' understanding of intervals, I frequently encounter a sense of helplessness, especially when students are placed under the conditions of tests and examinations. There may be several possible causes to this, including a lack of curiosity about the phenomenon, as if intervals are an incidental aspects of reading and performing; an acquired impression that intervals demand measurement, which gives the impression that they are viewed as quantities rather than as musical experiences; or just the generalised panic associated with fear of failure which itself leads to confusion.

A great many of the experiences of *Harmony Signing* and the games and tasks that led up to it have been devised to prepare students to overcome these fears and acquire an innate capacity to handle intervals in creative work and performance with purpose and confidence. This chapter represents a kind of focused revision on existing practical experience that should continue to inform individual students while they engage with activities intended to consolidate and extend their personal understanding. The collective fluency achievable through group practical experience will continue to support this.

The class may already have been introduced to practice related to the experience and discrimination of intervals through the exercise provided for Task 5 (chapter 5). This could be reintroduced for the whole class to experience as a reminder in preparation for individual work—it could be tried on instruments as well as voices. Individuals should then work at keyboards or other instruments and listen acutely and with sensitivity to affect and preference as much as to structure. The intervals should be tried out over different ranges, with the purpose of ascertaining what is distinctive and memorable about each one; and at different volume levels. Students should also continue to vocalise the intervals to establish their secure transference from the sound of the instrument to the inner ear.

In some respects, it is perhaps a shame that intervals are named after the means by which they are identified by size. I have an impression that if, as for colours (which share the feature that they represent emissions discriminated by differences in wavelength), we learned them as children through a set of arbitrary names, we might find that they 'stuck' more easily. To adopt a different analogy, we could view them as specific ingredients with different flavours that we can learn to recognise in their 'raw' state so that we can make sense of the recipes that combine them. As all good cooks know, one begins by knowing one's ingredients, obtaining the freshest and most tasty, and learning how the properties of each can work with others. All of this prepares for the subjective and student-centred approach we will take to developing confidence in handling intervals, and doing so with certainty. In particular, we will draw on variety of learning styles and associations for to achieving this.

The chart inFigure 13.1 allows the personal investigation of the properties and effects of each interval to commence a process of relating them to performing and listening experience. To be sure, the two left-hand columns represent precisely the sequential presentation (number of semitones; numerator; minor/major) that I have criticised as the only classification available. But it provides a visual layout against which we can distribute the centre and right-hand columns. These have been devised to allow students to customise and reflect on their own responses. Overall, the chart represents a multimodal recall system that can be employed over a period of time and refined until it becomes fail-safe.

The third column should be filled in by the student, who will provide four examples for each interval:

- one that spans two white notes;
- one that spans ('either way up') a white note and a flattened note;
- one that spans ('either way up') a white note and a sharpened note;
- one, if available, that spans two black notes.

It is essential that each student works this out for themselves, and does so as a result of performing them on an instrument: 'up', 'down', and if possible simultaneously through practising with a peer. They must acquire the experience of hearing each interval in these four arrangements as possessing the same properties, irrespective of how the interval is played. Without such focused homework and personal practice, the chart will be less effective in its application. In addition to understanding the sounds of intervals, students need to be secure in accurately mapping them onto the scale system.

This then leads on to the two right-hand columns. In the column labelled 'Character and Effect', students will enter adjectives that they feel they can reliably associate with the experience of each interval. They should choose these descriptive terms after carefully, repeatedly, and purposefully listening to intervals played over various ranges, dynamics, and durations. This can first be modelled in class. A useful starting point is the employment of opposites. The class should be asked to generate a list of descriptive opposites that might be drawn upon to achieve this. Here are some that students have proposed in the past:

Old	New
Near	Far
Safe	Threatening
Sharp	Blunt
Rough	Smooth
Familiar	Unfamiliar
Rude	Polite
Bright	Dark

It is infinitely more effective if this register of potential descriptors is the result of the students' own deliberations, since it will, as a result, generate a sense of ownership that will inform their confidence in applying these terms—and others—as they make the comparisons on which this process depends.

In addition to drawing on these opposites, other terms can prove useful. Some students may find that colours provide an unbreakable connection with certain sounds. If this works, so much the better, though it certainly may not work for everyone.

This column should be filled out with three to four precise terms that, taken together, represent the unique descriptor which, with practice, students can learn to apply so that each of the interval types (by their name, e.g., minor seventh, perfect fourth) can be both recognised and reproduced at will.

The final column, labelled 'Examples in Repertoire', represents known employment, both up and down, of each interval in available music. This column can be filled out over time through a mixture of collective contribution (especially where everyone in

Personal Interval Evaluation Chart

No. of semitones	Name of Interval	Examples (incl. # & b)	Character and Effect	Examples in Repertoire (both ascending and descending)
1				
2				
3				
4				
5				
6				
7				
8				
9				
10				
11				
12				

Figure 13.1 Template for a Personal Interval Chart.

the class has heard or performed the same works) and individual examples based on specific instrumental or vocal repertoire and listening experience that each individual can trawl for these. It is essential that students base these selections on their own experience, rather than on examples provided.

Students should be encouraged to keep these charts—perhaps customising larger-scale versions they can display in their own working environment for ready access—and build on them as their technical knowledge and repertoire experience grows. An additional feature that can seal this process is to compose solos for their instrument that employ each interval with the precise intentions presented by the student's personal selection of descriptors. This balancing, through subjective reflection and evaluation, of the conventional analytical/theoretical approach to interval recognition can harness creativity and consolidate the associations which permit progress in aural skills and a new understanding of the role of intervals in composition and performance.

Chant and Monophony

Building on the preceding work on intervals, this section addresses single-line improvisation and composition and the ways in which this develops aural and creative experience that carries into the handling of music in two or more parts. The principle adopted is that students devise pieces that they perform either vocally, instrumentally, or both.

One of the critical breakthroughs in early human evolution that led to musicality and language was the adaptation which permitted voluntary breathing. We employ this in harness with the neural response to aural feedback to confer the ability to perform a sustained monotone (Bannan 2012a). Many vocal styles around the world employ chant on a monotone as a means of performing text in a manner that conveys the intention that it is special. This form of performance is often associated with resonant buildings that provide an additional acoustic response. Chant of this kind can be performed solo, but also lends itself to collective identification with participation.

Chant is also often elaborated. While the central monotone is retained as a *reciting note*, there may be preceding and succeeding melodic motifs that denote and decorate the beginnings and endings of phrases. Creating and performing settings of selected words in this way can provide an insight into this ancient form of music-making. As a model, Figure 13.2 provides a verse from a Latin psalm sung to a chant that is believed to have survived from the ancient Hebrew origins of its text.

An initial exercise would be to take a poem or other text and work on setting it to music in this manner. What pitch of reciting-note best represents its performance within the range of one's voice? What initial and concluding motifs could be added? What are the challenges to effective performance? The trick in chanting is to make

Figure 13.2 Music notation of the *In exitu Israel* chant, Tonus Peregrinus.

the links between successive vowels as smooth and continuous as possible, allowing them to remain correctly pitched so that the consonants do not distort the sense of tonality. This is the basis of good singing technique, and chant performance illustrates this well. Voiced consonants (l, m, n, v, etc.) should be performed with as much attention to tuning as vowels. Pitched plosives (b, d, g) should also be tuned to match the succeeding vowel. Unvoiced consonants (f, k, p, t, s) should be placed as lightly and swiftly as possible so that they do not interrupt the airflow on which the sustained monotone depends. This experience provides a valuable insight into the function and potential of tonality as it became established in musical styles across the world.

How might single-line melody transfer from a chant basis to instrumental exploration? We might achieve this through reference to the evaluation of intervals with which we worked in the preceding section. While a sense of return to a specific reciting note could act as a unifying principle, our composition could introduce various ways of contrasting with this through melodic excursions that visit other salient pitches. We might experiment with different durations according to the relative significance of the pitches involved: some being brief stepping stones to temporary alternative reciting notes, and so on. We might set out, as in the Alap examples (chapter 10, figs. 10.1 and 10.2) to cover the feature of range in a systematic way. We might consider the effect of different levels of loudness, as in echo effects or contrasts between sustained notes of specific pitch.

A single-line composition achieved in this way provides a means of exploring the colour and range of one's instrument. These techniques represent an excellent means of working with 12-tone rows, which we will deal with in due course. The resulting composition can be retained for harmonic or polyphonic elaboration.

When students have performed and reflected on their monophonic pieces, they will be ready to consider parallels with a range of works they could listen to that deal, to an extent, with the same or similar constraints and possibilities:

William Barton	Didjeridu solo[1]
Japanese soloist	Shakuhachi performance[2]
Elke Baker	Traditional Scottish fiddle music[3]
Claude Debussy	Syrinx, for solo flute[4]
Edgard Varèse	Density 21.5[5]
Igor Stravinsky	Three pieces for clarinet solo
Benjamin Britten	Six Metamorphoses after Ovid, for oboe
Brian Ferneyhough	Time and Motion Study No. 1, for bass clarinet
Luciano Berio	Sequenzas (several different solo instruments)

[1] https://www.youtube.com/watch?v=26PpaNN08PI
[2] https://www.youtube.com/watch?v=spO-WvyoOgI
[3] https://www.youtube.com/watch?v=xu_QKs4m07A
[4] https://www.youtube.com/watch?v=a2DxZkkb2iE
[5] https://www.youtube.com/watch?v=0EkX_Qgrf2o

Further possibilities are represented by the solo stringed instrument repertoire of the Baroque period, though this exploits the harmonic underpinning of double-stopping that the instruments make available:

Heinrich Biber	Passacaglia for solo violin[6]
J. S. Bach	Chaconne in d minor[7] for solo violin
J. S. Bach	Prelude to the First Suite in G[8] for solo cello

Word-setting and More on the Vocal Template

This section takes a different look at the relationship between language and music that can stimulate a range of musical ideas which extend students' experience. Instead of setting texts in a chantlike manner, students aim at a melodic structure more typical of the song tradition. Those interested in writing songs can develop their skills in locating suitable texts and responding to the potential they offer for rhythmic interpretation and vocal contour. If, at first, these are set purely as single-line melodies, they can be set aside to be arranged or orchestrated at a later stage and can be treated as material for acquiring these skills through some of the more advanced aspects of *Harmony Signing* that we will introduce.

A further strategy that relates vocal working-out to composition, which can transfer to instrumental scoring and performance, is the use of graphic scores as a form of sketch. Here, we can refer back to some of the games we first introduced in order to employ the voice as a template for musical discovery, especially the material on voiced and unvoiced phonemes presented in 'Exercises to Remedy Poorly Developed Pitch-Matching' (see Chapter 7). Indeed, the task that follows builds on precisely these elements and represents the kind of higher-level creative task for which they were intended to prepare.

The graphic score in Figure 13.3 can be presented as an example to be performed by the class.

Different streams of sound are employed to create a polyphonic texture. The score is read from left to right, different individuals or groups performing different lines, with symbols in vertical alignment performed simultaneously. Depending on the assumption about how time is experienced, the piece may be as short as, say, fifteen seconds, or be spread out over a minute. For younger students, working with this material and creating their own versions in this way may be the first opportunity they have to engage with a multivoice score. Their ensuing creative response will be their first scored composition. They achieve this as individuals.

The acoustic elements in play here are sounds that can be represented by letters of the alphabet. A few blends and clusters can also be added (e.g., <ch>, <sh>, <ts>, <frr>). These can be placed and varied in the space available to suggest differences between long (sustained) and short sounds; sounds of different pitch, including glides up and

6 https://www.youtube.com/watch?v=sgcR183f8gA
7 https://www.youtube.com/watch?v=QqA3qQMKueA
8 https://www.youtube.com/watch?v=S6yuR8efotI

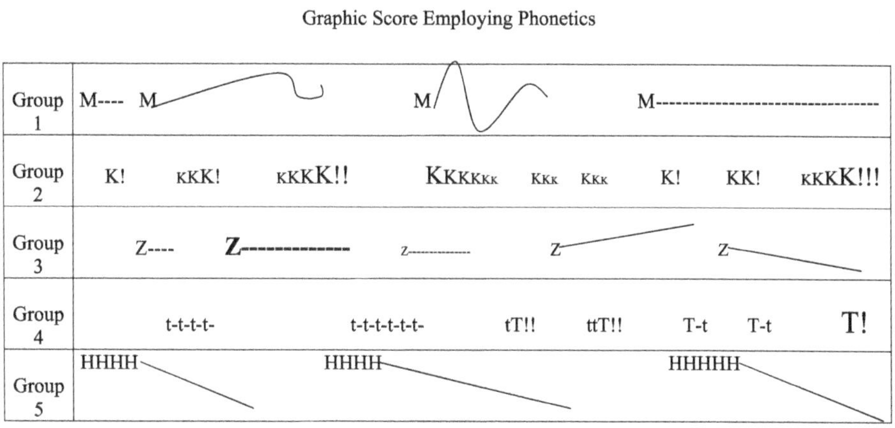

Graphic Score Employing Phonetics

Figure 13.3 An example of a graphic score conveying musical information through the use of phonetics.

down; sounds of different loudness (conveyed by size of font/grapheme); and so on. Decisions should be taken regarding the rate of performance, arising from the time-space notation (e.g., 1 cm = 1 second). The breadth and variety of compositions that can be achieved with these ingredients is enormous, and students should be encouraged to imagine a distinct sound world for their pieces that can be consistent with the titles they assign to them.

In a subsequent class, these individual compositions can be rehearsed and performed by groups of about five students. Once this has been achieved, an interesting next step can be one of the following:

(1) Pieces are passed from group to group for a second performance. This permits the class to evaluate whether interpretations of the notation remain stable, which is an interesting consideration with implications for all learning of notation.
(2) Pieces by different members are sequenced by the group that first performed them into continuous longer works that can represent a more varied achievement. A five-minute composition performed with conviction by a group can cross the threshold from classroom exercise to music presented to proud parents at a school concert.

These scores are then worth keeping, because at a later point they can be reemployed to form the basis of a different outcome. Having had an initial existence as vocal sketches, they can be performed on instruments. This may involve some adaptation, but the solutions to this challenge will be instructive. Depending on the age and experience of the participants, this can be done in one of two ways (or both):

(1) Students perform from the vocal version, employing instruments in ways that preserve the balance between elements of the original as far as possible;
(2) Prior to rehearsal, students re-score their piece for instruments in music notation, using a program such as Finale or Sibelius to achieve an accurate and well-presented fair copy.

As before, group versions that represent a collage of the individual contributions can emerge from both of these ways of building on the original material. A practice of this kind provides insight into how larger pieces can be structured.

This teaching and learning sequence based on the use of a graphic score elaborates on the value of developing work from a vocally based 'template' from which musical ideas can be shaped and elaborated. The repertoire abounds with cover versions and arrangements that cross the boundary between instrumental and vocal media in both directions.

Instrumental Music That has been Rendered Vocal

Instrumental works have often formed the basis of vocal realisations. The sustained, expressive texture attained by Samuel Barber in his *Adagio for Strings* (1936; itself an arrangement of a movement originally for string quartet, his Op. 11) was seen to lend itself to a vocal version, and Barber eventually adapted it to the words of the *Agnus Dei* (1967). Two works by Edward Elgar have entered the choral repertoire in similar fashion. Elgar approved the singing of Arthur Benson's words *Land of Hope and Glory* to the tune of *Pomp and Circumstance March No. 1* (1901). However, Elgar's *Nimrod*, from the *Enigma Variations* (1899) was adapted after the work came out of copyright to words such as *Lux aeterna* (for unaccompanied choir by John Cameron 1996) and *Requiem aeternam* (version for choir and orchestra by David Hill 2011).

In a similar way, songs were adapted by Robert Wright and George Forrest from the instrumental music of Borodin for the musical *Kismet* (e.g., 'Stranger in Paradise'; 'And This Is My Beloved'). Many listeners are unaware that these melodies for the 1953 Broadway show had an original life in the Russian concert hall a century before.

Putting words to existing music is one means of making it performable by singers. Another is to apply a technique that first emerged in jazz in the mid-twentieth century. Singers could improvise ('scat') like their instrumentalist colleagues, a practice that recalls the 'singing in tongues' with which ecstatic performers of Gospel music would inject variations on and between words. Performers such as Louis Armstrong,[9] Ella Fitzgerald, and Mel Torme[10] were leaders in the development of this technique, which became widespread in jazz vocal performance in the 1950s.

In the early 1960s, the American singer and arranger Ward Swingle worked with a group in Paris on applying scat to arrangements of pieces by Bach (e.g., *Badinerie*[11]). The international success of these Paris recordings led to compositions in this style for The Swingle Singers by Burt Bacharach (e.g., 'Bolivian Getaway', in the film score for *Butch Cassidy and the Sundance Kid*, 1969[12]), as well as to further arrangements by Swingle himself of music as varied as Rimsky-Korsakov's *Flight of the Bumble-Bee*[13] and Debussy's *Claire de Lune*.[14]

[9] https://www.youtube.com/watch?v=P3fGrQYHHBI
[10] https://www.youtube.com/watch?v=9CbVy1NnB4g
[11] https://www.youtube.com/watch?v=_NzIrMFW3m4
[12] https://www.youtube.com/watch?v=Jw_hee-7R_o
[13] https://www.youtube.com/watch?v=CZo1_BDn8Ew
[14] https://www.youtube.com/watch?v=vrxw3PraOeM

A great many groups have developed this approach to re-presenting instrumental classics, and versions have become available for school and community choirs. The trend has become increasingly virtuosic, as in the Cuban ensemble Vocal Sampling's version of Strauss's *Also Sprach Zarathustra*[15] and the solo cover by one of their members of Jimi Hendrix's guitar solo from Woodstock. The phenomenon of beat-boxing has given rise to a new generation of artists who perform unaccompanied vocal music that imitates instruments, such as the group Naturally 7.[16]

Vocal Music That has been Rendered Instrumental

Of course, the process also works well in the opposite direction. Songs have often become the basis of instrumental variation. Schubert turned his song 'Die Forelle' into the theme and variations movement of his Trout Quintet, and did the same in his String Quartet No. 14 in D minor with the song 'Death and the Maiden'.

A vocal 'Pavane' by Arbeau (1589) was arranged by Peter Warlock as a movement of his *Capriol Suite* (1926), though not every performance of the latter version captures the accentuation and lilt of the original text 'Be-lle, qui tiens ma vi-e capti-ve dans tes yeux'.

In addition to Schubert's incorporation of his own songs into other works, a practice also followed on several occasions by Gustav Mahler, they were also adapted as transcriptions for solo piano by Franz Liszt, alongside vocal music by composers as diverse as Allegri (the *Miserere*, no less, combined with Mozart's *Ave verum corpus*), Bellini, Délibes, Donizetti, Gounod, Handel, and Wagner. In a remarkable sequence on these lines, Liszt's piano arrangement of Mozart's choral gem *Ave verum corpus* was turned by Tchaikovsky into an orchestral version as part of his suite *Mozartiana*. Fauré's *Après un Rêve* is almost as well-known in the version for cello as it is in its original song form. Rachmaninoff's wordless *Vocalise* for voice and piano has also been adopted by instrumentalists.

Comparison between the vocal and instrumental versions of this wide selection of works can be highly instructive to the young musician seeking to understand the principles of scoring and the potential combination of sounds.

---

[15] https://www.youtube.com/watch?v=EpiyYI25xYg
[16] https://www.ted.com/talks/naturally_7_jams_fly_baby_with_an_orchestra_of_vocals

14

Working in Pairs

The rationale for encouraging students to work in pairs is twofold: to develop through collaboration an understanding of polyphonic music in two parts and to achieve this through experience of its performance. Any outcomes that two students work towards can also be performed with larger groups.

Precursors to the kind of paired work to be introduced here were provided in game 5 (rhythmic interaction; see Chapter 2), games 7 and 12 (a progressive approach to pitched singing; see Chapter 3), and in the emotionally motivated exercises of 'Facial Expression and Timbre' (see Chapter 4). In relation to the elaboration of *Harmony Signing*, a vital component of the understanding and presentation of signs can be provided by further experience of Kodály gestures that employ both hands to control two separate streams of sound. This builds on the combination of melody and drone we encountered in 'More on Aural Location' (see Chapter 10) and is best developed through mutually supportive pair work in which the relationship between sound and gesture can be practised prior to its transference to larger performing groups.

Consonant Beginnings

A strategy that can build well on existing skills while preparing for what comes next is the paired exchange of melodies over *moveable drones*. In this task, two participants face each other and decide on a tonic pitch that both sign as Doh. Having chosen which of the pair first acts as drone, one of them does so while the other performs a brief (single breath) melody, conscious of its relationship with the drone. Both sign both parts, adopting Kodály gestures to do so (fig. 14.1).

Figure 14.1 Music notation of a movable drone duet.

A more interactive response to the potential of two-part singing occurs where the participants take it in turns to act as drone while the other takes on a melodic function. When the first melody singer comes to a pitch that they can settle on as a drone, their partner moves off their drone note and takes over the melodic role. Such an exercise might sound like this:

Voice 1:   Doh – Ray – Me – Ray – Me – Fa – Soh - Fa – Me – Fa – Soh – La – Soh - - - - - -

Voice 2: Doh - Ti$^+$ – Doh – Ray – Me – Fa – Ray - - - - - - - - - - - - - - - - - - - Me – Doh

A new element that supports the embodiment of two-part music in the gestures used to convey it, and which relates to a strong pedagogical tradition within the history of European music, is *species counterpoint*. Developing an approach to this through classroom experience provides an insight into how all subsequent polyphonic practice can be traced to the conventions of sixteenth-century composition. This derives from an academic text, *Gradus ad Parnassum*, published by Johann Fux in 1725. Fux was a composer and teacher admired by his contemporary J. S. Bach. He was influential on every subsequent generation of composers and theorists from Beethoven, Brahms, and Debussy to Schenker, Hindemith, and Nadia Boulanger.

What Fux set out to provide was a comprehensive road map to the fluent composition of counterpoint. His intention was to aid students in writing music that would be effective in performance because it would make sense in rehearsal; to develop the inner ear, so that composition represented a fluent working out of the musical potential inherent in the material one first devised; and to help manage the interaction of separate streams of music as additional parts coalesce into coherent textures. The principle that was to make this possible is *voice leading*. This is a term we have employed from time to time in this text, but which now requires thorough examination.

We are all familiar with the concept of melody and accompaniment that governs how a great deal of music is composed: a tune is placed in a more pleasing acoustic framework through the provision of chords or material derived from them. There is, to an extent, at least in the simpler form of this arrangement (such as a singer playing chords on a guitar to accompany the melody they perform vocally), a clear hierarchical relationship; that is, the accompaniment serves the melody.

But musical styles evolved convergently in several different cultures in which, while this arrangement might also be present, an alternative to it emerged in the practice whereby two or more parts carry streams of sound that are *of equal importance and are independent of one another*. We will tease out the implications of this definition as we study the phenomenon through the perspective that Fux provided.

In moving as we have done from monophonic, single-line composition into pair work as a means of introducing polyphony, we can invoke a formula that I have distilled from this experience:

> *n*-part music is more like 2-part music
> than 2-part music is like monophony

What this formula is intended to stress is that, once we cross the threshold into two or more parts, the hierarchy whereby one part dominates needs to break down. This is achieved in the interests of presenting to the listener an experience that depends for its intelligibility on attention being drawn appropriately to all of the contributing components. This is an advanced skill, in which we need to learn to walk before we can run. It is Fux's achievement that he provided the means for learning the skills involved in a systematic manner which reveals the attainments of other composers while it presents the means for students to climb the same mountain—by steps, to Parnassus.

Since Fux's intention is that we train the inner ear so that habits are formed in the aural imagination that can provide instant solutions to compositional challenges, we start with very simple tasks. Recalling the work we derived from chant (the basis for much of the Renaissance music from which Fux took as his model), we begin by composing well-formed melodies that are limited to notes of equal length moving only up and down by step. As soon as we can cope with this, in performance and in signing such melodies to others, we will be ready to attempt, under guidance, their combination in two-part polyphony.

For example, the following is not a very memorable or expressive tune:

(i)   Doh – Ray – Me – Fah – Soh – La – Soh – Fa – Me – Ray – Doh

Why not? (it is certainly worth posing this question to a class and seeing what observations are made). One answer would be that it is predictable at two points in its journey: after Me we anticipate that it will continue rising; and after the second Fa it will continue to fall. Arguably, the only salient feature one might recall is the point (La) at which it changed direction. This is an idea we should hold in the back of our minds: What generates interest, why, and how?

How does the following melody compare?

(ii)   Doh – Ray – Me – Ray – Me – Fa – Soh – La – Soh – Fa – Me – Ray – Me

There are only three changes of direction, but they appear to be sufficient to create a sense of shape that is no longer predictable. These are the properties we imply in talking of a 'well-formed' melody, given the constraints first placed upon us (equal duration; moving only by step).

We know from previous experience that such a melody could be accompanied by a drone or by a progression of well-chosen chords. If it is instead to be one part of a polyphonic interaction with another voice, how do we write one that is both equal to it and independent?

This is where Fux's approach is so supportive. It teaches how to work simultaneously with the horizontal (the well-formedness of each individual melody) and the vertical (the relationship between the two when heard at the same time). This is where the goals of *equality* and *independence* define our intentions. The two tunes, at least at this stage, are made up of similar attributes and the relationship between them is arranged so that neither is slave or accompaniment to the other. Before we introduce the conventions Fux presents to achieve this, let's again consider a clearly bad example:

(iii)   Voice 1: Me – Fa – Soh – Fa – Soh – La – Ti – Doh – Ti – La – Soh – Fa – Soh

        Voice 2: Doh – Ray – Me – Ray – Me – Fa – Soh – La – Soh – Fa – Me – Ray – Me

Signed, or read from notation, the class should perform this in two parts. It will sound pleasant and achieving it will be a valuable exercise in choral performance. But what about the material itself?

Students will recognise that the two parts are in lock step. There is no sense of equality, in that the upper part seems to have been added as a slave of the lower that was introduced previously. Each is, of course, individually well-formed. But the unbroken *parallel motion* that binds them together removes any possibility of independence.

What, then, about the following?

(iv)   Voice 1: Soh – Fa – Soh – La – Soh – Fa – Me – Ray – Me – Fa – Soh – Fa – Me

         Voice 2: Doh – Ray – Me – Ray – Me – Fa – Soh – La – Soh – Fa – Me – Ray – Me

Again, this should be performed several times, 'each way around' (half the class singing the top first time, and the two groups swapping over at a later point). Once its properties have been fully experienced, they can be investigated. What is different about this phrase? Did it seem more satisfactory than (iii)—even if only marginally? Was it more interesting to perform?

Such deliberations will open up an understanding of what Fux's method, from which this is derived, has made available as procedure:

- where (iii) was limited to *parallel motion*, what governs the interaction of parts in (iv) is the equal presentation of parallel motion and *contrary motion*?
- where (iii) was limited to the interval of the third between parts, (iv) presents a variety of intervals, which is consistent with the achievement of independence.

If the class is providing answers and suggestions on these lines, they will be ready to absorb the conventions Fux provides:

(1) The relationship between parts should comprise an equal variety of qualities of movement (parallel and contrary motion).
(2) The resultant intervals between parts should be as follows:
   (a) in parallel motion: thirds (or sixths)[1];
   (b) in contrary motion *only*: unisons and fifths.
(3) The following intervals should not at this stage result between parts:
   seconds, fourths, and sevenths.

One can go back to (iv) and test these assumptions. Is the 'new' part in (iv) equally well-formed? Are the intervals used as described? Students can commence the valuable discipline of writing the interval between parts in the space above the lower stave (or between the lines of Kodály notation), so that they can learn how to check their work when composing their own solution to polyphonic exercises of this kind. And that is what they should do next, either in Kodály note names or in staff notation. For this

---

[1] We will very soon be able to employ sixths, but not quite yet.

purpose, the following examples and fig. 14.2 permit students to create the additional part(s) that can be combined together, still adopting the conventions introduced so far:

(v)   Me – Ray- Doh – Ray – Me – Fa – Soh – La – Soh – Fa – Me – Fa – Soh

(vi)   Doh⁺ – Ti – La – Soh – La – Soh – Fa – Soh – Fa – Me – Ray – Me – Fa

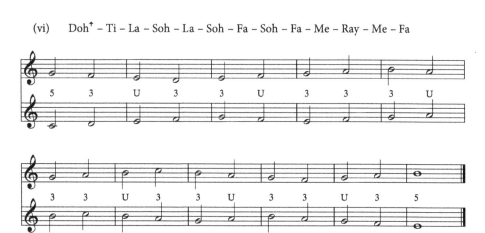

Figure 14.2 Music notation of two parts moving independently by step.

Once students have worked some examples of their own, they will become ready to take the next steps Fux provides. As revision of this stage in the species, an effective way of developing all-round competence with these exercises is to perform them in a variety of ways:

- reading both parts from notation, singing the Kodály note names;
- following two signers, each signing one of the parts, while signing one's own;
- singing the exercise to a legato <Aaahh>;
- following a single signer who uses both hands to direct both parts while all participants also sign both parts;
- performance on instruments;
- combinations of these.

A further possibility could also be tried. Can students improvise two-part passages compliant with these current conventions: (a) in pairs; (b) in paired leadership of the group as a whole; (c) with one leader using both hands? Even if attempts to achieve these aims do not meet with full success, they will provide formative experience.

The clarity that should be associated with this first level of species counterpoint confers aural recall that, if held in the inner ear, will contribute well to the development of creative musicianship. But to many students who achieve this, it may all seem somewhat limited at this point. The desire to move on is good, as long as each step is mastered securely. How could we confer a greater degree of freedom and of greater independence in the voices?

The next strategy is to loosen up the rhythmic lock step that permitted control of intervals within the forms of motion first introduced. The new convention is: *some notes can be twice as long*. This permits turns to be taken ('you move while I stay', but within a more rapid interdependent cycle than that of *moveable drones*), and the interval of the sixth to be introduced (it was latent in the earlier conventions, but inaccessible until this

Figure 14.3 Music notation of oblique motion.

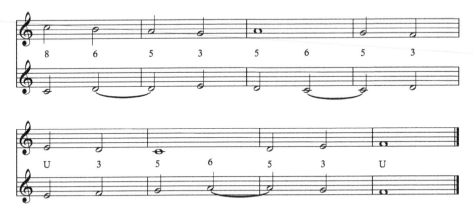

Figure 14.4 Two-part polyphony combining notes of different length.

rhythmic step was introduced because it was difficult to make use of it without the two parts diverging beyond the octave—which held the danger of 'top' and 'bottom' parts emerging in which the sense of equality would be lost—or of converging onto a fourth).

So, the following steps can now be inserted into a two-part texture, depending on whether they link together passages that diverge from being a third apart or converge on voices an octave apart (or vice versa). This new step opens up far greater possibilities of varying interval-type and overall range (fig. 14.3).

Here is an example of the new convention in a more extended context. As before, this should be performed in a variety of ways, with and without signing and note names (fig. 14.4).[2]

Students could practise the lower part given in Figure 14.5, before writing and rehearsing their own complementary upper part, practising their solution with a partner and checking it for application of the prevailing conventions prior to trying it out in performance with a larger group:

While we initially stressed the vital feature of independence of parts so as to establish the values that distinguish polyphonic voices from a mere accompanying role, we might now more properly refer to *interdependence*: as students work with examples such as these, they will find that good solutions often encounter a kind of cul-de-sac that is not open to unravelling and requires 'backing up' in search of a better route through the possible material. This patient trial-and-error working sharpens the musical perception and builds a sense of what fits. Once they are able to write or improvise solutions to exercises of this kind, students can compose their own two-part pieces for signing to

---

[2] Notice that the resulting intervals have been written in between the stave lines.

the class with both hands. The development of such skills is likely to take several weeks of gradual exposure to performing each other's exercises. The acquisition of fluency in this genre may usefully receive additional support through sight-reading examples of Renaissance two-part counterpoint from a collection such as Donald Tovey's anthology entitled *Laudate Pueri* (1910), and arranging these for performance on instruments.

As we introduce further liberating conventions to permit freer interdependent interaction between parts, we need to constantly monitor the well-formedness of individual voices. The signs we look for of one part being subservient to another include: 'ambulances', whereby a part oscillates between two pitches rather than attaining a sense of free contour, and ostinato, in which a part repeats a pattern in a manner that appears to fix its role. Similarly, holding or repeating notes consigns them to the function of temporary drone.

The unequal note lengths we have recently introduced afford further choices in terms of perceived rhythmic organisation. They provide the potential for the sensation of metre in three time. Initially, we can think of this as 3/2. Eventually we can employ an expanded range of durations to apply the conventions of counterpoint to 3/4 as well as compound meters based on a triple division of the beat such as 6/8. At this stage, let's try working with 3/2 in which the first two beats of the bar can either be a single whole note or two half notes (fig. 14.6).

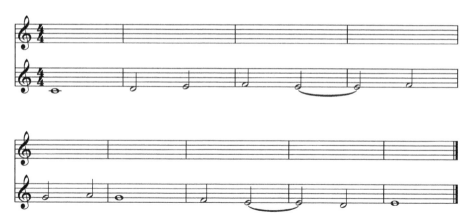

Figure 14.5 An exercise in adding a new part to an existing one.

Figure 14.6 A musical example of two-part polyphony in three time.

Our first strategy for liberating the sense of lock-step movement was achieved through a rhythmic modification. Our second is intervallic, with the introduction of leaps. But we will proceed carefully, both in range and in understanding the implications of working with intervals larger than a step. We will work at first only with thirds and we will treat them in a specific way that permits us to develop a confident aural image of the outcome. When we introduce a leap of a third, up or down, we will pursue the convention of 'coming back inside', moving by step to the note we have omitted by leaping over it. The purpose of this is to retain control of the consequences for our texture of vocal range and to become familiar with the harmonic possibilities made available. So, for each voice to represent a well-formed contribution, we must always check that, after a leap, we 'come back inside' (fig.14.7):

Doh - Me - Ray   Soh - Me - Fa

Figure 14.7 Music notation of a well-formed melody that employs leaps of a third.

Students should begin by improvising with their partners well-formed single-line melodies that conform to the available conventions, now embracing, if desired, notes of double length and leaps of a third. It is vital in doing so that strict rhythm is observed, so that this becomes a fully felt and recognised component of the style. Hesitancy is incompatible with achieving this. It is better that mistakes are made confidently than that rhythmic flow is not maintained. Such exercises could also be prepared in notation for performance by the whole class led through Kodály signs.

The following is an example of the kind of melody that might result:

Doh – Me – – Ray – Fa – Me – Soh – Fa – – La – So – Me – Fa – – Soh – Me – Fa – Soh

Figure 14.8 Music notation of a two-part texture that employs these conventions.

As shown in Figure 14.8, a melody of this kind can then be combined with a complementary voice of students' devising to create a two-part texture. In achieving this, both voices conform to the principles of well-formedness, while also giving rise to the same initial conventions by which intervals are permissible between parts: thirds and sixths in both parallel and contrary motion; unisons, fifths, and octaves in contrary motion only; and no seconds, fourths, or sevenths at all. In addition, to preserve independence, neither leaps nor long notes should occur simultaneously in both voices.

In Figure 14.9, a variety of solutions is provided to combining melodies: (i) and (ii) provide a different upper part over the same lower voice; (ii) and (iii) provide a different lower part beneath the same upper voice.

Students will rapidly realise how much greater the freedoms are that have become available at this stage by comparing the different solutions they arrive at for any task they might be set where they begin with the same material (see exercises i, ii, and iii in Figure 14.9). Equally, they may find it frustrating to continue to apply all the conventions successfully without encountering errors. As in learning any language, it pays to be scrupulous, gently illustrating that there are almost always solutions close to what students attempt that represent a more convincing application of one feature or another. One needs to work at exercises at this level over time as what they have to offer is not absorbed quickly.

Introducing Dissonance

A frustration for students familiar with any polyphonic music from the European Medieval period onwards, via Renaissance and Classical music to later styles that have continued to draw on the conventions that arose, will be the lack of *dissonance* in what we have covered so far in this chapter. This will be especially noticeable in that a degree of controlled dissonance has occurred in a great many of the games and exercises we encountered earlier, and it is a common property in much of the music that students will know through listening and performance. The only reason that we have avoided dissonance up to this point in our exploration of the species counterpoint derived from Fux is in order to be able to embrace it with confidence when we introduce it, as we are about to do. The assumption may well be that this is principally about employing the intervals that we have hitherto set aside—the seconds, fourths, and sevenths—and this is true. We will, at a stroke, almost double the number and variety of sounds that we can access simultaneously. This is one significant reason why we made a systematic study of the characteristics and effects of each interval (see Chapter 13, 'Working on Your Own: Understanding Intervals'). But it is of equal importance to recognise that the incorporation of dissonance plays as great a part in developing the rhythmic and temporal features of polyphonic style as does the timbral potential of new combinations of pitch. Dissonance within the conventions we are applying requires *resolution*, and this results in a heightened sense of the give-and-take which occurs between parts, that governs the overall sense of flow. We hear this as eliciting greater expressiveness. The setting up and fulfilment of expectations that determine both a more colourful sound world and a

Figure 14.9 Three examples in music notation: (i) and (ii) present two different versions based on the same starting point; (iii) builds a different solution out of the 'new' melody of (ii).

greater complexity of relationship between constituent voices. It was thus vital that we mastered consonant polyphony prior to taking the steps that follow.

The four classes of dissonance that we will explore are: (1) unaccented and (2) accented passing notes; (3) anticipations; and (4) suspensions. Of these, by far the most characteristic are suspensions, and we will accord them a section of their own.

Passing Notes and Anticipations

Passing notes fall into two categories: unaccented and accented. The difference between the two is a matter of harmonic colour and intention resulting from a combination of perceived rhythmic placement and the sense of dissonant function that demands resolution. One might think of unaccented passing notes as being disguised or unassuming whereas accented are overt and draw attention to their expressive function.

All of the dissonances to be introduced depend on the introduction of intervals between parts previously unavailable: seconds, fourths and sevenths. For each new function, an illustration will be provided that involves each of these dissonant intervals.

Unaccented passing notes arise largely as links that preserve stepwise movement in one part while another is sustained. This form of interaction may be associated with varied rates of movement between voices. For instance (fig. 14.10):

Voice 1   Doh – Ray – Me – – – – Fa – Soh – – – – – –

Voice 2   Doh – – – – – Ray – Me – – – – – Ray – Doh

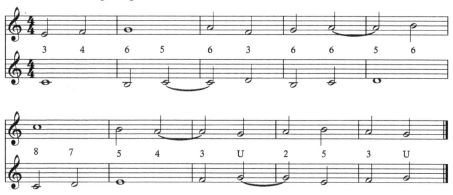

Figure 14.10 Music notation of a two-part passage (1) that features unaccented passing-notes.

Here, the movement between parts is neither in parallel nor contrary motion: we can refer to this as *oblique*, and this will tend to carry the association that passing notes are involved and that one part is moving while the other remains still (see 'Moveable Drones' at the start of this chapter). This permits us to have intervals such as seconds and fourths between parts. The voicing 'passes' through dissonances by step between consonances that mediate their effect. The dissonance in unaccented passing-notes normally falls on the weak beats between consonances that occupy the strong beats.

Accented passing notes present dissonance as a more salient feature of the relationship between parts: the dissonance occupies the strong beat, and resolves on the weak, usually downwards by step.

Examples of the use of passing notes are provided in fig. 14.11:

Figure 14.11 Music notation of: (2) a two-part passage that features accented passing-notes; (3) a short passage that mixes accented and unaccented passing-notes.

Presenting passing notes while the rhythmic choices available are limited to only two durations, while preserving all other features of well-formed two-part polyphony, is a valuable discipline, though the constraints one is working under make it difficult to fully bring them alive as a component of style. As we will see shortly, both types of passing note come into their own where greater choice of movement is made available through introducing notes of different durations, such as quarter notes and dotted rhythms.

Anticipations also relate more typically to styles in which there are greater differences available within individual voices. However, while in our introduction of dissonance we are focusing on the element of rhythmic control that they involve, it helps to experience them in comparison with the other features of species counterpoint that we have introduced which have all emerged within the same limited rhythmic practice. Anticipations are the complement of suspensions, the significant practice that we will deal with next: one deals with the arrival of a salient pitch ahead of its normal position in a phrase and the other delays its sounding, to both harmonic and rhythmic effect. Here is an example of anticipation:

Voice 1:   La – Ti – Doh⁺ Doh

Voice 2:   Ray – – – – Doh

At the point at which Voice 1 reaches the upper Doh, it forms a seventh with Voice 2. However, we tolerate this because we anticipate Voice 2 falling to the lower tonic to complete the sense of a well-formed cadence, in which this feature has expressively drawn attention to this outcome.

Figure 14.12 provides further examples of this phenomenon in which the other conventions of our current understanding of species counterpoint are preserved. Anticipations do not sound very comfortable in this rhythmic framework. They, too, emerge more successfully with freer access to rhythmic variety. But experiencing them here in comparison with the other aspects of dissonance we have introduced makes their function clear.

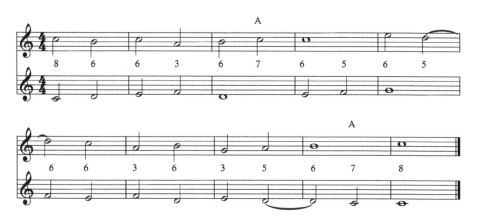

Figure 14.12 Music notation of a passage that features anticipation.

Suspensions

Suspensions have featured as expressive devices in polyphonic music from the early Renaissance to the present day, gracing the music of composers whose styles are otherwise as different as Josquin, Palestrina, Tallis, Monteverdi, Bach, Handel, Mozart, Schubert, Wagner, and Tchaikovsky. They are also common in popular music and jazz. It may seem odd to present such a list—and indeed, all of these names could be replaced by others—but the point that it stresses is that the way in which suspensions have figured in their music has for the most part conformed to the same conventions.

A suspension occurs where a part moves to a note which creates a dissonance with the other part that repeats or sustains the pitch it was previously sounding. This is the moment of suspension, which is resolved when the suspended part moves downwards by step.

Figure 14.13 Music notation of a passage that features suspensions.

The formula for this covers four stages:

Preparation (a consonance that includes the note to be suspended);
Suspension (the accompanying part moves to create a suspension with the note that
    is maintained or repeated at the same pitch as previously);
Resolution (the suspended note falls by a step);
Continuation (the music moves on) OR Cadence (the music comes to rest).

The mnemonic **PSRC** can be employed to analyse a range of cadences and to evaluate
one's own work (see fig. 14.13).

Note how each example could be viewed as a variant of the kinds of parallel motion
we have encountered previously, in which the suspension operates as a time delay to
achieve the harmonic effect. This is especially clear in the 'chain of suspensions', which is
like an out-of-phase sequence of parallel thirds. In this 'chain', each resolution becomes
the preparation for the next suspension.

Pairs of students should practise performing these examples, signing both parts
while each sings top and bottom by turn. They should then devise their own examples,
and also see if they can include suspensions handled in this way (tracing the PSRC
positions) in improvisation.

Leaps Greater Than a Third

A further liberating strategy is to include leaps greater than a third. In Renaissance
practice, leaps of fourths and fifths are common. Sixths and octaves are more rare. In
almost all cases, the convention of moving inside the leap to continue the phrase is
preserved (fig. 14.14):

Doh – Fa – Me   Doh – Soh – Fa   Doh – La – Soh   Doh – Doh[†] – Ti

Figure 14.14 Examples of the use of: (i) leaps greater than a third; (ii) these combined with suspensions.

Further Rhythmic Possibilities

In order to focus on the relationship between intervals—presented horizontally within melodies and vertically between parts—we have limited rhythmic durations to the minimum that has permitted oblique passing notes, suspensions, and anticipations to be introduced. All of these, and the overall sense of flow of the music we produce, become more characterful as a consequence of incorporating a wider range of durations.

The first step we can introduce is to make the sequence of half-note pulses unequal through including dotted half notes and the quarter notes that complement them. This can be achieved both within the bar and through the use of ties across the bar-line (fig. 14.15).

Figure 14.15 Examples employing 'dotted notes'.

Figure 14.16 Examples employing quarter notes.

Notice that the conventions for leaps and well-formed voice leading continue, irrespective of the rate of movement. This remains the case when we take the next logical step of introducing free use of quarter notes (fig. 14.16).

Working With Imitation and Complementary Phrases

Imitative counterpoint is a significant feature of Renaissance practice that, like suspension, has continued to inform subsequent composition. The discipline achieved through the conventions encountered so far is crystallised where the independence of parts conveys similarities that unify the compositional intention. Each part, as it enters, presents a near copy of its predecessor, modified so as to yield rhythmic and harmonic clarity and consistency through transposition or intervallic variation. Both performer and listener trace the relationship between parts as dependent on the memory of recent experience defining present and future unfolding. The exercises we have worked with until now have been built on the conventions introduced but resemble stepping stones on the way to mastering the continuation of the two-part texture. Working with the phrase lengths and sense of purpose that imitation requires takes our practice closer to composition proper. All existing conventions still apply, with one key exception: In order to separate and articulate the component phrases that make up the texture, we can introduce rests; periods of meaningful, measured silence. At certain moments, our two-part texture has only one sounding voice. A new sense of give and take, of light and shade, becomes part of the musical narrative. At the same time, the musical progression takes on the human dimension of allowing the performers to breathe and weaves this necessity into the expressive design.

Diagonal Movement

The Kodály gestures we have used to explore counterpoint provide a secure and precise representation of the component voices which make up the kinds of two-part texture we have traced through practice based on Fux's species counterpoint. Aspects of the way voices can be led in sounding together played a part in the games and tasks designed for the youngest and least experienced participants. We can consider the link between this foundation level, and the considerable sophistication of what we have dealt with in this chapter, as a means of illustrating the continuity of learning and experience that underpins the approach from which *Harmony Signing* has emerged.

The embodiment of forms of movement in space both communicates visual representation and supports aural recognition. We have focused in detail on the role that parallel, contrary, and oblique motion have in the various steps by which we outlined their function in counterpoint. Each of these can be conveyed more simply in gestures that capture the direction and rate of movement, employing two hands to convey these:

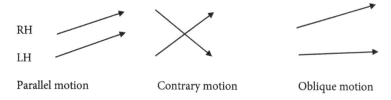

| RH | Parallel motion | Contrary motion | Oblique motion |
| LH | | | |

This approach works well in warm-ups and can be led successfully by primary school participants as a preparation for mastering more precise and complex gestures (see Chapter 3, Game 12). A further quality of movement is referred to as *similar motion*, where the voices move in the same direction by different sizes of interval:

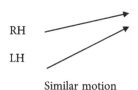

RH
LH

Similar motion

The term is clear enough, and it allows us to label two streams of sound that are neither oblique (both move) nor parallel (they move in different ways). But, while working with students on the properties of a particular arrangement between parts that arises from the harmonic series, we decided that the term *similar motion* was insufficient. So the term *diagonal motion* was coined, with their approval, to provide a unique label for this category of movement (fig. 14.17):

Voice 1:   Doh⁺ – Ray – Me – Ray – Me – Soh – Me – Ray – Me

Voice 2:   Me – Soh – Doh⁺– Soh – Doh – Me – Doh – Soh – Doh

Diagonal motion arises frequently in writing for pairs of horns from the Baroque and Classical periods and became a defining characteristic of German Romantic music. It seemed useful to have a specific term that could be employed to capture this effect when it is present in music that students encounter.

Figure 14.17 Examples of diagonal motion.

Summary: What We Have Achieved in Pairs

This chapter has focused at length on the value of working in pairs, both as a means of developing musical skills that can be shared in practice with a minimum of one other person, and as a suitable approach to acquiring the theoretical understanding derived from species counterpoint. The experience built in this way can act as the foundation for free improvisation in a variety of genres and styles. As we move on to the opportunities involved in working in larger groups, choirs, instrumental ensembles, paired work will continue to represent a valuable means of sketching and rehearsing musical ideas in preparation for creative and leadership roles.

The exploration of counterpoint has largely involved Kodály hand signs and the singing voice. These can be replaced or complemented by participants using instruments to perform the material covered and developing responses of their own to the possibilities it has opened up. As the consequences of employing Fux's approach become apparent for students' aural development—their capacity to track what is happening where two or more streams of sound are presented polyphonically—this will contribute to their understanding of tonality, and of consonant and dissonant function, on which we build next in work with larger groups and a return to focussing on harmonic progression.

15
Working in Groups

In this chapter we return to working with left-hand *Harmony Signing* gestures that permit us to extend the range of chords and tonal relationships through which we can lead participation by larger groups. Specifically, we will work with the combination of right-hand melodic signing with left-hand harmonic accompaniment as a means of developing the representation of musical works and the capacity of students to sketch and compose. We will again model this practice vocally, assuming the potential of leaders to work with whole classes. We should nevertheless recognise the value of working with groups as small as four participants, which could comprise 'pairs of pairs' extending into this practice the lessons learned in the previous chapter. Especially when working with instruments, groups of four led by a signer can carry a great deal of musical information that can be accessed through improvisation. This can both represent valuable musical experience in its own right and form a template for rehearsing material that can be transferred to much larger groups, whether vocal, instrumental, or a mixture of the two.

Combining Melody and Harmony

In Chapter 11, 'Collective Creativity', a variety of chord progressions employing the primary triads was introduced to illustrate their role in selected musical works. One was the opening bars of Schumann's song *Seiht ich ihn gesehen*, which can be represented as follows:

RH   Soh – La: Soh – Soh – La:

LH   I   IV: V   I   IV:

Similarly, we are able to lead the opening of Bernstein's 'One Hand, One Heart', from *West Side Story*:

RH   Me – Me – Me | Fa – – | Ray – – | Me – – |

LH   I   IV   V   I

This is as far as we can go right now because there are harmonic and tonal complexities to follow that we have not yet covered. Solutions will be made available as further harmonic possibilities are introduced.

However, some of the other progressions we introduced earlier are open to a complete interpretation in two-handed signing:

1   *Wimoweh*

(4-beat measures)

RH | | | |Doh – Ray-Me – Ray – Me | Fa – Me-Ray – Doh – Ray |

LH   I   IV   I   V   I   IV

LH   Me – Ray-Doh – Me-Ray-|- - - - - | ... and proceeding to ...

RH   I   V

RH   Doh – Ray-Me – Ray – Me | Fa – Me-Ray – Doh – Ray | Me – Soh⁺-Soh – Soh-Soh-|- - - -

LH   I   IV   I   V

From these ingredients, it should be possible to put the whole song together, with or without words and chorally. instrumentally. or with elements of both. The accompaniment can be carried by chordal vocalisation of the word *wimoweh*. It also works very well on wooden mallet instruments.

2   *Silent Night*

[3-beat measures]

RH   Soh - - La Soh - | Me - - - - - - | Soh - - La Soh - | Me - - - - - - | Ray⁺ – Ray | Ti - - - - - - |

LH   I   I   I   I   IV   V

RH   Doh⁺ – Doh |Soh - - - - - - | La – La | Doh - - Ti La - | Soh - - La Soh - | Me - - - - - - |

LH   I   I   IV   IV   I   I

RH   La – La | Doh - - Ti La - | Soh - - La Soh - | Me - - - - - - |

LH   IV   IV   I   I

RH   Ray⁺ – Ray | Fa⁺ - - Ray Ti - | Doh - - - - - - | Me - - - - - - | Doh – Soh⁺ – Me – |

LH   V   V   I   I   I

RH   Soh - - Fa Ray - | Doh - - - - - - | - - - - - - ||

LH   V   I   I

Readers may wonder why chord IV is employed to harmonise the note Ray. It is, in fact, a shortcut, giving access to chord ii⁷. It works, and no singer young or old has ever objected to or questioned it.

3   Chopin's *Etude in E major* Op. 10, no. 3 'Tristesse' (opening)

[4-beat measures]

RH   Soh⁺ | Doh – Ti Doh | Ray – – – | – Me Me Ray | Me – – – | – Fa Fa Me | La – – Soh |

LH   I   V⁷   V⁷   I   I   V

RH   Fa Me Ti⁺ Doh | Ray – – – | – Me Me Ray | Doh – – – | –

LH   I   V⁷   V⁷   I

(Note that the melody commences in the right-hand gesture prior to the first chord signed in the left hand.)

This experience of combining melody and harmony should act as a model for students to devise their own compositions and improvisations employing the triads with which they are familiar and the notes of the diatonic scale that they can sign with the right hand.

Next Steps: Chromaticism and Modulation

In this section, we introduce notes outside the diatonic array, and examine their potential for introducing journeys away from the Tonic through modulation. We have already glimpsed some possibilities through the use of minor replacements (i, iv, v) of the primary triads. These depend on the sounds and signs of Ma, Lor (which we sign identically to Si, and may if, we wish, also represent with the name Si[1]), and Ta, respectively.

We now investigate alongside these the pitches Di (sharpened tonic/flattened supertonic) and Fi (sharpened fourth).

---

[1] *Harmony Signing*, while observing the convention of movable Doh, concedes that it simplifies matters to employ an equally tempered approach to the pitches of the chromatic scale, thus limiting the number of names and signs to twelve.

Image 15.1a, b, and c Signs for Ma, Lor/Si, Ta.

Image 15.2a and b Signs for Di, Fi.

Here are some examples of combining chromatic right-hand gestures with primary triad harmony:

1   Joplin, *The Entertainer*

[4-beat measure]

RH   Ray-Ma | Me-Doh⁺– Me-Doh – Me | Doh – - Doh-Ray-Ma | Me-Doh-Ray-Me – Ti-Ray- | Doh

LH   V   I   IV   I   V   I

2   Beethoven, *Für Élise*

RH   [Soh⁺ -] Soh⁺-Fi-Soh-Fi-Soh-Ray-Fa-Ma | Doh – - Ma⁺-Soh-Doh | Ray – Soh⁺-Ti-Ray | Ma

LH   i   V   i

3   Monty Norman, Theme from *James Bond*

RH   Soh_____Si_____La_____Si_____ :||

LH   i_____ i_____ i_____ i____

(The right hand 'captures' the part that performs Soh in order for it to move to Si and La.)

Students should gain experience in adding chromatic melodies of their own devising to harmonic progressions in the major and minor. They would do well to develop their skills step-by-step alongside those of other participants, beginning with the primary triads and introducing the secondary and minor triads as everyone's confidence and capacity to respond develops.

Diminished Triads

Before we deal with modulation, we will introduce a family of chords that can contribute to achieving it and which represent a further, more sophisticated set of relationships with the array of the primary triads: the diminished triads. There are again three of these, and they can be seen to relate to the dominant, tonic, and subdominant positions and functions, respectively.

The sign for the diminished triad employs both hands, making a diagonal cross in front of the centre-line of the torso. Anyone familiar with the novels and films associated with the Dracula story will recognise the origin of this sign. Diminished triads have a long history of association with the Gothic, from settings of poetry and drama arising from Goethe's *Faust*; music depicting the supernatural from Mozart and Weber via Mendelssohn, Berlioz, and Wagner; to Mussorgsky, Mahler, Tchaikovsky, and the film music of the twentieth century.

The first diminished triad is a variant of chord vii and behaves like a colourful alternate to the dominant. We have not previously introduced chord vii because it outlines the Devil's Interval of the tritone rather than a perfect fifth. We can add to chord vii (Ti/Ray/Fa) the note Si, and this full four-note diminished triad contains two tritones, each of which can be viewed as divided into two component minor thirds:

Ti – Ray – Fa – Si

We can access this chord as follows, conveying the intention with crossing the forefingers in a space below the horizontal tonic position, with the backs of the fingers facing participants:

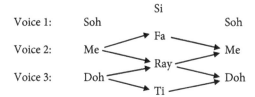

The graphic symbol for notating the diminished triad is <X>, which is consistent with figured bass usage in which it is also presented as 7. To distinguish between the three possibilities in chord-symbol notation, we can use the following: $7^↓$ for the 'dominant'; $7^=$ for the triad over the tonic; and $7^↑$ for that over the sharpened tonic. While all diminished triads can be employed in ambiguous ways that permit modulation in unexpected directions, the most common associations of each are captured by these symbols and gestures:

(1) $7^↓$ acts as a replacement dominant;
(2) $7^=$ acts as a chord with a subdominant flavour that can both lead to the dominant and return to the tonic;
(3) $7^↑$ leads via the sharpened tonic to chord ii, which is relative of the subdominant.

A version of <X> is used for all diminished triads, denoting the crossing of the index fingers in three positions: *below* the horizontal; *on* the horizontal; and *above* it. For $7^=$ and $7^↑$ it is more comfortable and visually clear if the backs of the hands face the signer. Graphically, because the gestures we use for them involve both hands, we place the <x> between the symbol for the shoulders, O, which still represents the position of the elbows in comparison with which the fingers are oriented:

(1)   O ∨ O   (Ti/Ray/Fa/Si)
          X

(2)   O –X– O   (Doh/Ma/Fi/La)

          X
(3)   O /\ O   (Di/Me/Soh/Ta)

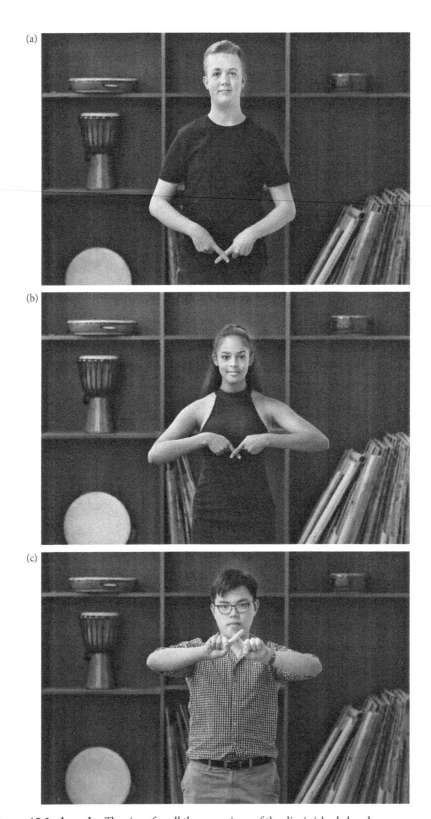

Image 15.3a, b, and c The signs for all three versions of the diminished chord.

The following progressions can now be led by a signer:

(1)   o———■   →   O ∨ O → o———■
                        X

                I   7⁺   I

(the voice-leading for this is given in the above diagram)

(2)   o———■   →   O –X– O → o———■

                I   7⁼   I

The voice-leading that achieves is:

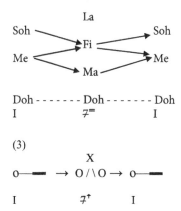

(3)
                          X
o———■   →   O / \ O → o———■

I   7⁺   I

This time, the voice-leading is:

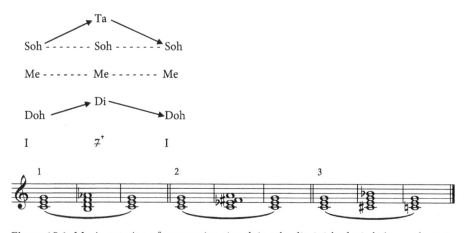

Figure 15.1 Music notation of progressions involving the diminished triads (examples 1, 2, and 3).

The notated progressions 1, 2 and 3 in fig. 15.1 capture the voice-leading that results in accessing each of the three diminished triads. Two further examples are as follows:

Progression 4 presents a descending sequence of diminished triads that can be led through the gestures illustrated in the diagrams above.

Progression 5 provides an example of the use of the diminished triads in a more varied progression (fig. 15.2).

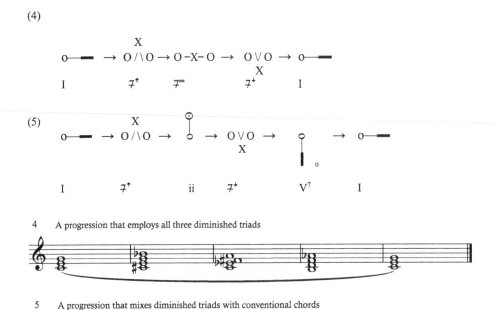

Figure 15.2 Music notation also of diminished triad examples 4 and 5.

Students can devise examples of their own that mix the diminished triads with any accessible chords for which the gestures are known and the voice-leading consequences familiar to participants.

A link that we will explore later is that between the diminished triads and the dominant minor ninth chords that are related to each. Where such chords are in play, they are often associated with the undermining of the prevailing tonic, the resolution of which involves modulation. 7^{+} is commonly employed to achieve movement away from the tonic towards the sharper keys of the cycle of fifths and $7^{=}$ opens links to keys that are on the flat side of the cycle.

Diminished triads work equally well in the minor. The following chord progression that figures strongly in the 'Sturm und Drang' music that composers such as Haydn and Mozart wrote in the minor mode:

Modulation

We have illustrated through a cut-and-paste technique that it is possible to drag chords to the tonic position. True modulation occurs when pitches from outside the prevailing tonality demand that one tonic is replaced by another as a means of resolving the tension created by the presence of nonscale pitches, especially when associated with dissonant harmony. This permits us to cross tonal space, a foundation for the structural developments of Baroque music through which longer and more sophisticated movements arose through the nesting of tonal relationships.

Whatever key tonal music is presented in, the pull to a prevailing tonic is dependent on the relationship between all three of the primary triads. This is where the tonicising sign ꚜ plays a significant role in *Harmony Signing*. It invites participants to contribute to the chord that they sense as presenting the tonic function. For this to be reliable, participants need to be listening to the harmonic implications of the music while they perform.

The most frequently encountered modulations in common-practice music are:

- to the subdominant;
- to the dominant; and
- to the relative minor.

Of these, modulation to the subdominant is the most straightforward. Simply adding a minor seventh to the tonic chord undermines the tonic and resolves to 'old' chord IV, which as a result becomes 'new' chord I.

The gesture for adding the seventh is the rounded finger-and-thumb 'OK' sign that adapts the left-hand chord currently sounding. The graphic for the result is o—■°, and it invites one or more participants to add the flattened seventh. This is followed by the right-hand tonicising sign ꚜ which alerts participants to anticipating that the next chord will be the new tonic. Since the tonic is always represented by the gesture o—■, settling confidently onto this will illustrate that a modulation has been completed. When acquiring confidence in achieving this, it is helpful immediately to visit the 'new' subdominant and dominant to assess whether the group has collectively heard the implications of the modulation.

Here is the progression in full (fig. 15.3):

I   I⁷   (new) I

Figure 15.3 Music notation of modulation to the subdominant.

When a group is ready to do so, a sequence of modulations towards the subdominant can be attempted.

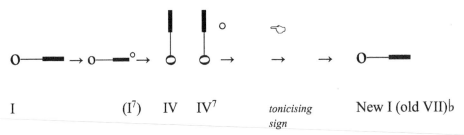

| I | | (I⁷) | IV | IV⁷ | tonicising sign | New I (old VII)♭ |

However, the 'return journey' will not be possible until everyone has mastered the next step.

Modulation to the dominant is more radical and is dependent on a 'pivot' chord outside the prevailing key: the major version of chord II, in which the fourth is sharpened (Fi) to act as a leading note that introduces the new tonic. The sign for chord II(#) exploits the association of the Kodály <Fi> gesture, which represents the entire chord when given with the left hand. Its position 'outside' the primary triads is conveyed through the radical step of its being outside the body, the movement to it akin to a tennis backhand. The 'thumbs-up' gesture of Fi is given with the arm horizontally away from the body, capturing the extent to which it differs in all ways from the tonic: ✎─ O. This can be followed by the tonicising sign, which ought to alert participants to the fact that the 'old' dominant will now occupy the tonic position. The voice leading for this is:

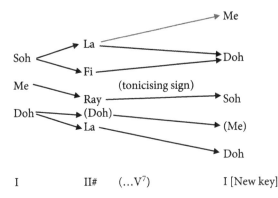

| I | II# | (...V⁷) | I [New key] |

Note that the option is presented here of adding a seventh to the II# chord, making it V⁷. This can be achieved by making the gesture 🖐 in the right hand prior to confirming this with the tonicising sign.

The graphic version of modulation to the dominant is:

O━━ → ✊━O 🖐   O━━ → O━━° ... 🖐 → O━━

| I | II# | tonicising Sign | I (new) | I⁷ | tonicising sign | I (old tonic returns) |

The 'return journey' is also illustrated here through adding a dominant seventh to the new tonic that allows the original tonality to be reinstated. Such a progression represents the skeleton of the Classical sonata form.

Since we can now deal with modulations 'in both directions', we can also take the opposite route (fig. 15.4):

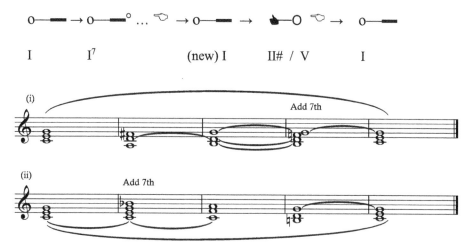

Figure 15.4 Music notation of: (i) modulation to the dominant and back; (ii) modulation to the subdominant and back.

The third most common modulation is to the relative minor. This is a less radical move than to the dominant because, with the exception of the introduction of the sharpened fifth that acts as pivot note, the accidentals remain the same. It is, after all, the relative (chord vi) of the original mode with which it shares the same key signature. However, it requires us to employ both hands to capture the harmonic pivot on which it depends, which is provided by the right hand making the <Si> gesture while the left hand makes <Ti>[2].

The procedure runs as follows (fig. 15.5):

Note that the new tonic is minor. If we were to follow the tonicising sign with the gesture for the tonic major, o—■, this would access a *Tièrce de Picardie*—the VI(#) of the original tonic. Since we have learned that both major and minor are available on all three primary positions, their interchangeability can also provide a variety of pathways into modulations.

---

[2] Where the two hands convey pitches through Kodály signs, whoever is performing the third part sustains the prevailing pitch, which acts as a pivot.

Figure 15.5 Music notation of modulation to the relative minor.

The three modulations covered in this section present the potential for a wide range of harmonic developments that a class or ensemble may take some time to assimilate. We will build further on these later in this chapter (see 'Advanced Harmony Signing: Dissonance, further modulatory short-cuts, and serialism'). However, another set of modulations is made possible by exploiting the properties of the diminished triads.

Further Properties of the Diminished Triads: Ambiguity and Unexpected Resolutions

The symmetry of the diminished triad, with its interlocking tritones and chain of minor thirds, presents choices between alternative resolutions. We have seen how the progression I → 7⁺→ V⁷ → I involved a pitch within the diminished triad needing to resolve by step so as to produce a dominant seventh chord that then resolves to the tonic. But what if this resolution of one of the voices occurred on a different constituent pitch of 7⁺? There are three to choose from. These alternatives are, by definition, going to take us somewhere new by a previously unexplored route.

Let's begin as before, but this time 'capture' <Fa> with the right hand and move it to <Me>. This will become recognisable as III⁷, a pivot similar to that via which we modulate to the relative minor. So, applying the tonicising sign,[3] we can effortlessly move to a new chord that will take the place of 'old' vi or VI (fig. 15.6).

RH: Fa → Me

I   7⁺   (V⁷)   'new' i (or I if preferred)

If this works for 7⁺, then it will for the other two diminished triads as well. This means that with these chromatic resources operating in this manner, we can get from any tonic to any other in just three steps, major or minor and across the entire chromatic

---

[3] Note: When using the right-hand tonicising sign in these progressions, it needs to *touch* the left hand that is still in the position for the prevailing 7. Otherwise there is a danger of confusing it with other Kodály signs now potentially in use.

Figure 15.6 Music notation of this modulating progression to the submediant.

spectrum. These moves were initiated in the late eighteenth and early nineteenth century by composers such as Mozart, Schubert, Weber, and Beethoven. The consequences of their employment to range more rapidly across distantly related harmonic fields is largely what is implied by the phrase 'dissolution of tonality'. No chord or key is more than two steps away from any other.

Here are the pathways for the remaining two options arising with chord $7^{\downarrow}$:

```
              RH: Ti → Ta              ☞
O——■    →    O ∨ O          =    ○    →    O——■
              X                    │
                                   │ ○
I            7⁺                   (V⁷)      'new' I
```

Can we ascertain where we have 'arrived'? Assuming we started in C major, the shift in the right hand of Ti to Ta turned $7^{\downarrow}$ into a dominant seventh on B♭, resolving to E flat major, so this provides an alternative means of modulating to III♭ (fig. 15.7).

Figure 15.7 Music notation of this modulating progression towards the flattened mediant.

Here is another possibility:

```
              RH: Ray → Di             ☞
O——■    →    O ∨ O          =    ○    →    O——■
              X                    │
                                   │ ○
I            7⁺                   (V⁷)      'new' I
```

This time, the move from Ray to Di turned the $7^{\downarrow}$ chord into a dominant seventh on D♭, and we have completed the most distant modulation we have yet achieved—indeed, the most distant possible. We have arrived in the key of G♭, itself a tritone away from where we started on a chord of C major (fig. 15.8).

Figure 15.8 Music notation of this modulating progression towards the key a tritone distant.

Here is the set of four modulations that can result from the pathway initiated by movement to 7̄:

(7̄/1) From the original tonic major, colourfully, to G major (the dominant) (fig. 15.9):

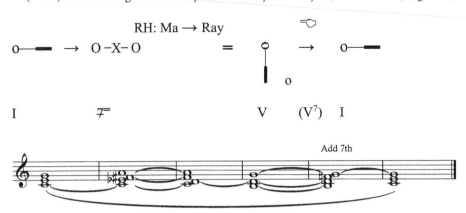

Figure 15.9 Music notation of this alternative modulation to the dominant.

(7̄/2) From the original tonic major to E major (III) (fig. 15.10):

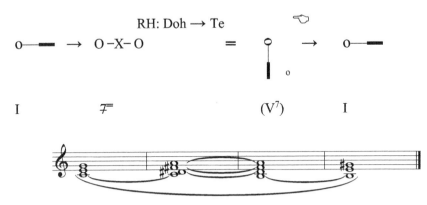

Figure 15.10 Music notation of this alternative modulating progression to the mediant.

(7̄/3) From the original tonic major to VII♭ (fig. 15.11):

RH: Fi → Fa

0—— → 0 –X– 0   =   0   →   0——
                              |
                              | o

I   7̄   (V⁷)   I

Figure 15.11 Music notation of this modulating progression towards the flattened leading note.

($\mathbf{7}$ /4) From the original tonic major to II♭ (fig. 15.12):

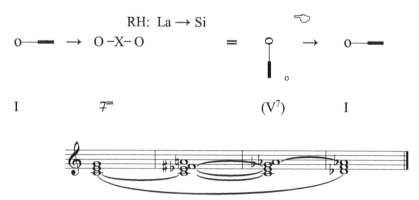

Figure 15.12 Music notation of this modulating progression towards the flattened supertonic.

Next come the four modulations that are initiated by movement to chord $7^\uparrow$.

($7^\uparrow$ /1) An easy one to start with—a colourful way of getting from the original tonic major to chord IV (fig. 15.13):

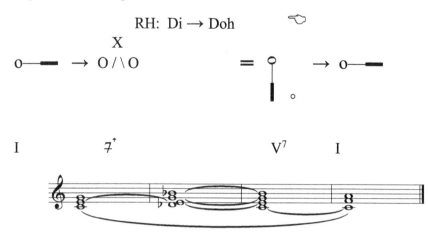

Figure 15.13 Music notation of this alternate modulating progression towards the subdominant.

($\overline{7}'$/2) From the original tonic major to chord VI♭ (fig. 15.14):

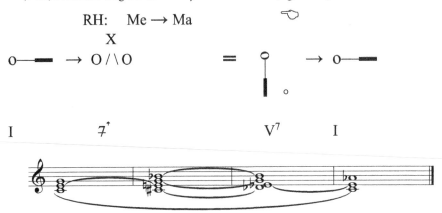

Figure 15.14 Music notation of this modulating progression towards the flattened submediant.

($\overline{7}'$/3) From the original tonic major to chord VII (fig. 15.15):

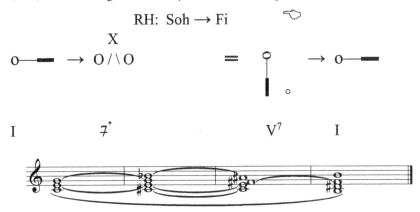

Figure 15.15 Music notation of this modulating progression toward the key of the leading note.

($\overline{7}'$/4) From the original tonic major to chord II (fig. 15.16):

Figure 15.16 Music notation of this modulating progression towards the key on the supertonic.

All twelve of these diminished triad modulation patterns could both commence and/ or terminate on the minor. A useful consolidating exercise would be for everyone in the class to devise their own patterns and lead them.

Four-Part Music

The pedagogical foundations of *Harmony Signing* were developed with and for primary school-aged children who are able to sing together and acquire the ability to participate in progressions. Theirs is vocally a treble clef world, similar to that of the instruments played by students of this age. For this reason, the assumption was made that experience of harmony would be most appropriately acquired in circumstances in which young voices could attain self-sufficient textures not dependent on bass notes. This has been advantageous in terms of providing interchangeable experience of the various voice-leading roles and pathways that have allowed what we have achieved so far to be possible.

There is a further reason that we have not previously dealt with basslines. There has, up to now, been a kind of equality or democracy of participation in negotiating the largely three-note chords that result from what has been presented. These are sufficient to generate the sense of harmonic function and colour that is central to the aural and creative development they enable. However, there comes a point at which successful engagement with musical styles and genres depends on the fuller texture and clearer sense of direction that basslines provide. The difficulty involved is that one can only have one bassline: as the theorists of the late sixteenth century such as Vincenzo Galilei argued, the bass determines the harmony it underpins. So, basslines require a new level of agreement and preparation and become the province of those allotted, for reasons of vocal range or instrument type, to perform them.

Male voice development between the ages of about twelve and fifteen makes its contribution. As voices deepen, they can simply drop an octave. If this eventually produces a rich six-part texture in which male and female, or changed and unchanged male voices, are combined, this is not a problem. Much of the development of *Harmony Signing* has been achieved in secondary and tertiary institutions in which this doubling at the octave is normal. Similarly, as students grow and mature, instruments such as the double bass, bassoon, bass clarinet, trombone, and others become available when handspan and other factors permit.

So one might propose focusing on bass function as these resources present themselves. Where students aged about fourteen combine sufficient experience of what we have studied so far with the capacity to perform in the bass clef, the two features will feed from each other, especially where *Harmony Signing* figures in choral and band or orchestral education.

There are two ways in which bass function can be introduced. The first and simplest is to introduce root-position notes to all chords. These can be doubled at the octave in female voices so as provide an insight into this role. For every chord signed, those given the responsibility of providing the bass sing the root. A good example is the Pachelbel *Canon*, which we encountered earlier (see Chapter 12, 'Signs about Signs: The Notation of Harmony Signing'). The original 1609 harmonisation of a chorale by Melchior Vulpius (opening line) provides a more subtle example:

[3-beat measures]

Melody	Doh	Ti	La	Soh	–	Soh	La	Ti	–	Doh
Chords	I	V	vi	iii		I	IV-vi	V		I

The second possibility is to lead the bass part with the right hand, just as we have already done with melody. This permits greater freedom, including the possibility of first and second inversion chords and passing notes. It provides a template for experiencing the bass as having an independent character, as foundation of the harmony and a melodic voice in its own right. For example, drawing on Purcell's *Evening Hymn*:

[3 beats per measure]   [Hemiola: 2-beat feel]

RH (Bass):   Doh-Ti$^+$-La | Ti-La-Soh | La-Soh-Fa | Soh-Fa Me-Fa Soh – |Doh (etc.)

LH:	I	V	IV	I	I	IV V	I

This is in fact a repeating bassline, and this pattern could be employed as an accompaniment to instrumental improvisation. So the feature of adding basslines can also lead to further avenues of creative exploration.

The Further Development of Basslines

The focus on providing independent basslines brings the signing of harmony into harness with the signing of melody in a manner that both recalls and can recapture the features of polyphony that we studied in the learning sequence derived from Fux's species counterpoint. One example of this that could be attempted by sufficiently experienced students presents only melody (RH) and bass (LH), requiring the remaining participants to develop their own inner parts (alto and tenor) through interpreting the implied harmony. Henry Ley's nineteenth-century harmonisation of the same Vulpius melody we just met redistributes the chords to interesting effect. This bassline needs to be signed as an independent melody. As an exercise, it would be instructive only to sign melody and bass and build in rehearsal the inner harmonies that are implied.

Melody	Doh	Ti	La		Soh – Soh	La	Ti		Doh
Chord	I	iii	IV	V - V⁷ I	IV	vii	I	
Bass line	Doh	Me	Fa		Soh Fa Me	Fa Me Ray	Doh	

The Alberti bassline would appear to pose problems for representation through *Harmony Signing*. The rapidity of movement is beyond what the sound-to-hand processing of the director and the vision-to-sound interpretation of participants are likely to manage. But there is a different solution. By taking the voice-leading patterns on which three-part *Harmony Signing* depends and spreading these into broken chords that can be sung to scat syllables by a single voice part, figures representing Alberti bass patterns become feasible as material for improvisation. Once those singing the bassline have understood that they are to respond with this Alberti pattern, they apply it to the chords (I, IV, V, etc.) required by the leader (see fig. 15.17).

Figure 15.17 Presenting Alberti bass figuration.

We encountered elements of walking bass in the Purcell and Henry Ley material that we signed with a combination of strategies. The technique is common both to Baroque practice and jazz. Taking the Pachelbel *Canon* chord progression as a model, we can link together notes of the original bassline with passing notes of various durations.

Figure 15.18 Making Pachelbel walk.

The quarter-note version could easily be signed in the right hand alongside the original left-hand chords in order to practise this technique. The eighth-note version will need to be done more slowly. After encountering these, students should devise their own chord progressions over a walking bass.

Advanced *Harmony Signing:* Dissonance, Further Modulatory Shortcuts, and Serialism

We will recall from above examples such as 'Moon River', 'One Hand, One Heart', and the adaptation of the Chopin E Major Prelude that we were unable to continue beyond their openings because of the limitations in our gestural vocabulary. A variety of dissonances colour music from the late nineteenth and twentieth centuries, leading eventually to 12-note serialism, and new ways of modulating (i.e., employing enharmonic pivot chords) provide a whole range of options.

Surrogate Subdominants: Journeys to the Flat Side

We have encountered the idea of chord substitutions at several points in our journey. The following varieties of chord emerged from relationships with the original primary triad positions:

Tonic-related	Subdominant-related	Dominant-related
I	IV	V
vi	ii	iii
i	iv	v
7⁺	7꞊	7⁺

The next steps we will introduce involve further shortcuts that expand the tonal connections beyond the primary triads and the conventional relationships that we have encountered previously. We have already met *chromatic inflection* through combining out-of-key notes with conventional harmony and by substituting minor for major and vice versa, as well as through adding sevenths to chords to accelerate and clarify modulation across tonal space. These techniques have prepared us for some colourful possibilities to which we will now turn:

(a)   the flattened submediant
(b)   the Neapolitan (flattened supertonic)
(c)   the flattened mediant, and its role as relative major of the tonic minor

The Flattened Submediant

Recall that the chord of the flattened submediant is the natural chord VI of the minor mode. We can access it by tonicising the minor, at which point it emerges as the appropriate response to the chord VI gesture rather than vi that would occur in the major:

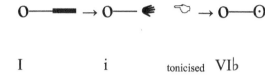

I   i   tonicised VI♭

Where participants are made aware of the location of chord VI in this way, it then becomes possible to introduce a shortcut to progress directly from I to VI♭, without needing to pass through i. The technique that is required parallels the modulation we learned for using two hands to progress from I to vi. Where in the major, the pivot chord required responds to the <Si> sign 🖐 for entering the relative minor, this time, the two hands sign, respectively, signal <ma> (left hand) and <si> (right hand): the pitch si we enharmonically represent with the sign 🖐 whether it is the sharpened fifth or, as in this case, the flattened sixth. So, we can get from I to VI♭ in a single step:

LH / RH

The pitch that 'anchors' these two chords is Doh, which can be sustained as a component of both. Once we have accessed an out-of-key chord in this way we can tonicise it to complete a modulation (fig. 15.19).

Figure 15.19 Music notation of this alternate pathway to the flattened submediant.

The Neapolitan (Flattened Supertonic)

The chord of the Neapolitan seems to have entered harmonic practice via the influence of Arabic scales on the treatment in Western music of the Phrygian mode. Both share a focus on the flattened supertonic: in the major, this is II♭. We can represent this degree of the scale with a half-fist sign that can indicate both the sharpening of Doh and the flattening of Ray. The graphic sign for these pitches <Di> is ⊣.

Harmonically, we can access the chord of the Neapolitan as a variant of the minor subdominant, using the ⊣ sign in the right hand to modify chord iv (fig. 15.20):

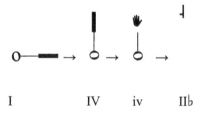

I   IV   iv   II♭

Figure 15.20 Music notation of this alternate pathway to the flattened supertonic.

The truly Neapolitan effect occurs in the 'escape' back to the tonic. No modulation has taken place, so this has not changed (fig. 15.21):

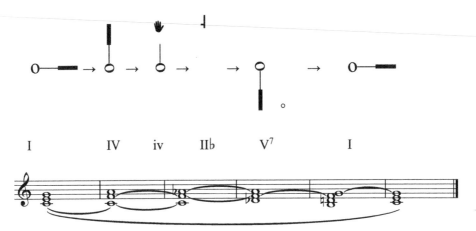

I   IV   iv   IIb   V⁷   I

Figure 15.21 Music notation of this chromatically inflected progression around the flattened supertonic.

Now that we have experienced this version of access to the Neapolitan, presenting IIb as a variant of iv, we can introduce the shortcut that employs the right-hand sign ⊣ simultaneously with iv, allowing the progression to proceed more fluently (fig. 15.22):

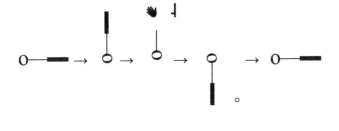

I   IV   IIb   V⁷   I

Figure 15.22 Music notation of this condensed progression around the flattened supertonic.

Alternatively, we can arrive on chord II♭ and tonicise it to complete a modulation up a semitone (fig. 15.23).

Figure 15.23 Music notation of this modulation up a semitone.

The Flattened Mediant and Its Role as Relative Major
of the Tonic Minor

The major chord on the flattened mediant (III♭) is a further chromatically accessible relative that has found a special place in some of the most beautiful music.[4] Here, the anchor note is Soh, as it is in the progression I - V, but with very different consequences for both tonal function and expressivity. It is the other two notes that we have to sign in order to achieve movement onto this chord, employing the left hand for the minor triad and the right hand for ta ♭ . It is vital that the sign for Ta ♭ has this clear, vertically downward quality to distinguish it from the *tonicising sign* ↶ that we are also about to employ. This has the outcome of replacing <Doh> with <Ta>, as in capturing the voice performing this role.

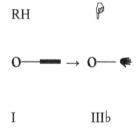

We can confirm this as a modulation through the use of the tonicising sign and proceed from there:

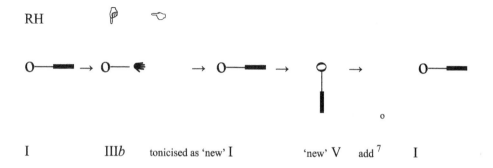

---

[4] We will analyse some well-known works that employ this relationship when we consider in more detail the features of *enharmony*.

(+7th)

Figure 15.24 Music notation of this progression around the flattened mediant.

As we can see, having reached this 'new' I, its own 'new' subdominant and dominant can come into play: the definition of a completed modulation (fig. 15.24).

Revising Modulation from the Minor to the Relative Major and Its Potential

We have already considered some possibilities arising from the interchangeability of tonic major and minor, and the ambiguous properties of the diminished triads.[5] As the variety of strategies that can be signed increases, there will inevitably be several ways to do the same thing. All such outcomes sharpen both theoretical experience, of benefit to aural skills (location), and creative opportunity—the library of available relationships from which students can devise their own music.

To modulate from i to IIIb, we access chord VIIb of the minor (which is modally the flat seventh), for which we now introduce the new sign ■— O. This is one of the only two gestures in *Harmony Signing* in which the left arm extends outwards to the left of the chest (the other is the sign for II[(♯)]). This is because, in both cases, we rely on the modulatory empowerment of a chord that is outside the triangular formulation of 'home' positions for i/I, iv/IV and v/V (the primary triads and their dependents). A crucial sign deserves a special place for its distinct function to be easily recognised.

i   VIIb

This also makes the following progression technically possible, in which we can start on the tonic major:

I   VIIb

However, the voice-leading for this should not normally move in parallel. Here is a proposal for the routes that voices might best take to perform this progression, presented here as a modulation:

---

[5] Where there may be ambiguity regarding whether the tonic is Major or minor, the tonicising sign can be employed, pointing directly at (or even touching) the left hand to confirm which is currently operating.

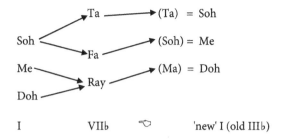

I   VIIb   ☞   'new' I (old IIIb)

So, the chord ▦—— O, as in the formulation in the following figure, presents a means of exploring movement away from the tonic that, together with the use of dominant sevenths initiated by adding the hand sign °, makes possible a variety of routes to keys, major and minor, on the flat side of the cycle of fifths (fig. 15.25).

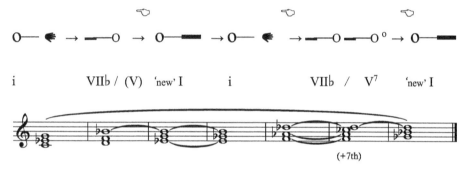

Figure 15.25 Music notation of this progression beyond the flattened leading note.

Such a pattern permits us to cross tonal space with great agility: here, we moved from one minor key to the major that is a tritone distance away. The first chord of the progression could equally well be the tonic major.

Here is a similar progression that employs VIIb as a modulatory pivot from a major starting chord (fig. 15.26):

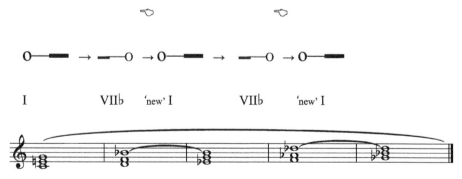

Figure 15.26 Music notation of this progression employing a sequence of flattened leading notes.

Further Examples of Modulation to New Regions

As we have noticed in considering the harmonic series and its consequences for the cycle of fifths, there is a natural grain by which changes of key occur. Music tends to move towards the subdominant. In order to cross tonal space, therefore, we need to find ways of moving as clearly and efficiently as possible in a sharpwards direction. Once we do this, the natural flatwards currents of the cycle of fifths will then bring us home.

Several of the progressions we will employ to achieve sharpwards shortcuts require conveying that *two* new pitches are outside the prevailing key, which requires us to sign with both hands. The voice-leading we can thus communicate, either directly or by implication, defines the means by which notes outside the tonic operate so as to initiate the modulation. These are, as we have seen, notated split left-right around a forward slash /. In all cases in which this method is used, the remaining pitch of the preceding triad acts as an *anchor note* and should continue to sound so as to maintain the tonal reference point around which the modulation revolves.

Starting with a reminder of the simplest modulation to the dominant followed by the return to the tonic, the following sequence illustrates a series of further steps to ever-more-distant positions in the sharpwards cycle of fifths (fig. 15.27):

(a) Modulation to the dominant and back[6]:

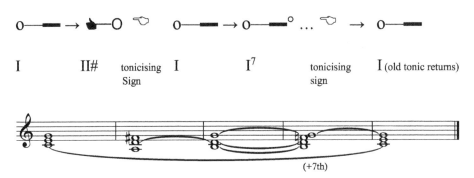

Figure 15.27 Music notation of this modulation to the dominant and back.

(b) Modulation to the supertonic, chord II (dominant of the dominant) and back (fig. 15.28):

O——■ → Di/La + ° → ꙮ   O——■ → O——■° ꙮ → O——■° ꙮ → O——■

I   V - V⁷ tonicising I   I⁷ (= V⁷) tonicising I   I⁷ (= V⁷) tonicising   I (original tonic)
                  sign   sign   sign

---

[6] In addition to the explanations already provided for how this progression works, one might add that when in Western common practice one hears two major triads with roots a major second apart, the tendency is to hear them as a subdominant and dominant of a tonic, to which the ear anticipates a resolution in seeking out a subsequent tonic.

Figure 15.28 Music notation of this excursion to the supertonic returning via the cycle-of-fifths.

(c) Modulation to chord VI (major submediant) and back (fig. 15.29):

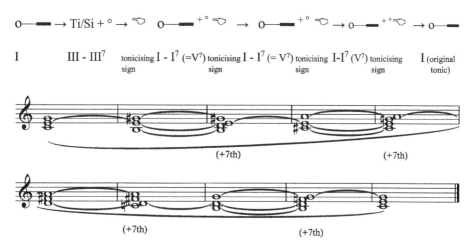

Figure 15.29 Music notation of this excursion to the major submediant returning via the cycle of fifths.

A similar set of operations can also 'bring us home' from excursions to chords III (major mediant) and VII (major leading note), though these more distant relationships *without anchor notes* are therefore far trickier to sign unambiguously. Participants who have mastered with fluency the implications of chord choice that can be conveyed with two hands should nevertheless be able to follow progressions that can be initiated as follows. In example (d), the voicing of chord VII, with its third signed in the left hand, is intended to avoid descending in parallel. This ought to work but will probably require a couple of attempts to be achieved confidently (fig. 15.30).

(d) Modulation to the mediant, chord III:

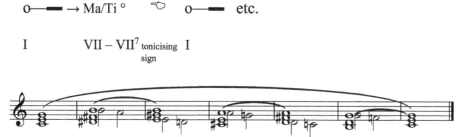

Figure 15.30 Music notation of this excursion to the major mediant returning via the cycle of fifths.

In this case, those performing note 5 (Soh) will need to recognise the implications of what is happening and fall to Fi.

The final single-step modulation we will attempt requires implying a 'round-the-world' progression that operates the chord a tritone away from the tonic as the essential pivot. Let's consider the voice-leading implications of this in advance:

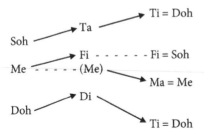

This modulation to chord VII (see (e), below) therefore requires conveying the significance of the sharpened fourth, **Fi** of the original tonic, and the signalling of the leading note, for which we can employ **Ta**. To make things as clear as possible, we will borrow for this purpose the left-hand sign for chord II, outside the body, with the expectation that the combination of this with the right-hand sign for **Ta** and the adding of a dominant seventh, will achieve this purpose. In this case, those performing note 2 (Ray) will need to recognise the implications of what is happening and fall to Di[7]:

(e) Modulation to the leading note (chord VII) (fig. 15.31)

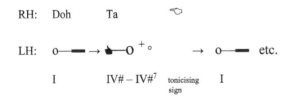

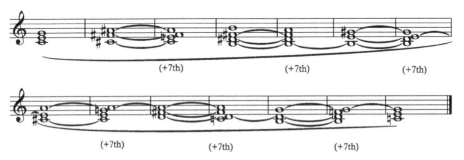

Figure 15.31 Music notation of this excursion to the key of the leading note, returning via the cycle of fifths.

---

[7] If the sign for a dominant seventh can be accessed early enough, it would permit some participants who performed the third of the original chord to sustain or return to it as the seventh of the new dominant.

A procedure of this kind is at the limit of what *Harmony Signing* can currently achieve,[8] and will only prove possible where participants have developed almost telepathic responses to leaders, and to each other, that such progressions demand. Therefore, we will proceed no further around the cycle of fifths. Experienced signers who have reached a level at which they can manage the modulations we have just introduced will, I have no doubt, be able to devise within the system further coherent ways of moving between unrelated tonal centres. Doing so in order to meet their creative needs as composers represents the true purpose of all that has been learned.

Some Harmonic Properties Derived from Modes, Old and New

Previously, we considered the ways in which modes such as the Dorian and Mixolydian could be accessed and employed using the basic gestures from which we could derive chords I, ii, iii, IV, V, and vi, selecting an appropriate *final* that characterised each particular mode. Two of the modes, the Phrygian and Lydian, have given rise to additional associations in a manner that provides further choices of harmonic effect and depends on new gestures being introduced that also indicate further creative possibilities.

Flamenco and the Phrygian Mode

The rich potential of the Phrygian mode for alternative harmonic progressions has been associated especially with Spanish music from the Flamenco culture of Andalusia. Sports fans will be familiar with the recorded trumpet samples employed to enliven crowds at events through eliciting the shouted response '*Olé*'! (fig. 15.32)[9]

Figure 15.32 Musical example of this popular Phrygian motif.

The Phrygian mode's opening semitone between notes 1 and 2 (Me and Fa) presents a characteristic that has given rise to harmonic treatment that especially suits guitar performance. The Phrygian is, besides, not well served by its weak natural dominant, vii. But it does lend itself well to harmonisation in parallel major triads:

Voice 1:	Ti	Doh	Ray	Doh	Ti
Voice 2:	Si	La	Ti	La	Si
Voice 3:	Me	Fa	Soh	Me	La

---

[8] Bearing in mind that students have often proved more proficient and fluent than me in leading groups through these more complex pathways, I have no doubt that suitably experienced practitioners will achieve further possibilities.

[9] https://www.youtube.com/watch?v=TZXOP1M6TuY

This progression will be familiar from the music for so-called spaghetti western films and from the music of composers such as Albeniz and Rodrigo. But the very parallelism of this example violates the voice-leading principles we have so carefully established. So, we need to introduce a new gesture to capture this kind of progression, both for this Phrygian example and for other cases in which we may wish to convey the requirement for parallel triads.

The double gesture ♩ ♭ signals that all performers move up a semitone, following the direction of movement of the hands. A semitone step is achieved by keeping the hands together. A whole-tone step is signalled by moving the hands apart and together again:

Both of these signs can be reversed in order to signal *downward* movement, with the same differentiation between semitone and whole-tone steps (fig. 15.33):

Figure 15.33 Musical example of a rhythmicised Flamenco pattern in parallel motion.

Having introduced the gesture ♩ ♭, we can employ it outside the genre of Flamenco Indeed, it becomes available for a variety of aural and creative purposes. It presents a potent strategy for choral and instrumental warm-ups in which we might want to tune adjacent chords. We could also use these double-handed gestures to perform the final bars of Stravinsky's *Firebird*[10]:

$$I - I\# - II - IV\# - II - I\# - I$$
$$\text{Drone} \quad I - - - - - - - - - - - - - - - - - -$$

The Whole-Tone Scale

Two new modes emerged out of the greater chromaticism of mid-nineteenth-century music: the whole-tone scale and the octatonic (also known in Messiaen's classification as the Second Mode of Limited Transposition). The whole-tone scale can be traced to an extension of the Lydian mode, in which the first four steps are all whole tones, together covering an augmented fourth. In our original diatonic array, these are the pitches on Fa - Soh - La - Ti. If we commence this mode on Doh, it maps onto Doh - Ray - Me - Fi. This feature was memorably exploited in Fauré's song in praise of a girl named *Lydia* (fig. 15.34).

---

[10] The 'stretched' move over a major third of the parallel chords II to IV# will need a little rehearsal. One needs to add the moves for a tone and a semitone together.

Figure 15.34 Musical example of the opening bars of the song *Lydia*.

Continuing from <Fi> with further whole-tone steps, we reach the octave without encountering the mediating function of a semitone, covering the octave span in only six steps:

Doh - Ray - Me - Fi - Si - Ta - Doh†

The aural sensation of omitting a semitone in a span of this range can be quite unsettling, so it is worth overcoming this by performing this scale with hand signs several times, shifting it around in range, and trying it in canon. A canon two notes apart elicits the characteristic major thirds that feature in the employment of harmony derived from this mode in the music of Debussy and Ravel (and a cliché of dream sequences in film music). This is even clearer in a three-part canon that gives rise to parallel *augmented triads*. The chord Doh/Me/Si can be moved up and down in parallel using the two-handed gestures we introduced in order to perform Flamenco: . The consequence can be an instant performance of a progression that features in Debussy's piano prelude, *Voiles* (fig. 15.35).

Figure 15.35 Musical example from the Debussy piano piece *Voiles*.

The Octotonic Scale

The octatonic scale would seem to have arisen in Middle Eastern and Asian cultures in which modes similar to the Phrygian gave rise to alternations of semitones and whole tones. It can exist in three forms (fig. 15.36):

(1)   Doh - Ray - Ma - Fa - Fi - Si - La - Ti - Doh
(2)   Doh - Di - Ma - Me - Fi - Soh - La - Ta - Doh
(3)   Ti - Di - Ray - Me - Fa - Soh - Si - Ta - Ti

Figure 15.36 Music notation of the three octotonic scales.

As with the whole-tone scale, this poses *location* problems for students habituated to performance of the major scale, and it is worth working step by step on accurate tuning for each of these three forms. Once this has been achieved, the harmonic potential of the mode can be explored through canons in two to four parts, again making entries two notes apart. This will result in parallel diminished triad chords, representing a further means of experiencing the properties of those.

Once this level of familiarity is in place, it becomes possible to explore some of the chromatic interactions that the octatonic scale presents. The following is derived from example (1) (fig.15.37):

Voice 1	La	La	Ti	Doh	Ti	Ray	Ma	
Voice 2	Fa	Fi	Si	La	La	Ti	Doh	
Voice 3	Ma	Ray	Fa	Fa	Fi	Si	Si	
Voice 4	Doh	Doh	Ray	Ma	Ma	Fa	Fi	etc.

Figure 15.37 Music notation of these chords derived from the octotonic scale.

The octatonic scale underpins a great deal of the chromatic harmony arising in the music of Mussorgsky, Rimsky-Korsakov and, especially, the three early ballets of Stravinsky (*The Firebird, Petroushka*, and *The Rite of Spring*), as well as much of the music of Olivier Messiaen.

Enharmony and 'Diagonal' Relationships

The feature of *enharmony* has been central to our development of aural discrimination through voice-leading experience right from the beginning. Enharmony bonds notes of the primary triads with which we began the establishment of *Harmony Signing*: the anchor notes shared by tonic and subdominant (Doh); and tonic and dominant (Soh). The feature of enharmony that permits more distant chords to be related through varieties of anchor notes has played an important part in our understanding of modulation. A rich and varied tapestry of progressions, modulation patterns and timbral colours can be accessed through elaboration on the simple foundations we first established.

We next explore some further examples of the potential of enharmonic connections in highly expressive linking passages from a variety of Baroque, Classical, and Romantic works.

The first example illustrates how a wide variety of different chords can be generated over the same unchanging bass line. It is the opening of the central choral *Crucifixus* from Bach's B Minor Mass. The movement is composed over a ground bass in the style of a chaconne. Bach's bassline weaves a chromatic descent that offers the opportunity for varied harmonic treatment. No two repetitions of the bassline are given the same harmonic realisation. The music even manages to pass briefly through different keys. Advanced students could analyse the original, seeking to enumerate the different keys that the music winds its way through, and the variety of chords that Bach employs, including an augmented triad and a dominant minor ninth (fig. 15.38).

Figure 15.38 *Crucifixus* from the B Minor Mass.

Henry Purcell also relished dissonance and chromatic inflection. In his wedding anthem *My Beloved Spake*, the section that depicts the cooing of the dove traces a harmonic progression that makes exceptional use of enharmonic change (fig. 15.39).

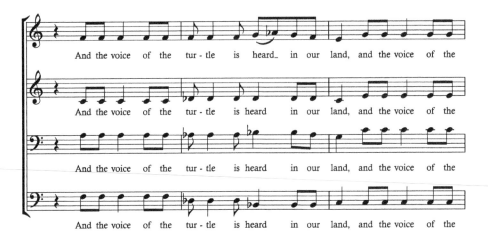

Figure 15.39 An excerpt from *My Beloved Spake*.

The particular feature of Purcell's opening phrase ('And the voice of the turtle'[11]) is that the movement to a distant tonal area is its exclusive expressive purpose. The note Doh within the tonic chord acts as the pivot, anchoring the pitch around which the other voices shift to the flattened submediant. Mozart exploited this same relationship to set the words 'Dona eis pacem' in the in the 'Agnus Dei' of his *Requiem* (fig. 15.40).

In his own *Requiem*, Fauré made use of this same shift, which leads to a sequence of magical enharmonic glides that extend his use of the technique (fig. 15.41).

Elgar adopted this same, calming turn as the link into 'Nimrod' from the *Enigma Variations* (fig. 15.42).

Why do these examples all have a similar effect: gently surprising, yet providing a sense of arrival or achievement? The secret is in the anchor note. We appear to move from one harmonic world to another, but this shared pitch acts as a bridge that makes the experience less jarring. The function of the anchor note in the two chords is significant.

---

[11] The turtle is a species of dove.

Figure 15.40 An excerpt from *Dona eis Pacem*.

Figure 15.41 An excerpt from *Lux Aeterna*.

Figure 15.42 An excerpt from the opening of *Nimrod*.

In the departure point, it is the Doh of the prevailing tonic. In the Fauré, Mozart, and Elgar, there is then a period in which this pitch is left unsupported. In the ensuing arrival point, this same pitch takes on the function of major third in the most distant key (the flattened submediant) for which such a bridge is available. This effect seems to be universally moving. Note that the inspiration of the four composers cited was of significance to them: a wedding, two funerals, and the depiction of friendship. Students should be encouraged to devise their own progressions incorporating enharmonic links of this kind and aiming for a similar capacity in their music to move and reassure.

Added Dissonant Notes: Sixths, Sevenths, and Ninths

We have already encountered the practice of adding a flattened seventh to chords by employing the 'OK' sign that we represent graphically as ^{O}. Followed by the tonicising gesture, this brings about modulation. But composers have also developed a variety of chords that colour harmony, not all of which lead to modulation.

Adding the sixth note of a chord is associated with jazz harmony, and the twentieth-century classical music that was influenced by jazz in the output of composers such as Kurt Weill and Darius Milhaud. We can represent this as follows:

RH:	La	Ray	Me	La
LH:	I	IV	V	I

Note that what the right hand signs here is not a melody but conveys that these additional pitches should feature in the voice-leading that provides the 'added sixth' harmony which characterises this progression. The voice-leading for these chords can be set out as follows (fig. 15.43):

Voice 1:	La	La	Soh	La
Voice 2:	Soh	Fa	Me	Soh
Voice 3:	Me	Ray	Ray	Me
Voice 4:	Doh	Doh	Ti	Doh
	$I^{6/5}$	$IV^{6/5}$	$V^{6/5}$	$I^{6/5}$

Figure 15.43 Progressions involving added sixths.

From these ingredients and employing a V^9 that stabilises the tonality, an accompaniment could be devised to Kurt Weill's 'Mack the Knife' (fig. 15.44).[12]

---

[12]   The YouTube clip https://www.youtube.com/watch?v=X7eO7MKEZAY features Weill's wife Lotte Lenya in an authentic performance of the original song.

Figure 15.44 The *Mack the Knife* accompaniment.

Adding notes to existing triads, especially in different inversions, masks their tonal origins and makes new connections available. By contrast, the diminished triad, constructed symmetrically from intervals of the minor third, is incapable of variation by inversion: all instances sound broadly the same, irrespective of range and the distribution of pitches. This presents the most marked contrast with the inversions available for the primary triads, each of which has a distinct colour and conventional function: the root position as final in perfect cadences; the $^6_3$ (first inversion) as introductory to recitative; the $^6_4$ (second inversion) heralding the concerto cadenza. The character of each inversion of a major or minor triad depends on its constituent intervals being varied (a mixture of major and minor thirds, and a fourth).

A class of chords emerged in nineteenth-century music that has been referred to as 'half-diminished', sharing some of the characteristics of major/minor triads—they invert asymmetrically—while suggesting the ambiguous tonal properties of diminished triads.

In the opening bars of his opera *Tristan and Isolde*, Wagner introduced such a chord, and employed it to achieve a new quality of restless, unresolved harmonic tension. A great deal has been written about the consequences of this. For our purposes, the best way to introduce the 'Tristan' chord is to perform a minor triad and add the sharpened (major) sixth (fig. 15.45).

LA⁺ - -

o— 👈

Figure 15.45 Music notation of this voicing of the *Tristan* chord.

However, it is in the specific distribution in which Wagner first employs it that the Tristan chord presents the unique timbre which Wagner exploited throughout his opera, and that other composers subsequently found irresistible (fig. 15.46).

Figure 15.46 The opening of the *Tristan* prelude.

Wagner himself resolves the Tristan chord in a variety of ways, most commonly through contrary motion voice-leading as in this initial phrase (fig. 15.46). But the Tristan chord is only one descending semitone step, in one voice, away from morphing into a diminished triad, which opens up several different chromatic pathways (fig. 15.47).

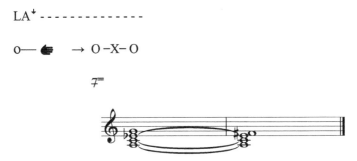

Figure 15.47 Music notation of this chromatic inflection of the *Tristan* chord.

The note Soh in the opening minor triad to which La (major sixth) has been added falls to <Fi> in order to create the diminished triad 7⁼. This opens up the full set of pathways available beyond the diminished triad (fig. 15.41) and permits modulation to a selection of possible tonal centres.

Tristanesque harmony abounds in the music of the generation that followed Wagner. The chord itself maintains its unique quality even when put to different uses in works by composers as varied as Tchaikovsky, Richard Strauss, and the young Schoenberg.

A related tradition in nineteenth-century harmony built on the chromatic alteration of the subdominant from major to minor in plagal cadences. This emerged in the music of Schubert was employed by Wagner as the final cadence of *Tristan and Isolde* and frequently crops up in the music of Ralph Vaughan Williams (fig. 15.48).

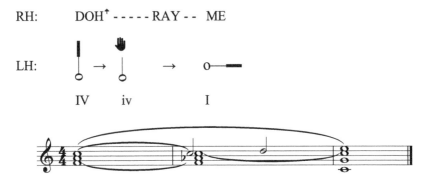

Figure 15.48 Music notation of this progression via the minor subdominant.

Further Varieties of Seventh Chord and the Signs for Them

We have already introduced the 'OK' sign ° in the left hand that allows us to build sevenths on major and minor triads. The sevenths derived in this way are minor.

o—■°   Tonic with seventh – I^7

Doh – Me – Soh –Ta

o— ✊ °   Tonic minor with (minor) seventh – i^7

Doh – Ma – Soh – Ta

Should we wish to add a major seventh to a chord, we need to employ the right hand using the Kodály sign for the appropriate degree of the scale. For example:

RH: Ti --- La – Ti – Doh

LH: O——■ - - - - - - - -

In the minor, this works as follows:

RH: Ti --- Doh↑

LH: O— ✊

This arresting dissonance features as the final cadence of Bach's *St Matthew Passion*, and also at the first trumpet entry in Mahler's Symphony No. 3 (fig. 15.49):

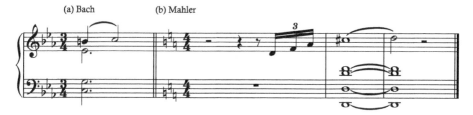

Figure 15.49 Musical examples of (a) Bach and (b) Mahler.

The first six partials of the harmonic series present the notes of the triad over the fundamental. As we have seen, the seventh harmonic presents the first pitch that we treat as a dissonance, and we have incorporated this and its treatment as foundational to the principles of *Harmony Signing*. The eighth harmonic presents the next octave arising in the sequence 1: 2: 4: 8. Immediately above this is the ninth harmonic, which generates a version of the supertonic, note 2 of the major scale. Adding this to the tonic triad, especially where the dominant seventh is already in place, presents a further mild yet colourful dissonance: the major, or dominant, ninth chord. We employed this as a decorated dominant in the Kurt Weill excerpt (fig. 15.44).

In order to signal this, we introduce a sign in the right hand that conveys that **two** notes are added over the prevailing triad: based on the victory sign ✌. The version we use for the dominant ninth is the one in which the fingers face towards the participants, with the back of the hand facing the signer, and it introduces the flattened seventh and major ninth:

RH:

LH: O———

Voice 1	Ray
Voice 2	Ta
Voice 3	Soh
Voice 4	Me
Voice 5	Doh

Like the dominant seventh on the tonic, this chord tends to resolve as a modulation to the subdominant. A version of this chord over a low B♭, set out as in the harmonic series with the note Doh doubled, forms the basis of Stockhausen's *Stimmung* for vocal sextet.

In the minor, the same procedure is also available, giving rise to a new chord with a more modal feel:

RH:

LH: O——— ✊

This time the voicing is as follows (fig. 15.50):

Voice 1	Ray
Voice 2	Ta
Voice 3	Soh
Voice 4	Ma
Voice 5	Doh

Figure 15.50 Music notation of this ninth chord.

Again, the resolution pattern tends towards the subdominant, though this (IV) may well be major,[13] depending on the prevailing sense of tonality. Where this is the case, it acts as a pivot that accesses the key of the flattened VII (fig. 15.51).

---

[13] It needs therefore to be signed carefully with the edge of the hand presented to the participants, rather than the palm that would convey <iv>.

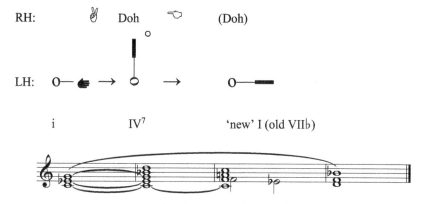

Figure 15.51 Music notation of this short-cut to the key of the flattened leading note.

As we have now discovered on so many occasions, semitonal inflections up and down are available that can vary the content and harmonic implications of chords. Turning the ✌ sign around so that the back of the hand faces the participants lowers the pitch of the ninth by a semitone, resulting in a dominant minor ninth chord. The sign for this is ✌, and the result is as follows (fig. 15.52):

RH: ✌

LH: O━━

Figure 15.52 Music notation of this dominant ninth chord.

The voicing for this is:

Voice 1	Di
Voice 2	Ta
Voice 3	Soh
Voice 4	Me
Voice 5	Doh

Again, this tends to resolve towards the subdominant region, either major or minor. Note, though, that the dominant minor ninth possesses, in the four pitches above the root, the attributes of the diminished triad.

One further possible combination of seventh and ninth above a root position triad is available, and it is instantly recognisable to anyone who has ever watched a James Bond film. The major seventh and major ninth are both added over the minor triad. We need to adapt our sign for this as follows:

It is essential that this is done with the fingers facing the participants and the back of the hand facing the signer, lest this gesture be confused with our cut-and-paste signal ✂ which we will soon being making use of for quite different purposes.

So, we can sign the James Bond chord as follows (fig. 15.53):

RH: 🖐

LH: O——👈

Figure 15.53 Music notation of this distinctive ninth chord.

The voicing for it is:

Voice 1	Ray
Voice 2	Ti
Voice 3	Soh
Voice 4	Ma
Voice 5	Doh

Removing the Root(s) of Added-Note Chords

A further set of harmonic possibilities arises when the root of added-note chords such as sevenths and ninths is removed. Lacking a root increases the ambiguity of chords and gives rise to new colours. In order to achieve this, we apply the 'cut' phase of the 'cut-and-paste' technique, but instead of moving the cut note to a new position we dispense with it altogether. We employ the sign represented by ✂.

If we take the dominant major ninth and remove the root, we end up with a four-note chord voiced as follows:

Voice 1	Ray
Voice 2	Ta
Voice 3	Soh
Voice 4	Me
(Voice 5 ceases performing)	

As before, this exerts a strong pull to the subdominant.

We can represent this as follows:

RH: ✌

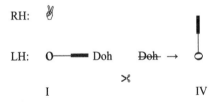

LH: O——▬ Doh   D̶o̶h̶ → O

I   IV

This progression features as the call of the Rhinemaidens in Wagner's *Das Rheingold* (fig. 15.54):

Figure 15.54 Musical example of the Rhinemaidens' call.

When applied to the dominant minor ninth, the process of dispensing with the root in this way reveals its close relationship with the diminished triad:

RH:

LH: O———■ Doh   ~~Doh~~ = 7 → etc.

The strategies outlined here have introduced a wide range of chromatic techniques. These featured in the styles of late-Romantic music from the second half of the nineteenth century remained common practice in the symphonic scores of twentieth- and twenty-first-century film music. While a great deal of complexity may be associated with the presentation and performance of these procedures, they empower students to gain creative experience of elements that characterise the music for films and video games that have introduced a new generation to this Romantic genre. Especially where students have mastered these strategies and can securely transfer them to instrumental performance and composition, they will be motivated to explore the potential of this magical sound world.

Signing 12-Note Rows

A new procedure emerged in the early years of the twentieth century in the music of Ives in America and Schoenberg and his circle in Austria—*total chromaticism*. Total chromaticism could be defined as the presence, in close proximity, of the entire set of pitches of the chromatic scale. This has been proposed as an inevitable result of the harmonic and melodic developments that followed the generations of Mozart and Schubert, accelerated by Wagner's new language and the orientalism introduced by the Russians. Liszt's use of the augmented triad in sequence resulted in a 12-note array in the opening of the *Faust* symphony (fig. 15.55).

An 11-note array occurs, almost in passing, in the music following the Prelude to Act 1 of *Tristan and Isolde* (fig. 15.56).

Some of the games and tasks in the early part of this book encouraged the development of *location* and the ability to hold independent parts by setting up textures in which any note could sound. When such textures are employed by composers to attain dense harmonic effects, they are referred to as *clusters*. These may be percussive, such as the violent chords in piano music from Bartok onwards, or more sustained, as in orchestral music by Penderecki and Xenakis. In the music of composers such as Ligeti and Ferneyhough, closely overlapping micropolyphony achieves a sense of movement within which totally chromatic harmony shifts in ripples and waves.

Figure 15.55 Music example from the *Faust* symphony.

Figure 15.56 Music example from the first act of *Tristan*.

Effects of this kind cannot be replicated in a controlled manner through *Harmony Signing*, which has explicitly developed around a clear sense of key. Nevertheless, the evolution of harmony that gave rise to them out of the complex orchestration of early twentieth-century music (Ives, Mahler, Strauss, Ruggles, Varèse) represents a distinct milestone in the development of musical language. Since this music is around and forms the foundation for what many composers across a range of styles are still achieving today, it would contribute to students' aural understanding to pay some attention to how it works. Achieving this will complement the investigation we have made into tonal harmony.

Schoenberg, emerging from the composition of works such as *Pierrot Lunaire* and *Erwartung* that are totally chromatic throughout, devised the principle of controlling for the polyphonic unfolding of pitch through the use of a 12-tone row. All musical material would be derived from iterations of the basic form of the row through repetition, inversion, retrograde, transposition, or a combination of these procedures. Clearly, the character of a piece of music would owe everything to the DNA, as it were, of the originally selected row.

Here are some rows with specific characteristics. They could be taken as the basis of improvisations or short compositions that explore their properties (fig. 15.57):

1	2	3	4	5	6	7	8	9	10	11	12

(a)   Fi – Soh – Fa – Si – Me – La – Ma – Ta – Ray – Ti – Di – Doh[†]

(b)   Doh – Ma – Di – Ray – Fa – Me – Soh – Fi – Si – Ti – Ta – La

The most effective way for students to gain insight into 12-tone composition is to devise their own rows and employ them in their own music. In order to develop the aural

Figure 15.57 Music notation of these 12-tone rows.

and practical skills that this involves, students should perform each other's rows, led by Kodály signing. Subsequent to this experience, they can compose short exercises, starting with single-line studies for an instrument of their choice. They may explore the properties of their rows through weighing up the rates of duration and movement appropriate to the presentation of the pitched material, as well as features such as range and dynamics. As in the sequence through which we studied species counterpoint, beginning with a single line before moving on to two-part polyphony and subsequently richer textures, a similar pattern of experience can endow confidence and fluency with serial procedures.

16

Working with Instrumental Classes and Bands

Our work in *Harmony Signing* so far has concentrated on the overlapping features of harmonic and polyphonic practice through which students can acquire creative experience in collective contexts. Alongside what these techniques are intended to teach, in terms of aural discrimination and creative choice, we have always emphasised the need to try out musical ideas in practice and make them relevant to students' ambitions as performers. This chapter alters our perspective on *Harmony Signing* in order to revisit some of what we have learned from the angle of its support for the development of music ensembles. We thus shift the focus from the classroom to the rehearsal studio. Progress will be much more confident and consistent for instrumentalists who have mastered these strategies through singing. Indeed, vocalisation remains an available means of consolidating experience alongside the transfer of practice to the use of instruments.

Where ensemble directors may value *Harmony Signing* as a complement to traditional practice based on reading from parts, they will be able to achieve a great deal through leading these activities themselves. In my own experience, though, participant understanding and response benefit from giving students the leadership role; especially where this may overlap with skills already established in the classroom. Teachers will have to make up their own minds as to the cost-benefit position this represents in terms of the amount of rehearsal time available.

The material that follows retains the characteristic of dealing with nonnotated music, with the intention of developing instinctive responses in a spirit of improvisation. Band directors and orchestral conductors will find that its value is in warming up and in the supportive features of practical theory that prepare performers for engaging with the repertoire they have selected. Links can be established among the kinds of challenges that specific scores present. The ideas that follow represent a library of practices that can be adapted for practical application.

Pitch Organisation: Keys and Tonality

All instrumentalists regularly practise scales, and this can also be done in unison by ensembles. But scales only contain the pitches that define a selection at any one point. Music modulates, sometimes to unexpected regions. Students at different stages in their development possess greater or lesser levels of proficiency related to the home keys with which they are most familiar, and these differ between instrumental families. *Harmony Signing* can provide an insight into both the likely voice-leading moves that performers will encounter in any key in which music is written and the sense of tonality that results, both of which are fundamental to secure sight-reading and functional tuning. Ensemble education achieves its initial goals when students begin to be independently aware that they are playing the right notes and are able to infer from previous experience of context and style the role that each pitch plays in melody, harmony, or texture. *Harmony Signing* can be employed to accelerate and consolidate this process through providing a flexible template for the development of listening skills. Participants' awareness is built partly through the acts of performance and listening, but the additional feature of following specific gestures deepens understanding of the role of the pitches they represent.

Chords and Functions

Scales

While scales can be played in unison, a sense of harmonic function is better developed where different notes sound together. Several strategies that we have already met can achieve this. They can be led by students or ensemble directors using Kodály hand signs and *Harmony Signing* gestures.

- Scales are played against the support of a drone. The drone can be sustained by bass instruments, or midrange instruments, or high-range instruments. The drone can also be rhythmicised as an ostinato to present an element that develops ensemble timing as well as tuning. Indeed, students can be given the opportunity to devise their own ostinati to fulfil this function (fig. 16.1).
- Scales are played in canon, parts entering to perform in parallel thirds and crossing at the octave. Durations can be either even or uneven (alternate half note and quarter notes; dotted rhythms). This can be led either by one director employing both hands or by two (or more), each of whom works with a subset of the ensemble (fig. 16.2).
- Scales are played in mensuration canon, parts performing in whole notes, half notes, quarter notes, or mixtures and alternations of these (fig. 16.3). This can be led by one or more signers.

These strategies can be implemented for all scales that are judged useful for an ensemble to attempt, both major and minor—especially the harmonic minor—and the range of modes that we have examined.

The Primary Triads

A selected student chooses a tonic and orchestrates its root position triad, which is then directed through *Harmony Signing* as chord I, permitting movement to the subdominant and dominant with all performers adopting the usual voice-leading principles. A bass part on the roots of I, IV, and V can be added.

When students are able to perform the major primary triads fluently in a variety of keys, they can introduce minor substitutions (i, iv, and v).

Figures 16.1, 16.2, and 16.3 Musical examples of scale exercises in augmentation and diminution.

Figures 16.1, 16.2, and 16.3 Continued.

Adding the Secondary Triads

The secondary triads form a family relationship with the primary triads that is captured in the signs that represent them, and which aids the recall and location of the pitches they comprise. Adding their use to experience of a particular key enhances knowledge of its tonal potential. When participants are ready, they can be introduced to the very different functions of the secondary triads in the minor mode.

Combining Melody with Harmony

Melody can be combined with harmony by conveying melody through Kodály hand signs in the right hand while employing *Harmony Signing* in the left hand as accompaniment. As before, students can learn from this opportunity either by presenting existing material that they have prepared or by improvisation.

Chromatic Alterations

The full range of gestures for chromatic inflection can be introduced in precisely the same way as described for vocalisation in the classroom (see chapter 5, Tasks 5-7):

- Minor versions of the primary triads (I/i; IV/iv; V/v)
- The diminished triads
- Chromatic melody against diatonic harmony, signed with both hands

Modes of All Kinds and Chords Derived from Them

The full range of mediaeval modes can be experienced against the drone associated with the *final* of each and through combining melody with harmony. This can be especially useful where existing repertoire is written in a mode rather than in the major/minor system. The two-handed pointing strategy for conveying parallel triadic texture associated with the Phrygian mode (see chapter 15, 'Flamenco and the Phrygian Mode') provides an additional means of developing tuning and balance.

Beyond the major/minor system are also:

- the whole tone scale;
- the octatonic scale; and
- the chromatic scale.

All of these can be led through signing, as well as through distribution canonically, which confers a feel for the special harmonic effects associated with each.

The signs for dominant sevenths, ninths, and other added-note chords (see chapter 15, 'Added Dissonant Notes: Sixths, Sevenths, and Ninths') can also be introduced in order to present the theory of their construction and build them into the repertoire of available harmonic devices.

Modulation

Once we have introduced diminished and dominant sevenths, participants will be ready to understand the role they can play in modulation. The *tonicising sign* will prove essential as a means of getting participants to listen for the implications of notes presented outside the prevailing key that enable modulation. As before, the first three modulations to introduce will be the most common: from the major to the subdominant, to the dominant, and to the relative minor. From the minor, we can modulate to the subdominant by adding a seventh to the tonic major; the move to the dominant (V or v) is via chord II#, as in the major. The third and most common modulation away from the minor is to the relative major through employing a seventh on chord VII.

As students acquire sufficient experience of both following signs and leading activities themselves, the full range of chromatic shortcuts introduced previously can be attempted, including the varied pathways available through the use of the diminished triads and enharmonic routes to the submediant and Neapolitan regions.

Rhythm and Ensemble

The goal of working with signs in this improvisatory manner is to encourage a level of musical understanding that is quite different to the experience of reading from an instrumental part. A significant aspect of this is the development of instinctive responses: the playing of constituent parts that depends on listening to others and sharing in responsibility for the overall outcome. Where *Harmony Signing* is achieved through the development of a strong rhythmic sense, it helps to overcome the hesitancy that can feature in the approach to group performance of inexperienced instrumentalists. In turn, this lays down values that can be transferred to the sight-performing context.

The range of pitch-related and harmonic material referred to in the preceding sections is brought to life through association with patterns of rhythmic, articulatory, and dynamic variation. Taking a simple progression as the basis for this, one can employ gestural techniques to adapt it in a variety of ways (fig. 16.4).

This is just one of the many options available. Students themselves will be the best source of ideas for developing varieties of texture, tempo, articulation, and orchestration that can express the range of possibilities available. Even while such material is in play, a director can impose modulation or harmonic variants (major for minor, etc.) that the ensemble negotiates without 'breaking stride'. Equally, such passages can be employed as 'backing tracks' over which improvisations or signed melodies can be added.

Texture and Orchestration

The varied presentation of a chord progression introduced in the preceding section also opens up the potential for illustrating the properties of texture and orchestration. For instance, what would happen in, say, a big band if the music of each of the three passages presented in Figure 16.4 were given to a different section to be played simultaneously?—the reeds on #1, the brass on #2, piano and guitars on #3, for instance—or in a different combination? How could what each player or section does, that contributes to the overall effect, be subject to variation in this way? A valuable lesson in orchestration could be based on practical experience gained through 'filling out' a texture through experimentation on these lines.

Skilled band directors who have absorbed the gestural language of *Harmony Signing* and shared it with participants will be able to lead complex musical activity in both rehearsal and performance. Assigning a leadership role to members of the ensemble

Figure 16.4 An ensemble progression with varied rhythm and articulation.

would be even more educationally valuable. Whether directed by a teacher or a student, ensembles can explore links between notated repertoire and improvised material. Such analytical and creative strategies provide an insight into the workings of the music their band performs. The pedagogical potential of *Harmony Signing* supports both the elements of technical mastery that benefit performing ensembles and the aesthetic response that captures the imagination of members.

17

Working With Vocal Classes and Choirs

The original rationale of *Harmony Signing* was derived from realising that young children could absorb musical theory in practice through collective participation that many of them would not be ready for conceptually or through notation. As a consequence, the approach lays down experiences that can inform all subsequent musical learning. It has proved equally suitable as a means of introducing adult beginners to singing in choirs.

Choirs in modern society are often in an anomalous position. There seems to have been a divergence in practice that has resulted in groups in some parts of the world being capable of exceptional levels of education and achievement, whereas in others they are a dying phenomenon. This appears particularly true in the case of the skill of music reading, which of course confers lifelong advantages for sustaining choral involvement. I have encountered schools on three continents in which the instrumentalists learn to read music but singers do not. Teachers tell me that it might spoil the fun and that the students prefer just to learn songs by rote. Choirs, even in mixed schools, have a repertoire of karaoke unison material. The boys do not participate. In all too many schools students do not sing at all.

Parallel to this is the trend towards a separation between young choirs and the larger adult groups that sing traditional repertoire, and which find it difficult to recruit members under the age of about forty. More than appears to be the case for instrumentalists, choral singers become conscious of social conditions that govern with whom they sing.

These factors are worth considering because, broadly defined, education is the only solution to the possibility that choirs and community singing in some parts of the world are under threat. Pedagogy that can support the learning of a variety of repertoire, that explores the very means by which choral blend is achieved, and that can meet the needs of both young and older singers, may be able to contribute to a framework of practice that allows the development of sustainable singing communities. An initiative on these lines will foster informed audiences as much as performers and present the joy of polyphonic singing as a means to broaden the base of the pyramid from which active, lifelong participants can emerge.

In extending our understanding of the potential of *Harmony Signing* into the regular practice of choirs, we will focus on the role that the pedagogy can play in choral education and its potential for creative activity that accelerates musicianship through the exercise of imagination. Both aims can be attempted with choirs of all conditions and ages.

Tuning and Blend

The improvisatory nature of the musical experience accessible through *Harmony Signing* offers a means of introducing students to how harmony works, including how to contribute the pitch one is performing oneself so as to combine it with others. In establishing the vocal practice on which the pedagogy is based in Part I, we explored means of developing vocal confidence through exercises intended to develop breathing, phonation, and pitch-matching. In addition, the strategies that explored listening to vowel sounds as components of the harmonic series provide a highly effective means of achieving two desirable outcomes. First, they endow an understanding of the natural intervals that arise from whole-number frequency ratios and are detectable when we sing with care. Second, they promote the consequent clarity of vowel-matching that is associated with the spectral signature of the voice when it is adapted to respond to others in respect of loudness and timbre as well as pitch. This kind of exercise is fundamental to teaching singers to listen to themselves, as well as to relate what they sing to the voices of others, rather than to a nonvocal model such as the piano.

In exercises such as singing melodies against a drone, singing scales in canon, and performing the initial primary triad progressions of *Harmony Signing*, musicians learn to differentiate accurately between whole-tone and semitone steps. In doing so, they acquire sensitivity to the effect of well-tuned harmony. This occurs when voices align themselves in mutual resonance that is only obtainable through acute and practised listening skills. Choral singers report the discernment of this outcome as amongst the most fulfilling goals of their participation, representing an intrinsic achievement: Harmony makes you feel good.

As we have seen, *Harmony Signing* can be achieved over a wide range of age and ability that embraces children's and adults' voices as well as both genders at all stages of development: there is no problem in doubling voices an octave apart. However, teachers should be mindful of the fact that boys need to readjust to the roles they play in harmonic vocalisation over the period in which their voices mature between the ages of about twelve to fifteen. Where boys have experienced and understood part-singing as trebles, they are far more likely to make the aural allowances that permit them to continue singing through voice change and beyond. Indeed, the free voice-leading principles on which *Harmony Signing* is based lend themselves to providing a means by which there is always a part a boy can manage, however temporarily limited his range may become as maturation occurs. Teachers need to monitor this carefully, not expecting the phenomenon to play out in a tidy or predictable manner but always keen to encourage a vocal contribution and to arrange notated music where necessary to make this possible. Again, the voice-leading principles of *Harmony Signing* represent a handy template for achieving this.

So, all of the vocal warm-ups and games covered at the beginning of this book remain available as strategies for preparing choirs for specific challenges in the notated music they may encounter. Beyond this, *Harmony Signing* also provides a means of generating new music. This is possible for all musical media, as was proposed in dealing with bands and instrumental ensembles. Where singers differ is that they can also communicate music based on words.

Texts

A variant of the use of two hands to convey musical information can be employed to set texts to music. This can provide experience of homophonic texture that develops part-singing and can initiate approaches to choral composition. The right hand conveys the flow of the text syllable by syllable, while the left communicates chord selection.

We can illustrate this initially with two words that are commonly set in church music: *Amen* and *Alleluia*. In Figure 17.1, each new syllable of the three repetitions of *Amen* is signalled with a clear right hand downbeat.

The word *Amen* is replaced in Figure 17.2 with the Australian place-name *Boggabilla*[1].

A more elaborate setting in three time of the word *Alleluia* is given in Figure 17.3. Each syllable is spread across a melisma of three beats.

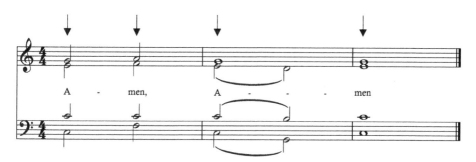

Figure 17.1 *Harmony Signing* with words Ex. 1.

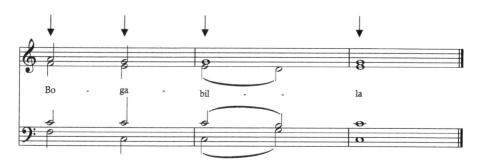

Figure 17.2 *Harmony Signing* with words Ex. 2.

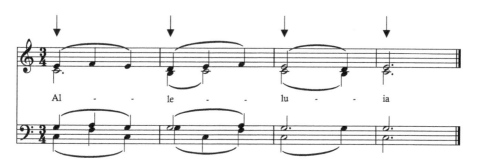

Figure 17.3 *Harmony Signing* with words Ex. 3.

---

[1] A town in New South Wales. I acknowledge Janice Chapman as the advocate of the potential of this word in the development of vocal technique.

Figure 17.4 *Harmony Signing* with words Ex. 4.

Figure 17.5 *Harmony Signing* with words Ex. 5.

Short snippets of memorable text can be played with in this way and participants will have to commit words to memory in order to be able to respond to musical leadership. Students can collect phrases suitable for vocalisation or write their own. The palindrome 'Rats live on no evil star' could be set as shown in Figure 17.4.

In Figure 17.5, a mixture of single syllables and melisma sets a short text ('Brazil, where the nuts come from') taken from the play *Charley's Aunt*.

Students and teachers can obtain texts suitable for treatment in this way from a wide array of literature and material: from public service announcements, proverbs, and newspaper headlines to poems and passages from plays. While polyphonic setting is difficult to convey given our limitation to two hands, in which one controls the distribution of the words, an exercise of this kind can form a springboard for notated work that introduces more idiomatic choral procedures.

PART IV
BUILDING CREATIVELY
ON HARMONY SIGNING

18

What Are Students Expressing Musically?

The focus in this book has been to employ creativity in the service of developing instinctive musicianship and expressivity through collective interaction. Students will often wish to extend work achieved in this manner into performable compositions that represent a finished product which fully reflects their own individual intentions.

The challenge in stimulating creative work that has its foundations in conventional procedures is meeting the needs of individuals. Especially where assessment is involved, students can feel constrained by the need to illustrate mastery of a convention, rather than breaking free of it in the pursuit of originality. One would hope that the full array of games and tasks presented will have illustrated the breadth of compositional ingredients that can be drawn upon in finding a personal voice. These have included the range of rhythmic procedures that deal with the organisation of time and the principles of voice-leading that permit the controlled exploration of varied tonal worlds, including dissonant and chromatic possibilities. Above all, in step with the kinds of experience this book has dealt with, students will have adopted their own role models through wide and varied listening and through performing a range of repertoire in choirs and ensembles.

Stimuli and Starting Points

A difficulty for student composers can be developing craft—adequate and suitable notation skills, a sense of structure, and knowledge of what instruments and voices can achieve—while simultaneously exploring the musical purposes that capture their interest and motivate them to complete performable pieces. A curriculum that presents a series of constrained tasks may fail to address the individual needs or interests of students, leading to a divergence between what they do as part of a music course and what they attempt away from the classroom, possibly in secret. This is by no means a new phenomenon, but teachers are highly likely to encounter it if they have a genuine interest in supporting students in becoming composers.

One solution can be to separate the technical features of craft development from the aesthetic stimuli of supported opportunity. In my own experience, students can be considerably motivated by the appeal of writing music that they know will be performed as part of a school project or community programme as opposed to an academic exercise. Writing for video or for collaboration with student choreographers for a dance event can provide this kind of opportunity. The commission that specifies a purpose, including information regarding how long the piece of music required needs to be and what resources are available to perform it, can act as an effective stimulus to students, just as it does to professional composers.

Building towards the capacity to fulfil a 'commission' is, then, a useful way of balancing the development of craft and musicianship skills with a sense of personal growth as a potential composer. This is the mind-set that participants in *Harmony Signing* are intended to experience, especially when they have the opportunity to lead activities and make creative decisions. It is useful to retain a view of the aesthetic associations that relate to the outcomes of improvised music-making, such as the emotions evoked by procedures or the titles or narratives that might be linked to their sound world.

From time to time, it may therefore be suitable to propose that work with the class, or in a small group, addresses a response to stimuli on these lines. For example, instead of introducing a new theoretical element, the existing level of ability of the class can be explored through composing for a 'commission' conveyed through verbal or pictorial means. Ideas could include:

Titles

The ghost ship
Sunrise over the ruined city
Rainbows and snowflakes

Narratives

The hot air balloon and the submarine: a love story
The maze and its secrets
Rescue from the forbidden island

Pictures

Reproductions from art history worldwide
Famous newspaper photographs
Pictures taken by students themselves

These suggestions illustrate the kinds of stimulus that provide a sense of purpose to a group setting out on a project that needs to carry their enthusiasm over a period of time. Teachers and students can devise their own starting points. What these will represent are a means of conceptualising the work to be done and the work in progress in a holistic manner that will contribute to shaping and completing the process.

Musical Archetypes and Links Between Genres

In relation to the concern with stimulus and process we have considered, another association with the creative potential arising out of *Harmony Signing* is to explore musical archetypes. Australian composer Percy Grainger was an exponent of the similarities between culturally separate forms of music. Grainger proposed 'A common-sense view of all music' in a series of radio broadcasts that he wrote and delivered in 1934 (Blacking 1987). Grainger espoused a universalist view of the development of musicality in the human species and a fascination for the similarities and differences available to musicians in expressing different emotional states through a variety of means.

His lectures explored such features as rhythm, echo, homophony, polyphony, and the use of instruments, through comparing recorded examples of music of diverse geographical and historical origin.

A focus on *archetype*—a musical procedure that can be shown to manifest itself in different traditions with similar purpose or effect—can help to support musical creativity through developing thinking that is not dominated by the conventional features of a particular genre or style. Let's imagine a musical event: a loud, arresting sound, followed by silence, and then another loud, arresting sound. The reasons that this might occur could be considered. In nature, for example, it might be the conditions prior to a lightning storm. But where the sounds would be assumed to be of human origin, it might be a signal that something is about to happen. Might a rock concert begin in this manner? Or the title sequence of a feature film? Or a classical symphony?

Thinking in terms of archetypes involves an important component of why we create music; that is, its effect on the listener. We could regard such events, similar across different styles, musical periods, and genres, as *gestures*, or as musical material that communicates parallel intentions irrespective of the precise means employed (notes, chords, instruments). Such a viewpoint ought to have emerged from the educational experiences we have shared from the outset. Throughout the procedures of *Harmony Signing*, participants will have been listening. They will have developed musical fluency and the capacity to join in successfully through awareness of the intention of the signer, even where the unexpected has been required of them; and this experience is available both through vocal and instrumental participation. The response between signer and participants is founded on this shared journey through material and experience, and this is what prepares them for surmounting the structural challenge of writing pieces of music. A library of procedures has been built up:

- Repeat identically
- Repeat with modification
- Introduce an unexpected contrast
- Change one parameter only (pitch, duration, timbre, volume)
- Develop the outcome as a dialogue between the previous version and the new one

These methods are a consequence of thinking about musical archetypes. While some may occur more frequently in one style than another, they are not here expressed in relation to any specific music. And yet, musicians who love to play or sing in order to express themselves will immediately call to mind—to their mind's ear—examples of these ideas in practice. An outcome of *Harmony Signing* is the capacity for musical spontaneity.

The Teacher as Collaborator

Our exploration of the potential of *Harmony Signing* concludes with further reflection on the role of the teacher and the specific opportunities provided by the multimodal nature of this pedagogical system. We will focus especially on the intention that it proceeds at all times through appealing to the creative responses of students. A great many music educators around the world have, over the last fifty years or so, assumed a student-centred approach to teaching, especially where contemporary music and student composition feature in the curriculum (Folkestad 2006; Laycock 2005; Green 2002; Maxwell Davies 1963). The workshop context they construct largely breaks down the functions of instructing and learning that are often associated with more traditional approaches, with the teacher aiming to facilitate student progress through shared aims and mutual interaction.

Yet *Harmony Signing* has been designed to access and demystify the very aspects of traditional learning—theory and aural—that students are often taken to view as the least satisfying aspects of their musical development. In the learning sequence presented in this book, the constant expectation has been that students will take from the experience and skills required elements that they can customise to their own needs. Aspects of *Harmony Signing* have drawn on Mediaeval chant, Renaissance counterpoint, common-practice tonal harmony, Romantic idioms, and 12-tone technique, as well as influences from a variety of world musics, jazz, and contemporary genres. These have been pursued with a view to students finding in their understanding musical components that fire the imagination while extending technical proficiency. The standpoint throughout has been that creative music education reveals the music of tomorrow. The approach permits teachers to interact with their students both as components of classes and ensembles in which collective performance enhances a sense of community achievement and as individuals with unique musical personalities.

The collaborative approach that *Harmony Signing* embodies permits a means of experiencing the development of explicit and implicit knowledge in tandem. Explicit knowledge, which is 'knowing about' or embracing music theory and stylistic analysis, can seem remote from the aesthetic experience of music that comprises 'knowing how', which students associate with performing. The multimodal techniques *Harmony Signing* employs encourage 'thinking in sound' that allows ideas to be tested and elaborated through practice. Performance and musical analysis converge in collective exchange. This lessens the sense that musical information is provided through the teacher's instruction. Rather, musical possibilities are examined through shared experiment within the language of music itself.

Nevertheless, for all their availability to the students they teach as peer and collaborator, there are several remaining respects in which teachers need to develop the skills of expert guides. Some of these represent features of the teacher's greater experience that can be placed at the service of students: wider repertoire knowledge, for instance, or the ability to offer themselves as performer or director in bringing students' creative work to life. Other aspects relate to responsibility for the use of time and resources in arriving at a balanced curriculum of which *Harmony Signing* may play only a small part.

A good example of an activity derived from *Harmony Signing* in which a teacher can take a leadership role is that of developing aural response through *tracking*. Either employing Kodály hand signs or *Harmony Signing* gestures, students display what they hear in response to music played by a teacher on the piano[1] or from a selected recording. Participants may either sing along or listen silently. Here, there are right answers. This

---

[1] Either devised in advance or improvised.

activity builds accuracy and speed of response in developing the skills of discrimination and musical memory on which dictation depends.

A couple of suitable examples of recordings that lend themselves well to student tracking would be:

(1) Graeme Koehne's *Forty Reasons to be Cheerful (Festive Fanfare.)*[2] This is an exhilarating 2013 orchestral work that just happens to be based on chord relationships of the kind that *Harmony Signing* makes accessible.

(2) Billy Joel's *And So It Goes*, especially in the a cappella arrangement that Bob Chilcott composed for The King's Singers.[3]

To the extent that teachers diagnose the strengths and weaknesses of individual students and seek to meet their needs, pedagogy of this kind lends the opportunity to operate a classroom in which, for some of the time at least, students can direct their own activities while a teacher works one-on-one by rotation. Students' level of skill and confidence, especially in aural activities, varies, as do the learning styles through which they can make progress. In order to ascertain how a student is processing music and what sense they are making of particular tasks, teachers need to have the opportunity to interact with them closely. Otherwise, how can one know what students understand and how the sounds in their heads are becoming confidently and coherently handled? Test results only reveal a small part of this; one needs a more nuanced picture of whether they 'get' the relationship between theory and sound/practice. Once this begins to be ascertained, remedial possibilities can be considered. A range of suggestions for these can build on the games and tasks presented in parts I and II of this book. Within the framework of *Harmony Signing*, there is much to be gained by revising foundational activities as a means of restoring and building confidence.

Teachers will make their own decisions regarding the balance of activities with which, in the context of their classroom and rehearsal studios, they combine *Harmony Signing*. A curriculum in the twenty-first century is likely to involve instrumental and/ or vocal tuition, music technology and ensemble performance, and listening work that develops repertoire knowledge and cultural awareness. How much time can be allocated to *Harmony Signing* as a new element? It is most likely to be effective 'a little and often'. Begun early in students' lives and carried on so that progress to new levels is consistent with other musical demands, *Harmony Signing* can be employed over time to enrich and support other core activities, with the new pedagogy weaving into related aspects of the existing curriculum.

The aim is to accelerate the means by which students become independent, self-motivated, and creative learners working within a musical community in which they respect the work of others. This informs the very earliest experience of the *Harmony Signing* approach and remains present over years as these foundations yield to higher-level work that responds to the complementary influences of instrumental and vocal learning, membership of ensembles, and the development of personal tastes and preferences. Working with students whose curiosity about music is aroused in this way,

---

[2] https://www.youtube.com/watch?v=urdL2UfouQc
[3] https://www.youtube.com/watch?v=gTt3ZUmfPm0

teachers stand to sustain their own openness to new musical experience and renew their sense of professional fulfilment through realising the uniqueness of the work they are engaged in. Where this is the case, they may be rejuvenated through making music in a spirit of free play that results from knowing that they are celebrating the achievements of the next generation.

Three rounds that complement the *Harmony Signing* approach

The three rounds provided here complement the games and tasks through which confident singing in parts was introduced in Part I. They have been written to lend themselves to choreography that underpins and makes explicit the relationship between text and music. In No. 1, the contrasting forms of movement can be represented through steps, while the heartbeat ('lub-dup'—the expression by which doctors code the sound of the pulse they hear through a stethoscope) can be mimed, as can the idea of growth through binary fission. In No. 2, the contrasting steps can also be danced, while No. 3 permits a more music-theatre form of response, acting the meaning of the phrases in sequence. 'Choralography' of this kind can deepen the experience of singing the rounds polyphonically, the timed interaction between groups of performers taking on a visual and kinaesthetic quality in addition to the musical counterpoint. Such multimodal experience is at the heart of *Harmony Signing* and forms a stimulus to students to compose their own material adopting similar characteristics.

Bibliography

Ball, P. (2011). *The music instinct: How music works and why we can't do without it.* New York, NY: Random House.

Bannan, N. (1997). The consequences for singing teaching of an adaptationist approach to vocal development. In D. J. Schneck & J. K. Schneck (Eds.), *Music in human adaptation* (pp. 39–46). Blacksburg: Virginia Polytechnic Institute and State University.

Bannan, N. (1998). Aural feedback, vocal technique, and creativity. *Phenomenon of Singing, 1*, 11–19.

Bannan, N. (2000). Instinctive singing: Lifelong development of 'the child within'. *British Journal of Music Education, 17*(3), 295–301.

Bannan, N. (2003). Reverse-engineering the human voice: Examining the adaptive prerequisites for song and language. In *Proceedings of the Fifth Triennial Conference of the European Society for the Cognitive Sciences of Music, CD-ROM.* Hanover, Germany: Hochschule für Musik und Theater.

Bannan, N. (2005). Music teaching without words. In *Proceedings of the 1st International Symposium on Cognition and the Musical Arts* (pp. 400–405). Curitiba, Brazil: Departamento de Artes da Universidade Federal do Paraná.

Bannan, N. (2008). Language out of music: The four dimensions of vocal learning. *Australian Journal of Anthropology, 19*(3), 272–293.

Bannan, N. (2009). Priming the musically instinctive: New pedagogy for creative improvisation and aural development. *Musicworks 14*(1), 39–52.

Bannan, N. (2010). Embodied music theory: New pedagogy for creative and aural development. *Journal of Music Theory, 24,* 197–216.

Bannan, N. (2012a). Harmony and its role in human evolution. In *Music, language, and human evolution* (pp. 288–339). Oxford, U.K.: Oxford University Press.

Bannan, N. (Ed.). (2012b). *Music, language, and human evolution.* Oxford, U.K.: Oxford University Press.

Bannan, N. (2014). Music, play and Darwin's children: Pedagogical reflections of and on the ontogeny/phylogeny relationship. *International Journal of Music Education, 32*(1), 98–118.

Bannan, N. (2017). Darwin, music and evolution: New insights from family correspondence on *The Descent of Man. Musicae Scientiae, 21*(1), 3–25.

Bannan, N. (2019). *Every child a composer: Music education in an evolutionary perspective.* Oxford, U.K.: Peter Lang.

Bannan, N., & Montgomery-Smith, C. (2008). 'Singing for the brain': Reflections on the human capacity for music arising from a pilot study of group singing with Alzheimer's patients. *Journal of the Royal Society for the Promotion of Health, 128*(2), 73–78.

Bannan, N., & Woodward S. (2009). Spontaneity in the musicality and music learning of children. In C. Trevarthen & S. Malloch (Eds.), *Communicative musicality* (pp. 465–494). Oxford, U.K.: Oxford University Press.

Benzon, W. (2001). *Beethoven's anvil: Music in mind and culture.* New York, NY: Basic Books.

Bickerton, D. (1991). *Language and species.* Chicago, IL: University of Chicago Press.

Blacking, J. (1987). *'A commonsense view of all music': Reflections on Percy Grainger's contribution to ethnomusicology and music education.* Cambridge, U.K.: Cambridge University Press.

Burnard, P. (1995). Task design and experience in composition. *Research Studies in Music Education, 5*(1), 32–46.

Campbell, P. S. (1998). *Songs in their heads: Music and its meaning in children's lives.* Oxford, U.K.: Oxford University Press.

Cardew, C. (1972). *Scratch music.* Latimer New Dimensions.

Chagall, I. (Director). (2014). *Let's get the rhythm: The life and times of Miss Mary Mack.* New York: Women Make Movies/City Lore & Public Art Films.

Changizi, M. (2013). *Harnessed: How language and music mimicked nature and transformed ape to man.* Dallas, TX: BenBella Books.

Cook, G. (2000). *Language play, language learning.* Oxford, U.K.: Oxford University Press.

Cross, I. (1999). Is music the most important thing we ever did? Music, development and evolution. In Y. Suk Won (Ed.), *Music, mind and science* (pp. 10–39). Seoul, South Korea: Seoul National University Press.

Damasio, A. (1994). *Descartes' error: Emotion, reason, and the human brain.* New York, NY: Putnam.

Dargie, D. (1988). *Xhosa music: Its techniques and instruments, with a collection of songs.* Cape Town, South Africa: David Philip.

Dargie, D. (1996). African methods of music education: Some reflections. *African Music 7*(3), 30–43.

Darwin, C. (1872). *The expression of the emotions in man and animals.* London, U.K.: John Murray.

Davies, C. (1992). Listen to my song: A study of songs invented by children aged 5 to 7 years. *British Journal of Music Education, 9*(1), 19–48.

Dawkins, R. (2004). *The ancestor's tale: A pilgrimage to the dawn of life.* London, U.K.: Weidenfeld & Nicolson.

Dissanayake, E. (2000). Antecedents of the temporal arts in early mother-infant interaction. In N. Wallin, B. Merker, & S. Brown (Eds.), *The origins of music* (pp. 389–410). Cambridge, MA: MIT Press.

Dunn, R., & Dunn, K. (1978). *Teaching students through their individual learning styles: A practical approach.* Reston, VA: Prentice Hall.

Ekman, P. (1973). *Darwin and facial expression.* New York, NY: Academic Press.

Espi-Sanchis, P., & Bannan, N. (2012). Found objects in the musical practices of hunter-gatherers: Implications for the evolution of instrumental music. In N. Bannan (Ed.), *Music, language, and human evolution* (pp. 173–198). Oxford, U.K.: Oxford University Press.

Falk, D. (2004). Prelinguistic evolution in early hominins: Whence motherese? *Behavioral and Brain Sciences, 27*(4), 491–503.

Fanshawe, D. (1993). *Spirit of Polynesia* [CD]. Badminton, U.K.: SayDisc Records.

Fernald, A. (1992). Meaningful melodies in mothers' speech to infants. In Papousek, U. Jürgens, & M. Papoušek. (Eds.). *Nonverbal vocal communication: Comparative and developmental approaches,* (pp. 262–282). Cambridge, U.K.: Cambridge University Press.

Folkestad, G. (2006). Formal and informal learning situations or practices vs formal and informal ways of learning. *British Journal of Music Education, 23*(2), 135–145.

Fréour, V., & Scavone, G. P. (2010). Vocal-tract influence in trombone performance. In *Proceedings of the International Symposium on Music Acoustics,* Sydney & Katoomba, Australia.

Gackle, L. (2000). Female adolescent transforming voices: Voice classification, voice skill development, and music literature selection. In L. Thurman & G. Welch (Eds.), *Bodymind and voice: Foundations of voice education,* (pp. 814–820). Collegeville, MN: VoiceCare Network.

Gardner, H. (1983). *Frames of mind: The theory of multiple intelligences.* New York: Basic Books.

Gehlhaar, R. (1991). Sound = Space: An interactive musical environment. *Contemporary Music Review, 6*(1), 59–72.

Grauer, V. (2011). *Sounding the depths: Tradition and the voices of history.* CreateSpace.

Green, L. (2002). *How popular musicians learn: A way ahead for music education.* Aldershot, U.K.: Ashgate.

Hallam, S. (2002). Musical motivation: Towards a model synthesising the research. *Music Education Research, 4*(2), 225–244.

Halliday, M. A. (1979). One child's protolanguage. In M. Bullowa (Ed.), *Before speech: The beginning of interpersonal communication* (pp. 171–190). Cambridge, U.K.: Cambridge University Press.

Harvey, A. (2017). *Music, evolution, and the harmony of souls*. Oxford, U.K.: Oxford University Press.

Hodges, D. A. (1989). Why are we musical? Speculations on the evolutionary plausibility of musical behavior. *Bulletin of the Council for Research in Music Education, 7–22.*

Howard, D. M. (1995). Variation of electrolaryngographically derived closed quotient for trained and untrained adult female singers. *Journal of Voice, 9* (2), 163–172.

Iacoboni, M. (2009). Imitation, empathy, and mirror neurons. *Annual Review of Psychology, 60,* 653–670.

Jordania, J. (2011). *Why do people sing? Music in human evolution*. Bellingham, WA: Logos.

Kanellopoulos, P. A. (2007). Children's early reflection on improvised music-making as the wellspring of musico-philosophical thinking. *Philosophy of Music Education Review, 15*(2), 119–141.

Kayes, G. (2000). *Singing and the actor*. Abingdon, U.K.: Psychology Press.

Knight, S. (2011). Adults identifying as 'non-singers' in childhood: Cultural, social, and pedagogical implications. In *Proceedings of the International Symposium on Performance Science. Utrecht, The Netherlands: European Association of Conservatoires*.

Knight, S. (2013). Exploring a cultural myth: What adult non-singers may reveal about the nature of singing. *Phenomenon of Singing, 2,* 144–154.

Kohler, E., Keysers, C., Umilta, M. A., Fogassi, L., Gallese, V., & Rizzolatti, G. (2002). Hearing sounds, understanding actions: action representation in mirror neurons. *Science, 297* (5582), 846–848.

Kohn, A. (1999). *Punished by rewards: The trouble with gold stars, incentive plans, A's, praise, and other bribes*. New York, NY: Houghton Mifflin Harcourt.

Kratus, J. (1990). Structuring the music curriculum for creative learning. *Music Educators Journal, 76*(9), 33–37.

Krause, B. (2012). *The great animal orchestra: finding the origins of music in the world's wild places*. New York: Little, Brown.

Laycock, J. (2005). *A changing role for the composer in society: a study of the historical background and current methodologies of creative music-making*. Oxford, U.K.: Peter Lang.

Lecanuet, J. P. (1996). Prenatal auditory experience. In I. Deliège & J. A. Sloboda (Eds.), *Musical beginnings: Origins and development of musical competence* (pp. 3–34). Oxford, U.K.: Oxford University Press.

Lerdahl, F., & Jackendoff, R. S. (1985). *A generative theory of tonal music*. Boston, MA: MIT Press.

Levitin, D. J. (2006). *This is your brain on music: The science of a human obsession*. New York: Dutton.

Livingstone, R. S., & Thompson, W. F. (2009). The emergence of music from the Theory of Mind. *Musicae Scientiae, 13* (2 suppl.), 83–115.

Locke, J. L. (1996). Why do infants begin to talk? Language as an unintended consequence. *Journal of Child Language, 23*(2), 251–268.

Malloch, S., & Trevarthen, C. (Eds.). (2009). *Communicative musicality: Exploring the basis of human companionship*. New York, NY: Oxford University Press.

Manén, L. (1974). *The art of singing: A manual of bel canto*. London, U.K.: Faber Music.

Maxwell Davies, P. (1963). Music composition by children. In W. Grant (Ed.), *Music in education* (pp. 108–124). Colston Papers, Vol. 14. Oxford, U.K.: Butterworth.

Merker, B. (2000). Synchronous chorusing and the origins of music. *Musicae Scientiae, 3*(suppl.), 59–73.

Mithen, S. (1996). *The prehistory of the mind: The cognitive origins of art and science*. London, U.K.: Thames & Hudson.

Mithen, S. (2005). *The singing Neanderthals: The origins of music, language, mind, and body*. London, U.K.: Weidenfeld & Nicolson.

Molnar-Szakacs, I., & Overy, K. (2006). Music and mirror neurons: From motion to 'e'motion. *Social Cognitive and Affective Neuroscience, 1*(3), 235–241.

Morley, I. (2013). *The prehistory of music: Evolutionary origins and archaeology of human musicality*. Oxford, U.K.: Oxford University Press.

Nelson, J. (1997). Lullabies as Human Adaptation: A Cross-Cultural Analysis of Children's Bedtime Songs. In D. J. Schneck & J. K. Schneck (Eds.), *Music in human adaptation* (pp. 61–78). Blacksburg: Virginia Polytechnic Institute and State University.

Opie, I. A., & Opie, P. (1985). *The singing game*. Oxford, U.K.: Oxford University Press.

Paynter, J. (2000). Making progress with composing. *British Journal of Music Education, 17*(1), 5–31.

Paynter, J., & Aston, P. (1970). *Sound and silence: Classroom projects in creative music*. Cambridge, U.K.: Cambridge University Press.

Plutchik, R. (1980). A general psychoevolutionary theory of emotion. *Theories of Emotion, 1*, 3–31.

Podlipniak, P. (2016). The evolutionary origin of pitch centre recognition. *Psychology of Music, 44*(3), 527–543.

Powys, V., Taylor, H., & Probets, C. (2013). A little flute music: Mimicry, memory, and narrativity. *Environmental Humanities, 3*(1), 43–70.

Romet, C. (1992). Song acquisition in culture: A West Javanese study in children's song development. In H. Lees (Ed.), *Music Education: Sharing Musics of the World. Proceedings of the Twentieth World Conference of the International Society for Music Education, Seoul, Korea* (pp. 164–173). Christchurch, New Zealand: ISME/University of Canterbury.

Ruddock, E. (2008). It's a bit harsh, isn't it! Judgemental teaching practice corrupts instinctive musicality. In *Proceedings of the Thirtieth Annual Conference: Innovation and Tradition; Music Education Research* (p. 226). Australian and New Zealand Association for Research in Music Education.

Rutherford, A. (2016). *A brief history of everyone who ever lived*. London, U.K.: Weidenfeld & Nicolson.

Sacks, O. (1998). *The man who mistook his wife for a hat and other clinical tales*. New York, NY: Simon and Schuster.

Sacks, O. (1990). *Seeing voices: A journey into the world of the deaf*. New York, NY: Harper.

Sacks, O. (2007). *Musicophilia*. New York, NY: Alfred A. Knopf.

Scavone, G. P., Lefebvre, A., & da Silva, A. R. (2008). Measurement of vocal-tract influence during saxophone performance. *Journal of the Acoustical Society of America, 123*(4), 2391–2400.

Schafer, R. M. (1975). *The rhinoceros in the classroom*. London, U.K.: Universal Edition.

Schafer, R. M. (1977). *The tuning of the world*. New York, NY: Alfred A. Knopf.

Scherer, K. R. (1992). Vocal affect expression as symptom, symbol, and appeal. In U. Jürgens, H. Papoušek, & M. Papoušek (Eds.), *Nonverbal vocal communication: Comparative and developmental approaches,* (pp. 43–60). Cambridge: Cambridge University Press.

Small, C. (1999). Musicking: The meanings of performing and listening—A lecture. *Music Education Research, 1*(1), 9–22.

Street, A., Young, S., Tafuri, J., & Ilari, B. (2003). Mothers' attitudes to singing to their infants. In *Proceedings of the 5th ESCOM conference, Hanover University of Music and Drama, Germany*.

Taylor, H. (2008). Decoding the song of the pied butcherbird: An initial survey. *Transcultural Music Review, 12*, 1–30.

Tinbergen, N. (1951). *The study of instinct*. Oxford, U.K.: Clarendon Press.

Titze, I. R. (1989). A four-parameter model of the glottis and vocal fold contact area. *Speech Communication, 8*(3), 191–201.

Tomlinson, G. (2015). *A million years of music: The emergence of human modernity*. Cambridge, MA: MIT Press.

Tovey. D. (1910). *Laudate Pueri: Sacred music of the XVIth century for high voices, being the first part of the Northlands singing book*. London, U.K.: Augener.

Trehub, S. E. (2001). Musical predispositions in infancy. *Annals of the New York Academy of Sciences, 930*(1), 1–16.

Trevarthen, C. (1979). Communication and cooperation in early infancy: A description of primary intersubjectivity. In M. Bullowa. (Ed.), *Before speech: The beginning of interpersonal communication* (pp. 321–347). Cambridge, U.K.: Cambridge University Press.

Trevarthen, C. (1994). Infant semiosis. In W. Nöth (Ed.), *Origins of semiosis: Sign evolution in nature and culture* (Vol. 116, pp. 219–252). Berlin, Germany: Walter de Gruyter.

Wallin, N. L. (1991). *Biomusicology: Neurophysiological, neuropsychological, and evolutionary perspectives on the origins and purposes of music*. New York, NY: Pendragon Press.

Wallin, N., Merker, B., & Brown, S. (Eds.). (2000). *The origins of music*. Cambridge, MA: MIT Press.

Webster, P. R. (1990). Creativity as creative thinking. *Music Educators Journal, 76*(9), 22–28.

Welch, G. F., & Murao, T. (Eds.). (1994). *Onchi and singing development: A cross-cultural perspective*. London: David Fulton Publishers.

Williams, J. (2013). *Teaching singing to children and young adults*. Braunton, U.K.: Compton Publishing.

Winnicott, D. W. (1971). *Playing and reality*. Abingdon, U.K.: Psychology Press.

Wishart, T. (1977). *Sounds fun: A book of musical games, Vol. 2*. London, U.K.: Universal Edition.

Wishart, T. (1996). *On sonic art*. Abingdon, U.K.: Psychology Press.

Wolfe, J., Garnier, M., & Smith, J. (2009). Vocal tract resonances in speech, singing, and playing musical instruments. *HFSP Journal, 3*(1), 6–23.

Woodward, S. C. (1993). *The transmission of music into the human uterus and the response to music of the human fetus and neonate* (Doctoral dissertation). Cape Town, South Africa: University of Cape Town.

Index